## A DOCTOR'S YEAR IN VIETNAM

"How many times had I seen these kids wake up and look for their missing extremities? How many of these kids had we put to sleep in this room who never woke up? How many times had I been awakened in the middle of the night to see a severely wounded casualty and had actually been relieved to see that he was already dead and required no extensive care?

"I had played no role in his death, and I would have broken my ass to save him had there been a chance, but I was glad that circumstances had taken the responsibility of hours of work and emotional strain away from me before I could start. The value of life and limb decreases when you see them wasted day after day, and night after night. The dead were not our business, and nonviable, unsalvageable arms and legs could not occupy our time.".

# 12, 20 & 5

## A Doctor's Year in Vietnam

### JOHN A. PARRISH, M.D.

**BANTAM BOOKS**

TORONTO · NEW YORK · LONDON · SYDNEY · AUCKLAND

*This low-priced Bantam Book
has been completely reset in a type face
designed for easy reading, and was printed
from new plates. It contains the complete
text of the original hard-cover edition.*
NOT ONE WORD HAS BEEN OMITTED.

12, 20 & 5: A DOCTOR'S YEAR IN VIETNAM
*A Bantam Book / published by arrangement with
the author*

PRINTING HISTORY
*First published in 1972
Bantam edition / October 1986*

*Illustrations by Greg Beecham.*

*Maps by Alan McKnight.*

*All rights reserved.
Copyright © 1972 by John Parrish.
Cover art copyright © 1986 by Bantam Books, Inc.
This book may not be reproduced in whole or in part, by
mimeograph or any other means, without permission.
For information address: Bantam Books, Inc.*

ISBN 0-553-26029-4

*Published simultaneously in the United States and Canada*

*To Joan*

# ACKNOWLEDGMENTS

I am indebted to Susan Rothfuss for repeatedly transforming stacks of illegible legal pads, notebooks, cardboards, and worn, folded papers into typed manuscript, and to Dr. Michael Jarratt for his advice and support. I am grateful for the encouragement and enthusiasm of Gerry McCauley who convinced me of the importance of making this very personal story available to the public and then proceeded to make it happen. I appreciate the helpful and critical suggestions of Mr. Hal Scharlatt of E. P. Dutton & Co.

My greatest debt is to Joan, my wife, for her support, tolerance and unfailing faith in me and for the understanding it took to give up a husband for two years of nights and weekends after work to write a book after giving him up for a year of separation at war. She knew that both tasks were something I had to do.

The events in this story are true.

Names have been changed and sequences have been somewhat altered. Some characters have been altered, combined or recast. In fact, many of the characters' physical forms have been altered by removal of arms and legs. Some have been made totally unrecognizable because they have been blown away.

JOHN A. PARRISH M.D.

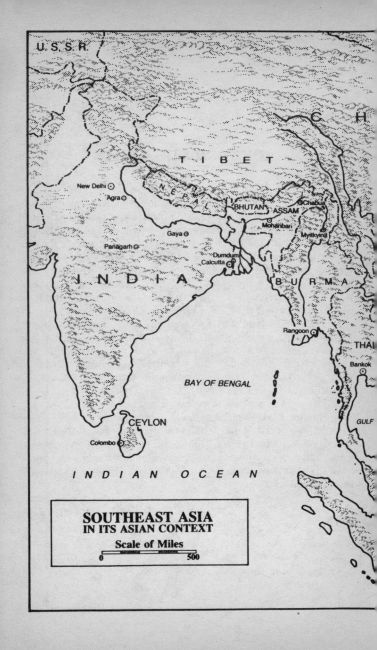

SOUTHEAST ASIA
IN ITS ASIAN CONTEXT

Scale of Miles
0          500

# ONE

*Tho I walk thru the valley of the Shadow of Death,
I will fear no evil—cuz I'm the toughest mutha' in
the Valley.*

The sign was hand printed beneath a picture of a rugged,
unshaven, World War II, John Wayne-type marine with fixed
bayonet and fixed stare. The poster was the focal point of a
clean, simple, and functional room. The bayonet pointed past
filing cabinets and chairs toward a vacant desk labeled "Officer of the Day." Three enlisted men draped over wooden
chairs looked up with an absence of enthusiasm that told us
that our arrival was not making their evening any less boring.

I was beginning my military career by checking in at
Camp Pendleton, a marine training base in southern California being used primarily as a staging area for personnel en
route to Vietnam. It had been over a year since I received
some friendly advice from my government suggesting that I
"volunteer" for a commission as a navy doctor. As added
encouragement, the same letter reminded me that student
deferment days were over and enclosed a date to report for
an induction physical as a 1-A buck private candidate should I
choose not to serve my country as an officer and a gentleman.

When I accepted my commission, the navy agreed to
permit me to spend another year of internal medical residency training at the University Hospital in Ann Arbor, Michigan. About halfway through that additional year I found out
that my first year in the navy would be spent with the
marines in the Republic of South Vietnam. From that point
on it was difficult to remain completely enthusiastic about the
academic discussions on metabolic or renal rounds, and the

1

collection of esoteric pearls from medical journals seemed somewhat less important.

The obvious good health of the yawning enlisted men scattered about the Officer of the Day's room was pleasant in itself. My last few weeks of civilian life had been spent in the hematology service where many of my patients were teenagers dying of leukemia. While investing much of my emotional energy in telling white lies of empty optimism, I had been the helpless observer of the waste and death of the young victims. I was fortunate that my work at the hospital had kept me extremely busy and left me little time for introspection and worry about the future.

During the ten-minute ride from the front gate to our checkpoint I was accompanied by a dentist and another doctor. We quickly sketched in our backgrounds and discussed our feelings about the impending 12,000-mile trip to South Vietnam. The dentist had become the father of his firstborn child three days earlier, and he seemed inappropriately brave, optimistic, and almost happy. The other doctor was an orthopedic surgeon and former football player who did not seem to mind the return to the physical life of an all-male atmosphere. Repairing broken bones and dismembered bodies would be excellent practice for him. Their confidence and excitement made me almost embarrassed about my anxieties over treating badly wounded people and my fears of personal physical injury.

We signed some forms in triplicate with a minimum of conversation. A sleepy marine threw our bags into a pickup truck, and we followed him to an old, two-story, white building. Inside we found thirty or more newly-arrived doctors and dentists in a state of partial undress staking claims on bunks and lockers and nervously making small talk. I found an empty lower bunk near the corner of the large room and began to unpack my new leather suitcase.

What sort of things does one take to a war on the other side of the world? Books? Stethoscope? Candy bars? Sneakers? Sports jacket? Tennis racket? Bathing suit? Jock strap? Camera? Aftershave? I looked over the information booklet about our two week basic training course and counted how many hours of sleep I would get before our orientation session the next morning. It had been dark for several hours, but the California August heat persisted. An upright, slightly dirty water fountain vibrated quietly in the hallway and cradled one hard ball of pink chewing gum in the drain. Four long rows of wooden, double-deck beds were evenly spaced along the worn, but well-polished wooden floor. The room was otherwise empty except for gray metal lockers, human forms, and suitcases.

I took a shower, listened to a few secondhand war stories, and made appropriate small talk with my new neighbors. A transient, slightly nauseating, nostalgic pain in my lower chest made me reach for a cigarette.

The guy in the next bed had the muscle tone of wet toilet paper. His skin was snow white, and his sweaty chest had no hair on it. He talked constantly.

"I don't know what the hell they want with me," he complained. "I just finished my internship, and I'm planning on going into obstetrics. What's your bag?"

My eyes were still scanning the room. "I'm about halfway through a residency in internal medicine, and I don't know exactly why I'm here either." There was no emotion in my voice.

"I volunteered to go," said a voice behind me.

I turned to see who Frank Meriwell was, and was surprised to find a reasonable-looking person. He proceeded to tell us at length about American boys getting sick and wounded and needing help. Although it wasn't a very impressive speech, it did cause me to think about the new job I had accepted with a corny little hand-raised oath. It looked as if I were really going through with it—I was going to war. Why? How could I justify taking a year from my life to go to a war on the other side of the world?

Immature wanderlust? A search for manhood and excitement? Did I want to be a hero? This war seemed to have no heroes. Was I patriotic? Regardless of my feelings about this war, it was true that American boys were getting sick and wounded. And there must be someone to take care of them. That someone might as well be me. Was my reason for going simply to have gone? To have done it? To experience war? To live through it? To flirt with death and win? Or, perhaps more importantly, to rob death and disease of their victims? Maybe this was my reason for becoming a doctor in the first place. And now I was going to be the doctor in his most trying and finest hour.

Maybe I believed that going to war was the right thing to do. I had been asked to go. It was expected of me. As a child I had learned that being good meant doing what was expected of me; at first by my parents, then by teachers and society. Then by the more mobile but sometimes less flexible superego or God they created for, or passed onto, me.

Living up to expectations was an unusually important part of my life. I was the son of a Baptist minister and a sacrificial, upright, full-time mother. My older brother had died when I was seven, making me the eldest of the remaining three children. My first society beyond the home had been the church. Much was expected of me and I had always made it my business to deliver.

I was a good boy. I silently sublimated away my youth being the quiet achiever. Fair play. Good grades. Nice guy. Hard work. And now war?

Maybe I was still competing. My childhood in Miami with its close, patriarchal family and the comfortable answers provided by religion had been challenged by an interest in science and biology and exposure to a wider range of outlooks at Duke University. My late-blooming ego was threatened. Small successes in the academic world reinforced escape into long nights and weekends of study. The time-limited, goal-oriented, tested, conquest of knowledge and identity seemed to lead logically into competing for a place in a good medical school, and the idea of being a doctor served a reasonable combination of independence and academic life yet leaving room to fulfill the need to serve my fellowman. Yale Medical School had been tough, interesting, and had required almost a full-time effort. Maybe war was another course, a graduate school, an even tougher test. I could compete and achieve and surpass expectations.

Or maybe I accepted going because I felt that for an American doctor, Vietnam was where the single greatest need existed. It was in Ann Arbor, Michigan as an intern and resident in internal medicine that I learned what being a doctor was all about. Medical school had been a prep school, a playground for my mind with no responsibility except to myself and my desire to learn. It was as an intern that I learned to be involved, to be responsible, to be completely immersed and irreversibly connected to the care of the sick.

It was there that I learned to concentrate all my thinking, time, and emotional and physical energy into the one patient that I happened to be taking care of at any one particular time. For two years my own fatigue, interests, problems, life, wife, and babies were completely subjected to the every call of my ward full of very sick people. I became conditioned to the point that there was never any decision to make as to whether I worked or didn't work. If one of my patients needed me, I was there. The response was automatic, unheroic, undramatic, nonphilosophical, nonpious, and quick. It was expected. Maybe my response now, when called to go to war, was just another automatic appearance at the bedside when needed.

On the other hand, maybe I needed to go to war for the same reason I had lifted weights when I was a teen-ager. The same reason I ran distance races at Miami High School as a second best miler. The same reason I worked construction jobs every summer. Maybe I didn't like being the tall, skinny, good, serious scholar with glasses. I wanted to be a professional football player. This war was my chance at travel, excitement, foreign ports, women, booze, danger, evil, and manhood. Besides, I was sick and tired of study and hard work.

Anyway, I had to go. It was too late to volunteer for the Public Health Service, too late to trump up a research project for the National Institute of Health, too late even to claim conscientious objection to the war. The alternatives were clear—jail for three years, Canada for life, or Vietnam for one year. The best choice seemed to be the gamble of surviving a year at war. The stakes were high, but the odds for a doctor were good. I did not realize then that physical survival was only a part of winning the gamble.

Since my residency training had been much too encompassing to allow any interest in politics, I did not have a clear picture of why this particular war was necessary. As best I could tell, some dictator in Saigon had taken advantage of the confusion of an exploding nationalism and the American fear of spreading "communism," and had enlisted our financial and military support in keeping a Vietnamese national hero from finishing off his revolution. To someone in the United States government, finishing a revolution seemed too bloody, too unstable, and too "un-American." And, furthermore, North Vietnam was becoming too closely aligned with her "Red Communist" neighbor.

When the Saigon dictator proved to be too unpopular with the Vietnamese people to survive—even with the United States' support—we switched allegiance to his successor. To keep the Vietnamese from killing one another and to make the countryside safe for the peasants, we moved in to bring peace and quiet. The fact that we now needed so many doctors to administer to broken bones and dismembered bodies suggested that our goals were not yet realized. It wasn't really a war in the legal sense. But somehow it was a really big league police action with bombing raids, napalm, search-and-destroy missions—the works. Involvement kept expanding just to maintain some dubious and illusionary American objective.

The whole scene was confusing. I only hoped that the political scientists and the politicians knew our best interests. The Southeast Asia experts told us that Southeast Asia mattered. Its 250 million people were entitled to free and independent development. The nations of Southeast Asia were threatened by the ambitions of North Vietnam and Communist China. America had "commitments" and had to demonstrate to the world that she would and could fulfill them. Finally, it would be nice to demonstrate that the communist technique of a "people's war of national liberation" could fail. We would try to make it fail. But, despite the opinions of the experts, I did not want to help stop a revolution, to get involved in a civil war, to stabilize an unpopular dictator, to fight "communism," or to provide free elections to an uneducated and unconcerned populace of farming peasants who could frankly care less as to who sat behind the oversized rosewood desk in the Saigon Governor's Palace. And the country was on the other side of the world! I did not want to leave home to force our brand of "freedom" on a distant, unfamiliar people. Despite our government's benevolent cries of freedom for the Asians, I could not help but think of my own freedom as well.

My free country was forcing me to leave home for an undeclared war in a distant country. To what lengths was I honor bound to serve my country? Pledge allegiance? Sure. Obey the law? Yes. Pay taxes? Okay. But go to an unpopular war? I was dubious. Where was my freedom of choice?

Where were my rights as an enlightened citizen in an enlightened society?

My country had given me a lot. I remembered my years of education, my safe home, and my family. I enjoyed an abundance of food, television, and a General Motors car. The security and abundance of American life had not come easily. The price had been paid in past wars, and now my generation was paying once again. But was this war too expensive for what we were asking from it? Maybe war is overpayment. Is war necessary anymore? Maybe I would find out. Little did I realize, I was going to learn *all* about war.

Next morning I made it through breakfast, coffee, and defecation without a cigarette. Six of us rode to the classroom area with the orthopedic surgeon who had one of the few cars available. We spent the first third of the trip shaking hands in all kinds of awkward positions, the middle third in total silence, and the last few blocks all talking at once. Camp Pendleton by day was a flat land bounded by a highway, a few hills, an endless fence, and an ocean. It took about ten minutes to reach the classroom area. Barracks, storage buildings, parking lots, and roads were scattered everywhere. Automobiles outnumbered jeeps and helicopters, but military uniforms far outnumbered civilian clothes. The marines at the gates and intersections were sharply dressed, brightly polished, and impressively erect. They snapped off what looked like a nine-position salute with the right hand, and directed traffic with snappy, determined movements of the left. Elbows and hands were everywhere.

We went to our first class in civilian clothes and looked like a group transplanted directly from a Miami Beach hotel. In dress ranging from bermudas and T-shirts to three-piece suits, we filled out more forms in triplicate.

Our instructor was a tall, tanned, and well-built marine captain. Even in the classroom setting, it was obvious that he was in excellent physical condition. There was spring in his step. He totally disregarded the hundreds of subconsciously-dictated energy saving tricks that less fit humans employ in their everyday body movements. He had a very short military haircut and wore a freshly pressed short-sleeved khaki uniform. He was the only person in the room not perspiring. Having already completed a thirteen-month tour in Vietnam, he was considering going back after a year as instructor at

Camp Pendleton. He ran for an hour at noon each day. He did not drink or smoke. He was a victim of rigid self-discipline. He actually seemed to believe in all the things he taught us. Consequently, I was not surprised when I saw him in Vietnam eight months later. By that time I was not surprised even by the wound in his neck and his lifeless body.

Several bored officers and enlisted men assisted the marine captain in giving a series of lectures designed to orient doctors to military life. Some used poor grammar out of ignorance—others on purpose for effect.

Much of the classroom material was worthless, some of it was interesting. A large part of it was simply common sense. Very little time was spent talking ideology or politics. No one felt obligated to justify the war effort, to discuss morality or freedom, or to argue democracy versus communism. The politicians made the war. The military just fought it. The only human qualities discussed were the stubbornness of the enemy and the comradeship of the marines. No talk of honor, country, truth, or heroes. The facts were simple. There was a war going on in which Americans were getting sick, wounded, and killed. Doctors were needed to care for them. We were the doctors.

Advice was given in the form of orders. Instructors who had served in Vietnam gave their advice with a sense of true self-satisfaction. Some led us to assume that their physically intact state after a tour in the war zone was the result of their training, ruggedness, and cleverness. Others admitted that they were also very lucky. No one discussed preservation of mental health.

The rules for self-survival were simple and logical. Responses had to become habit, because the stresses of the moment could preclude logical thinking. "Rules for responses that become habit make soldiers."

"We like rules," the marine captain would say. "You will learn to like rules." It was hard to tell if he was stating a fact or giving an order. "Rules will keep you alive.

"You are here to learn how to be soldiers in two weeks. That's impossible. So you might best learn some of the rules by which soldiers stay alive and, therefore, win wars. In winning wars it is helpful, but not completely necessary, to be alive. It is helpful, but not necessary, to escape injury. Your responses must be automatic and fast. There is no time for hesitation. A quick, highly-trained response may save your life. We train combat marines to make quick, highly-practiced moves that also take the lives of the enemy. You people must be satisfied with those moves that save your own skin. Rules for responses that become habits make soldiers.

"Never stand in groups or gather too closely together when in open country. One incoming round could get you all!

"On field maneuvers, don't give or return salutes, or wear any rank insignia, because snipers can use these signs as cues to select out officers for assassination.

"Immediately 'hit the deck' when any loud, unexpected noise occurs. Don't run for a bunker until there is a pause in the incoming shells. An upright, running body is more likely to be struck by flying shrapnel than a prone body. Shrapnel goes up and out.

"Sleep as near the ground as possible. Sleep under the ground if possible."

The rule that best summarized the laws of survival in a war zone was, "Keep your ass down."

We were taught field sterilization of water, selection of food for jungle survival, self-treatment of wounds, conduct when captured, necessity of salt pills. We had a brief discussion of tropical medicine including malaria prophylaxis and treatment. Military theory was presented quickly and unenthusiastically. Even the military mind had enough insight to know that without time to condition our responses to accept each rule in its logical, or illogical, sequence, we could not be expected to automatically respond to a command structure which necessitated assuming unreasonably dangerous positions. Not being volunteers molded by months of vigorous mind and body conditioning, we were not expected to react as young and eager second lieutenants.

Making doctors into soldiers was difficult, maybe impossible, because of the value judgments learned in our schooling and in our caring for the ill. Making doctors of soldiers would probably be easier. But since we were going to live by the rules of the military for a year, and since we would be treating the end result of many of the tactical failures and successes (even successes have casualties), we were given a brief outline of ground and helicopter warfare in Southeast Asia. It did not matter if we believed in the theory.

Marines are taught that when they are ambushed in

jungle terrain, the first response is to advance immediately toward the enemy automatic weapons implacement. The reasoning is that fewer will die if the enemy guns are extinguished quickly than if the unit is pinned down, encircled, and picked off one man at a time. The tactic makes sense to the company commander, the gunny sergeant, the marine unit as a whole. What is so unbelievable about the marines is that it also makes sense to the kids who are in the unhappy position of being up front ("Up front with the most.")—the kids who have to charge the machine guns. Such physical and emotional training makes the marines an efficient killing machine. Such rearranging of young men's thinking secures success for the group and wins battles.

On the other hand, the same overwhelming group identity, when carried to its pathologic extreme, paradoxically makes each man in the unit important—important as a marine, not as a certain John Doe. A marine becomes especially important if he is wounded, or even dead, and left behind. The group good is then sacrificed for the individual. The group makes unreasonable sacrifices, and takes predictable heavy casualties to retrieve him. The logic is only as sick as the game they play so well.

Nobody mentioned the fact that military historians have pointed out for decades that a traditional ground war in Southeast Asia cannot be won. Instead of a lecture on Diem Bien Phu, we saw a propaganda movie on the most heroic of heroes—the reconnaissance unit. Diagrams of behind-the-lines helicopter drops, cross fires, blocking forces, and ambushes were presented. They seemed so effective it was amazing that the war had not been won long ago.

"But then every football play, as designed, is a touchdown," reminded the marine captain. "It doesn't work everytime, because someone doesn't follow orders, doesn't do his job correctly, or isn't trained adequately."

One of the less articulate and more direct sergeant lecturers stated it a little differently. "Somebody always fucks up. The first rule of life in the service is that if a thing can possibly be fucked up, it will be. Camp Pendleton is here to eliminate the ones who fuck up the most—unless they are doctors."

It was pointed out to us that the doctor's role in a war zone is to conserve military manpower through proper selection of troops, preventive medicine, and care of the sick and wounded. The primary responsibility on the front lines is to prevent adverse effects of unevacuated casualties on combat efficiency. Also, the doctor conducts health inspections and acts as advisor to the commanding officer regarding preventive medicine. He offers advice in regard to sites for the mess hall and latrines and determines evacuation routes and water sources.

Only several hours of each long, dry, and hot southern California day were spent on classroom education. The rest of the time was devoted to some kind of a two-week miracle designed to make doctors look and act like soldiers. Our field training was directed by two marine sergeants. One was tall, slow, and cool, with the endurance of a long-distance runner. The other was short, energetic, and dumb. Both were friendly and patient. It was amusing to them, and embarrassing for me, to see the poor physical condition of the caretakers of the human body.

The first organized run was a disaster. After several hundred yards, the formation was broken by vomiting, wheezing stragglers who managed to laugh at their own discomfort. All of us realized that it was to our advantage to improve our endurance and to adjust to a more rigorous physical life. Two weeks was a short time to change one's physiology; however, most of us began to show signs of adjustment. Others were poorer specimens, and a few were irretrievable.

In our practice sessions out in the field, the same clumsy oaf tripped over every simulated land mine, fell in every pit, gave away every ambush, and stepped in the single daily dung deposit of the only dog on the compound.

"If that man was in my patrol in Vietnam, I'd have to kill him on the first day out, or none of us would get back," mumbled the drill instructor to himself as the hero of City Hospital fell off another cliff and broke his glasses. His holster slipped to his ankles as he tried to rise, and again he went down with canteen clanking and helmet drilling into the bridge of the sunburned nose which used to carry black, horn-rimmed glasses. When he finally recovered his upright stance, his .45 lay in the sand noticed only by the drill instructor. "Your weapon, Sir," the sergeant whispered respectfully.

We learned to shoot, break down, and re-assemble a .45 pistol and an M14 rifle. My first close call in the war came when my friend from City Hospital shot at us backward over his right shoulder when in the "ready" position at the target range.

I was point, or scout, on the first field maneuver. I was killed when I walked into an ambush set by the dental officers. I did manage, however, to see the poorly hidden dentists in time to warn the doctors to take cover and be saved. I was rewarded that night with a pitcher of beer.

We wore green fatigues and boots at all times. "Stateside" boots were heavy black leather boots that gave authority to the step. After two weeks, civilian shoes made my feet feel naked. We were told how lucky we would be to get the canvass jungle boots and the lightweight jungle fatigues in our new home in Southeast Asia. I could hardly wait.

After classes several of us went down to an oval, 440-yard track and raced one mile. Being tall, thin, and willing to voluntarily accept the necessary pain, I frequently won. I created in my own mind some importance in winning those silly races. One of the psychological defenses everybody learned, whether consciously or not, was to upgrade unrealistically the relative importance of the activities in our new life. Life's order of priorities had to be rearranged. Such mental gymnastics made it much easier to accept what we were doing and where we were headed.

The green fatigues, weapons, and military environment began to convince us that we were part of a giant machine assembled for the business

M 14

of war. Its very existence was a waste if there were no enemy to conquer. The constant reminder of a very real physical threat to our lives from some enemy kindled a hate for people we did not even know.

A .45 on the hip and two bars on the collar gave rise to a sense of personal prestige and power analyzed by a few, accepted by most, and needed by some. Boys who watched World War II movies, read war comics, and played war games in vacant lots were men now. They were being taught by professionals to play the game of war with real weapons. And here at Camp Pendleton, it seemed like nothing more than a very serious game. The rules were clear and simple. Involvement was contagious and inescapable. The game became important by definition, because each player's time was completely invested in it. The frustrations of civilian life were left behind. Long-range planning was unnecessary. In the war game, life for the moment was all-important.

Rapidly the collective attitude changed from that of complete confusion, to that of a boy-scout camp, and then to that of a high school football training camp where selected comradeships and internal competition became important. Gradually introspective thinking began to separate the individual from the group. The impending prolonged separation from country, family, and friends and the impending threat to life and limb added a quality of helplessness and pride— unappreciated modern gladiators. And, of course, like in any other developmental process, many of the rapidly created new soldiers got "hung up" at various stages and wore unresolved conflicts on their belts like canteens.

Little thought was given to freedom, love of country, or saving Asians from communism. The game was going to be a very personal, short-term war of individual survival. The goals were to live through it with four extremities, and remain uninvolved. We were forced to make this trip. We would be big boys and go. Then we would come home and resume our lives. If anybody talked of "winning" the war, few listened. Making the war a time-limited test of personal survival was not taught to us by any of our instructors, but somehow was adopted as a goal by all of us before we left Camp Pendleton. "Stay alert. Stay alive." The emphasis was definitely on the latter.

Our evenings were spent drinking beer at the Officers'

Club (or "O" Club), reading, writing letters, disassembling and reassembling weapons, or taking lonely walks around the compound. Camp Pendleton was a small country in itself with villages, simulated battlegrounds, and small towns. The industry of this country was making ready for war. We were new inhabitants from the outside world.

During the last night of our stay at Camp Pendleton, we force-marched eight miles into "jungle country," set up tents for our overnight stay, and practiced compass marches in the dark. On the long walk back, sleeplessness and full back packs overwhelmed a few of our less hardy comrades. As they rode past us in jeeps, laughing and beckoning us to join them, they were answered with frowns, curses, and finger gestures in the universal language. Despite it all, most of us had come a long way in two weeks.

Next morning, we cleaned our weapons before turning them in. Each time the marine sergeant inspected my weapon, he sent me back to clean it again. I oiled, cleaned, and wiped over and over again, but each time the sergeant looked down the barrel and refused it. Finally, I walked around the sergeant, turned in my weapon to the lance corporal, and disgustedly returned to my quarters.

After the two week introduction to military life, I packed all the belongings I had previously selected for my year abroad and shipped them in the new suitcase to my wife. I did not need or want any of them. I stuffed a few books, lots of underwear and socks, green fatigues, and my new boots in a seabag. I carefully, almost proudly, printed my name in indelible ink on the side of the green canvass bag.

Lt. John Parrish 690677
3rd Marine Division

I left the camp slightly more prepared, but much more anxious, than when I had arrived.

We were given two-and-a-half days to get from Camp Pendleton to Travis Air Force Base, which is a one-hour drive north of San Francisco. For most, the time was a frantic, alcoholic orgy that took different forms depending on morality, marital status, amount of denial, and amount of ready cash. For some it was another chance to say good-bye.

I had already said goodbye to my wife, Joan. I didn't

think I could bear to say it again. I had actually been saying goodbye to her for weeks. Ever since I had received my orders months earlier I had been thinking goodbye to myself every time I looked at her. From that point on, happy times made me sad and sad times made me angry.

When Joan and I began to realize the full meaning of my orders a strange involuntary distance grew between us as if we were bracing ourselves knowing that if the stress of the news caused too much dependence and intimacy, the separation would be that much more painful.

No social or intellectual encounter with any group could remove the thought of impending separation. Even the personal interactions, and sexual intimacy with my wife could not escape the chronic anxiety of loss. Waiting to leave was a sad and helpless contest with time that could not be won. There was never enough time together and too much of that time was spent thinking farewell.

For emotional support and because of financial necessity, Joan had decided to spend the year of separation with her parents in Miami, Florida where we had both grown up. Upon completion of my work in Ann Arbor, Michigan we had put our two girls, ages one and three into our Chevrolet station wagon and driven to Florida for more goodbyes. My folks in Orlando and then Joan's in Miami.

As we drove down the East Coast I kept looking over at the happy redhead who had been my college sweetheart. She looked older now and her small features were somewhat hardened by the fatigue of two babies and the ominous purpose of our trip, but her beautiful person-soul still broke through. She had decided to leave her exciting New York City job to move to New Haven, take my name, sleep with me every night, work my way through school, and bear my two children. As a reward she spent two cold and lonely years in Ann Arbor among strangers with two babies and a husband who was never home. Alone for meals, days and late nights, bottles, diapers, and bedtime. Now she was being returned to her parents for a year. Not a real bargain.

We had actually looked forward to the two years in service that most doctors serve. During my last year in Michigan I earned $3,600, not the kind of money that permitted luxuries for a wife and two kids. The service was to be our years of money, rest, and the revitalizing of our relationship.

My flight from Miami to California to begin training had left in the afternoon. Joan's mother had kept the kids outside so that we could sit in the den and say goodbye again. Heavy silences grew so long that it became difficult to find a word or phrase appropriate or important enough to interrupt the thickening quiet. Finally, after a very painful goodbye to my two little girls who fortunately did not understand my departure, it was time for Joan to drive me to the airport. She dropped me off and stood next to the car while I got my luggage from the trunk.

"Take care of yourself, baby" was all that I could manage to say before I kissed her once and turned to walk away. I didn't want to see her cry.

The two weeks at Camp Pendleton seemed too long to be apart. I weakened. I called from Camp Pendleton and told Joan to fly to meet me for that last weekend in San Francisco. I was willing to endure another goodbye to see her again.

I felt clumsy and a little out of character when I met my wife at the airport in dress khakis. I was surprised and a little bit frightened to find myself eager to tell her of the dangers and importance of my new job. I had barely started being a soldier and I already took pride in a kind of war story.

I wanted to leave and be on with it. Enough goodbyes. My tour had to start before it could end. Our separation was not concerned with victories or defeats. It had nothing to do with causes or campaigns. It had to do with the calendar and it could not end unless it started.

We could not face another official goodbye. Joan got up early on the morning of my departure date, called a cab, and left me in the hotel room to fly back home. Without speaking I kissed her lightly on the cheek as she left. If I had grabbed her then, I may have never let go. "We'll start again in a year," I thought to myself.

A friend from medical school days drove me around the bay area all day and then delivered me to Travis Air Force Base. Finally my own goodbyes were over. I began to see the other doctors from my Camp Pendleton group arrive. Two of our crew who were either too intoxicated or too sober did not show up at flight time. They were rumored to have fled to Canada.

Our Transworld Airline flight from Travis to Okinawa was scheduled to leave at 10 P.M., but did not get away until 6

A.M. the next day. The wait made our departure even more painful for those who had brought wives, sweethearts, or families. One doctor and his wife stood against the wall holding hands like junior high school kids. A little girl kept striking her father with closed fist and sobbing quietly. Daddy must want to leave. Nobody could make her all-powerful daddy go away if he did not want to leave. Mom was scolding and embarrassed. Tarbaby dad had uncontrolled tears rolling down his cheek. He made no attempt to conceal them or to protect himself.

My mind tried to close out my emotions. A dental officer stared at his beer bottle as if he were seeing his past and future through its off-brown mirrors. One man was already writing letters home. Another was reviewing the wallet pictures of family and loved ones, while a man seated at the same table read a recently acquired pocket book. Each had the frown of deep thought, confusion, and anxiety. The pain of last night's drinking was slow to yield to tonight's slowly rising blood level of alcohol.

Why hadn't I joined the U.S. Public Health Service? Or run away to Canada? Or been a conscientious objector? Was I going to die? As I lit my first cigarette in three days, four notes of a Sibelius theme began to play somewhere in the back of my brain. The notes grew louder as I looked at the slow-motion play surrounding me. I could not make the music in my head stop. As its volume increased, it slipped to a minor key, and then off key, and with each drum beat five hundred little girls beat on my heart.

I watched the second hand of my watch creep around and fully realized for the first time that I would not be returning for one year—twelve months—365 days. Maybe I would not come back at all. I was trapped now. Who could help me?

The music that was pushing outward on my eardrums suddenly stopped. The quiet was frightening. All of the goodbyes were in such slow motion now that wives and sweethearts and children and parents were frozen in grief. Did they realize that some of these goodbyes were forever?

I sat down on a bench next to a sleeping sailor and closed my eyes. An image of my dad's uncontrolled tears and my mother's brave, trembling lip made me open them again. My Sunday school teacher, scout master, principal, homeroom teacher, coach, and dean began telling me to go to the other side of the world and face danger like a good boy, but I wanted a bad cold to keep me home. Maybe my mom could write a note to my commanding officer.

A beautiful woman beckoned me to her bed, but I stomped out of the house nude except for my combat boots. She was holding her breasts and crying. I could not turn back, because people were cheering and throwing streams of paper and confetti. I could not hear her crying above the band music.

I lit up again. My throat hurt. Some fool son-of-a-bitch played "I Left My Heart in San Francisco" on the jukebox. I did not cry. An air force enlisted man asked me for a cigarette, and I gave him the whole pack. My stomach hurt, and I had to urinate.

"War is good business, invest your sons" was written among the usual sex-starved and homosexual graffiti on the walls of the men's room. A marine first lieutenant was vomiting in the stall. I looked in the mirror at my dress uniform and also became nauseated. I had even bought some colored ribbons for my square shouldered costume. I was the cutest boy at the party. I was a turkey dressed up for Thanksgiving. I was an eight-year-old boy kneeling by my bed and impressing my mother and God by praying for "our boys overseas."

I needed a cigarette, a beer, a woman, a mother. I needed to bolt from this airport and run. Were all those stupid doctors going to allow themselves to be herded into that airplane? Were we volunteering to leave home, to go to war, to see man at his worst, and maybe to die?

By sunrise, anxiety and fatigue had turned us into unresisting zombies. We shuffled slowly toward the aircraft without hesitation, without conversation. Was there no revolt?

The goodbye nightmare kept repeating itself as I slept intermittently on the flight. A lieutenant commander-post ROTC-GP-anus sitting next to me kept telling ridiculous secondhand war stories. He had volunteered to go to Vietnam. I was not impressed.

# TWO

Our dress khakis went into storage as soon as we arrived in Okinawa. This meant that we had bought these costumes for over one hundred dollars just for our flight. We received two or more injections in each arm, and I had malaise, low-grade fever, and headache for our entire two-day stay on the island. We checked in and out of several places, stood in lots of lines, and filled out more forms in triplicate. I exercised once in the gymnasium, which was full of muscled young men who spent most of their time talking about various theories of muscle building all of which were unscientific and untrue.

Most of the Americans I saw on Okinawa were either going to or coming from the Republic of Vietnam. The prostitutes were experts at making the distinction. They focused their attentions on the wide-eyed, nineteen-year-old boys away from home for the first time, afraid they may not live to return, and determined to show off their manhood in front of their colleagues. The returning seasoned twenty-year-old men of the world were more interested in drinking and telling war stories. They did not want to risk getting VD so close to homecoming. They would, however, usually get drunk and carefree enough to change their minds by late night.

Dancing with the girls and buying them drinks, the neophytes were considerate, almost courteous. They would pay higher prices for the girls' services, and the clever bargirl could usually fast talk her way into leaving them after one or two fast "tricks" in a small, nearby room (which the GI also paid for). The girls would then return to the bar to be picked up by the veterans who paid less, insisted on "all night," and

19

generally drank enough to sleep for at least most of the night.
Most girls could work in one or more "short-timers" before
their moderately drunk, "all night" trick. Many of these girls
were the major source of income for their family.

Another commercial airliner took us to Da Nang. Miles
of runaway were surrounded by tin-roofed hangars, concrete
blast walls, and sandbag reinforced, wooden-frame buildings.
Hundreds of helicopers sat in rows with blades folded. Commercial jets shared the runways with fighter jets and large,
propeller-driven, military transport planes.

Beyond the airport was more flat land crowded with huts
of wood, plaster, flattened tin cans, bamboo, and straw. A
single green mountain rose far in the distance. It was clear,
and hot, and so bright that the heat waves created by the
baking sun and evaporating fuels gave an unreal quality to the
landscape. Americans were everywhere, in jeeps and aircraft,
on heavy machinery loading and unloading war materials, and
in and about the terminal buildings. A few, short-statured,
Vietnamese soldiers were scattered about, standing quietly,
smoking Salems, and looking out of place. There were no
civilians and no women of any race.

My short-sleeved shirt was soaked before I had carried
my seabag the thirty meters from the aircraft to the large
open warehouse of soldiers called Marine Air Freight. My
instructions sounded easy enough. Go to Marine Air Freight
and "muster" to go to a place called Phu Bai.

For the next six hours I stood in various lines, put my
name on numerous lists, and waited. And waited. No one
knew or cared who I was. No one knew exactly how to help
me. It seemed that if I never appeared in Phu Bai, no one
would know. Could I go back home? I even tried to call Phu
Bai on the wall phone, but since I did not know whom I was
calling, the code name of the operator, or the switchboard
system, the attempts proved to be another exercise in frustration. I waited.

I finally got to the front of another line. The lance
corporal behind the counter was hot, and bored, and tired of
answering questions.

"Hi, I'm Doctor Parrish. I'd like to go to Phu Bai."

"No more flights today, Sir." He never looked up from
his clipboard.

"But I have to report there."

"Sorry, Sir."

"How can I get to Phu Bai?"

"I don't know."

Silence.

"Maybe there'll be an emergency flight up that way tonight," he resumed. He finally looked up.

"Can I get on it?"

"I don't know."

"Who does?"

"Nobody. You'll have to wait and see."

"How long do I wait?"

"I don't know."

Silence.

"My orders say to go to Phu Bai."

"I guess you'd better go there then, Sir."

"How do I get there?"

"Wait for a flight. No more today though. Your best bet is to be here at 0600 tomorrow. Good chance of getting on an early flight."

"Right here?"

"Line up right where you are now at 0600."

"Where do I sleep tonight?"

"I don't know."

Silence. The lance corporal was finally looking at me. He sensed that my frustration was on the verge of turning to anger. Not that he gave a damn. He did not make the rules. He was gathering up his lists and preparing to leave.

"Most of the marines sleep right here on the floor. There's a Transient Officers' Quarters about a mile and a half down the road."

"How do I get down there?"

"I don't know. Walk. Thumb. Call a navy taxi, Mosbey 100. If you want to wait, a truck comes by here at 1900 to take any officers up there for the night. It'll bring you back at 6 A.M."

"Where does it stop?"

"Right out there on the side of the road."

"Is there a mess hall around?"

"No."

"Is there a men's room?"

"There's a piss tube behind this building. The shitter is across the road."

"I beg your pardon."

"There is a piss tube behind this building. The shitter is across the road."

"Well, I just have to urinate."

"I guess you'd better do it, then, Sir. Piss tube behind the building."

"Thanks."

"Yes, Sir."

A full seabag propped up against a wall makes a fairly comfortable back rest. I sat and watched the aircraft take off and land. It would be an hour before the truck came by. Nothing to drink or eat since breakfast, and it was almost six o'clock. At least I could sit. No more lines shuffling along at zero pace.

I saw two marines drinking cokes walk out of a small building in the distance. I walked into the building and was overjoyed to find a soldier selling cokes, cigarettes, peanuts, and crackers. I took two warm cokes and a handful of assorted trash to eat.

"Forty-five cents, Sir."

I pulled out a one-dollar bill and handed it to the enlisted man.

"Oh, sorry, Sir. I can't take American green. That's illegal here, you know."

"Well, could I trade it for some military money?"

"Not here, Sir."

"Where, then?"

"I don't know."

"Who does?"

"I don't know. MPC window at the air base is closed by now."

"I really want a coke."

"Sorry, Sir, can't take green."

"May I have a drink of water?"

"There's a water buffalo around behind this building, Sir."

"Yes, but——"

"Right around back."

Behind the building was a small, tank-shaped, two-wheeled trailer with several faucets on one side. I returned to the building. "May I borrow a glass, or cup, or something?"

"I don't have any, Sir. The trash barrel is filled with empty coke cans."

Three coke-cans full of water and one bummed cigarette later, I leaned back against my seabag and felt much better. I waited.

This day counted! I had started my tour in Vietnam. One day was almost over. I was one day shorter. After months of anxiety, weeks of planning, and hours of travel, my tour was finally underway. War zone. Combat pay. I had earned over thirty dollars today standing in lines. It wasn't worth it, but what was really important was that this day counted.

It seemed to get dark rather suddenly. Then it started raining, but managed somehow to remain hot. I crowded my body and seabag back into the marine forms which filled the Marine Air Freight building. No one seemed to notice the rain. When the truck came, I lifted my seabag and walked out into the rain. Unfortunately, about thirty other soldiers did the same thing, and it appeared obvious to me that we were not all going to fit on the dump-truck sized vehicle.

Without any conversation, the driver and his helper threw the suitcases, seabags, and back packs into the truck. Soldiers climbed in on top of them.

It was raining very heavily, and the roadside had already turned to mud. It was dark enough that the traffic on the road needed headlights to travel. We could have been on any dirt road in the world.

When we stopped, our bodies actually spilled over the sides and out of the back of the truck. All of the gear was thrown off into a giant mud puddle, and the truck was gone.

In the darkness it was impossible to tell which of the mud-covered seabags bore the white ink printing I had so carefully placed there in California. I felt the bottoms of several bags before I found a bulge which felt like a 2,052 page Harrison's fourth edition of *Principles of Internal Medicine*. I carried my gear into a poorly-lighted room that looked identical to the Marine Air Freight building. It was equally filled with waiting soldiers. Some of them had formed a line at the far end of the room.

My first day in Vietnam had not been a total loss as far as a learning experience goes. I immediately got in the line without any idea of where it led and why.

Over the next hour, as the line inched forward, I slowly edged out of the building into the rain again, and then into the front door of a small wooden hut. When I finally reached the front of the line, there was a lance corporal seated behind a table with a clipboard and paper.

"Hi, I'm——"

"Orders?"

"Yes, here they are," I pulled two dripping wet papers from my shirt pocket. "I'm Doctor——"

"Hooch fourteen, rack twenty. We're out of blankets and towels. Next!"

"Which way is——"

"Wooden planks down to your right. Last hooch up against the runway. Next!"

"Thanks."

"Next."

Bed twenty was occupied, so I found an empty cot in the corner of the wooden-framed, screen-enclosed, tin-roofed structure and leaned my muddy seabag against it as a symbol of squatter's rights.

"Hi, I'm Doctor Parrish. I'm new in Vietnam."

"That's too bad. I've only got thirteen days left, and I'm going on R and R tomorrow."

"Where can I get something to eat?"

"Chow hall is closed."

I began removing my wet clothes.

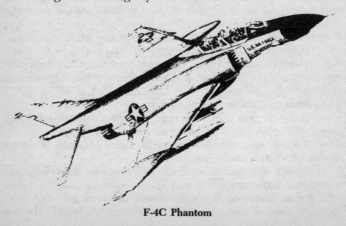

**F-4C Phantom**

"Hey, Doc, that's my rack you got there."

"Sorry." I moved again to another empty cot.

"Hey, Doc, ya want to go into Da Nang with us? We got a vehicle."

"No thanks. I think I could use some sleep. You see, I——"

"Well, you won't get any here. When the phantoms start..."

"The what?"

"The fucking phantom jets. They take off right down this runway all night long."

Dry shorts, T-shirt, and the prone position were so great that I could almost forget my hunger and fatigue. My cot was gritty with moist sand, and mosquitoes were battling over territory on my ankles. People continued to walk in and out of the room without communicating. I closed my eyes hoping that sleep would come before loneliness.

At first, I thought it was thunder. But it lasted too long, and, then, it headed straight toward me. It sounded like a freight train whistling in a tunnel, but it approached at unbelievable speed. Streaking, screaming, rumbling. Just before it hit my bed, it blasted into a controlled explosion which streaked past me and tore at my eardrums. At first, I was just startled. Then I was frozen with a fear that pushed in my neck and head and created a vacuum in my chest and stomach. Suddenly I remembered where I was. I remembered Camp Pendleton. I rolled off the bed onto the floor and covered my head.

I waited. Was that laughter around me now?

"Hey, Doc, you okay?"

"Hey, Doc, that was a phantom jet taking off. An F-4C. When it takes off, it turns on its afterburner and makes a hell of a noise."

"Just a jet taking off, Doc."

"If you roll out of bed everytime a phantom takes off, you'll get sore elbows. That goes on all night long."

"Well, that's kind of embarrassing. I thought we were being hit. I'm new here, and——"

"That's too bad. I've only got thirteen days left, and tomorrow I'm going on R and R."

I was prepared the next time a jet took off. But even then it seemed that the pilot had gotten confused. He was

headed right for my bed. I was done for. The afterburners
exploded past me. I had survived again. My fingers slowly
began to loosen their vicelike grip on the sides of the cot. I
was ready to go home. Enough war zone. To hell with combat
pay.

Scratchy canvass, mosquitoes, and phantom jets took
turns keeping me awake until daylight. With the early-
morning, sleep-deprivation shakes, I managed to cut my neck
in several places trying to shave without a mirror. The chow
hall opened at five thirty, and, for the price of standing in line
again, provided a good hot meal and coffee to brace me for
more lines back at Marine Air Freight.

One hour of line-standing and two hours of waiting got
me into a large, four engine, turboprop for the fifty-minute
ride to Phu Bai. We walked in through the tail section and
toward the front of the big C-130. People kept coming and
coming. We were packed in like sardines. Then, someone
told us all to sit down. Since the human form takes up much
more floor space when sitting than when standing, we were
all over each other. Everyone whose hands could reach the
floor held onto a series of straps that crisscrossed the deck.
After some effort the first engine started. The noise and
vibration were transmitted directly to our tangled jungle of
bodies. The effect was additive as each engine, in turn,
congested, sputtered, tried, and exploded. This monster was
going to fall apart before it even started rolling!

The big rear door began to close, seemed to get stuck,
and then closed further. The craft jerked forward crushing
those in the rear as we were thrown back. The noise of
metallic stress and strain, and the hiss of escaping exhaust,
and the squeaks of effort were more frightening than the
uncertain chatter of the engines. I did not want to chance my
life on this bird's ability to fly.

We sat sweating, waiting, and vibrating at the end of the
runway. Suddenly, we lurched forward and began to pick up
speed. Everyone fell backward on his neighbors. We were
going faster and faster—but, obviously, not fast enough. This
thing would never get off the ground! An awful hiss spewed
from the roof. Steam was escaping into the cabin. Were we
losing altitude? No one looked frightened.

Cross-legged. Cramped. Vibrating. The pain in my lower
back had to be ignored. I wanted to sleep. I did.

We were falling! No one looked frightened. Vibrating more than ever, we were flying slightly nose down. Our wheels touched. Why hadn't someone warned me about these frightening noises? Pressurized cabins, air conditioners, and padded seats had made me forget that it's always just you and a big machine and carefully bent metals way up in the sky making it. The C-130 did not let me forget.

I found my seabag and walked toward a big red cross painted on a blast wall next to the airstrip. Just beyond a helicopter landing pad, several white, wooden, one-story structures were grouped at one edge of the airstrip. A sign read, "A Medical Company. Third Medical Battalion. Third Marine Division." Inside the nearest structure a Medical Service Corps (MSC) officer sat behind a metal desk.

"Hi, I'm Doctor Parrish. I'm new here, and I——"

"Oh, yes, you'll have to go over to the Division Surgeon's office to check in. He's the number one doctor for the whole Third Marine Division. I'll get you a vehicle and a driver." He went out the back door of the hut and returned with a marine.

"This driver will take you to the Division Surgeon's office. There you will receive your first assignment. Maybe it will be with us here at A Med. I hope so. Don't forget that military doctors above the rank of lieutenant commander are to be addressed by their rank instead of as 'doctor.' The Division Surgeon is a navy captain. Captain Street."

Somehow, during that monologue, he had managed to light up a cigarette, pour a cup of coffee, and offer me both. "You can leave your gear here. Just put it over in the corner. It will be all right here."

It was a pleasure to put down that seabag.

"But on the other hand, you may not be back here if you get assigned to another outfit. Guess you'd better take it with you."

The driver picked up my bag and took it out to his jeep.

"Thanks very much," I said, as I left the MSC office.

"Oh, you're more than welcome. Anytime we can help, just let us know. That's what we're here for. The driver will . . ."

He was still talking when the jeep started up and left. We drove into the flat, sandy complex, which had countless rows of identical wood-framed structures with screen walls and tin-peaked roofs. One of them read, "Division Surgeon. Third Marine Division. Capt. Charles S. Street. USN."

Captain Street was in his late forties, prematurely gray, and generally unimpressive. He was addressing seven of my former Camp Pendleton "classmates" when I arrived.

We introduced ourselves and stated our home states and places of training. Any special training beyond internship was listed beneath our names on the blackboard. There were four doctors straight from internship, one anesthesiologist, one general surgeon, and two partially trained internists. The four without specialty training were immediately assigned to infantry battalions, three of which were out in the field on maneuvers. The remaining four of us were assigned to the hospital company in Phu Bai.

Captain Street walked with us to the hospital compound to show us our new place of work. He was in no hurry. He had spent his entire tour of duty in Phu Bai except when in Da Nang on business. He was going home in eighty more days, and anything that would take up a few hours, or even minutes, was welcome. We were his most recent time passers.

The hospital company was on the edge of the compound situated next to the airstrip. The location not only made it easy to receive casualties, but also placed the hospital directly adjacent to the prime target for enemy mortars or rockets. The airstrip was always an early target during any kind of enemy attack.

The building farthest from the airstrip was a single, wooden "hooch" with a large, mobile, refrigeration unit attached to the rear of the building. Three layers of sandbags protected each side. The sign on the front read, "Graves Registration."

Street did not even slow down as we passed. "This is Graves," he said, as we walked by the front of the building. "This is the only part of the hospital company completely staffed by marines. From the field, the dead come directly here where they are washed down, identified, and put in the freezer until the next flight south. They are embalmed in Da Nang or Saigon before shipment back to the States. The marines who staff this place are 'grunts' (foot soldiers) who volunteer for this duty, usually because they are cowards. Some are being punished. Others may be mentally ill or may want to be embalmers someday. On a hot, busy day this place smells terrible." Street seemed disgusted not only with the marines who worked in Graves, but also with anybody who would be stupid or inconsiderate enough to get killed on a hot and busy day.

We passed two large portable units that looked like large inflated tubes. "These are the MUST (Medical Unit Self-Contained Transportable) units; one is used as a medical ward, and the other as a surgery ward. The smaller units are attached to the main building. They house our operating rooms. We have six O.R.'s and an X-ray unit. Helicopters land here on the edge of the airstrip, and the casualties go directly to the main casualty sorting area called triage."

As Captain Street was talking, a helicopter settled down beyond us. Several marines ran out from the main building to meet the craft. They were handed a stretcher with a wounded marine, and the helicopter was gone. The stretcher bearers ran past us carrying a big Negro kid. He was completely nude. His M16 hung over the stretcher handle, and his boots rode between his legs. He was so black that the mud on his skin was light by comparison. He was long and muscular, and his spidery fingers curled tightly around the sides of the bouncing litter. His whole body was glistening with sweat that reflected highlights of the bright morning sun. The sweat on his forehead did not drip. It remained like tiny drops of oil and glue fastened tightly to his skin.

His eyelids were forced widely apart, and his stare was straight ahead into nowhere, seeing nothing, having seen too much. He threw back his head, and his white teeth parted as

M 16

if he were trying to speak, to curse, to cry. A spasm of
intolerable pain wrenched the muscles of his face into a mask
that hid a grinning skeleton beneath. His chest heaved
rapidly. The muscles of his steel arms bulged as he grasped
the muddy stretcher. A small hole in his rigid abdomen
permitted a steady snake of red and brown to spill onto the
litter. The fluids created red blacks and brown purples on the
green canvass. His left knee was flexed, and his long,
uncircumsized penis lay over on his right upper thigh. His
left foot arched as his toes grasped for the litter.

As he passed by, he raised his head almost involuntarily.
It seemed as if the contracting straps of his neck muscles
would tear off his jaw should his head not rise. His neck veins
swelled in protest. His mouth began to open, at first for air,
but then as a silent plea for help. He extended his dirty hand
directly toward me, and I turned to follow him into triage.

Captain Street had not noticed him go by. He was still
talking about the compound—something about the marines
putting the retaining wall in the wrong place. He was ready
to show us triage.

It was a large, open room measuring fifteen by twenty
meters. Reinforced on the outside with sandbags, the walls
protected floor-to-ceiling shelves filled with bandages, first-
aid gear, and bottles of intraveous fluids. An unprotected tin
roof was supported by four-by-fours. At the time, there were
six men lined up on stretchers supported at either end by two
lightweight metal sawhorses. Several doctors and corpsmen
were quickly, but unexcitedly, working over the wounded.
Captain Street was still talking, but I couldn't listen any
longer.

On the first stretcher lay a boy whom, earlier in the day,
any coach would have wanted as a tackle or a defensive end.
But now, as he lay on his back, his left thigh pointed skyward
and ended in a red brown, meaty mass of twisted ligaments,
jellylike muscle, blood clots, and long bony splinters. There
was no knee, and parts of the lower leg hung loosely by skin
strips and fascial strings. A tourniquet had been placed
around his thigh, and a corpsman was cutting through the
strips of tissue with shears to remove the unviable dangling
calf. Lying separately on the stretcher was a boot from which
the lower leg still protruded.

In the second position a sweating doctor was administering

closed cardiac massage on a flaccid, pale, thin boy with multiple wounds. A second doctor was bag breathing the boy. The vigorous chest compression seemed to be producing only the audible cracking of ribs.

In position three was the boy who minutes earlier had been carried past us. He already had intravenous fluids running into his arm, and a bandage was in place over his abdomen. He was vigorously protesting efforts to turn him over in order to examine his back. Positions four and five were occupied by two nude bodies quietly awaiting treatment. Their wounds were not serious. The next few positions for litters were empty. Off in the corner (position ten) lay a young man with his head wrapped tightly in blood-soaked, white bandages. No part of his body moved except for the slow, unsteady respiratory efforts of his chest. He had an endotracheal tube emerging from his nose, and each respiration made a grunting snort. No one was paying any attention to this man—a hopelessly damaged brain was awaiting death.

Captain Street never looked directly at any of the casualties. He showed us the rest of the hospital compound and left us with the hospital commander, a general surgeon who proved to be an intolerable, immature, egotistical, Napoleonic SOB, and an excellent surgeon. I liked him from the very first.

"Welcome to Vietnam," he said.

# THREE

The hospital commander showed us every building on the compound and introduced us to the other doctors. A concrete, covered walkway joined all the wooden one-story structures. Each small hut had screen walls, wooden floor, and a tin roof. Some contained rows of simple, collapsible metal beds; some were set up with tables and equipment for debriding and dressing minor wounds; others were used as operating rooms or housed X-ray equipment.

About fifty meters beyond this tightly grouped complex of buildings was the doctors' quarters. Five men lived in each of ten small wooden huts, or hooches. It was there I met my new "hoochmates"—the four men who would become my new family. For the next six months I would live in Hooch 75 and together we would go through some of the most physically stressful and emotionally tiring experiences of our lives.

It was clear that number 75 was an important hooch. Its members included the Third Marine Division's only fully-trained internist, the only psychiatrist, the Chief of Surgery for the hospital compound, and the marine captain in charge of Motor Transport for the hospital company and in charge of all of the marines assigned to the hospital company acting as drivers, litter bearers, and local labor force. I was outranked and outpowered, but no one seemed to pay much attention to such matters. They did, however, constantly remind me that they had been "in country" (in Vietnam) before my arrival and would rotate to CONUS (Continental USA) before I did. I soon became aware of my hoochmates' everyday activities, personal likes, dislikes, and peculiarities, and, usually, of each one's whereabouts at any time during the day.

If there was a father image in the hooch it was Prince

Edwards, the Division Psychiatrist. He was a thirty-six-year-old bachelor who was bright, opinionated, and slightly asexual. His average-sized body was flabby without being fat, and the only descriptive feature of his face was his short, bushy Hitler mustache. Only a psychiatrist could get away with being as "nonmilitary" as was Prince. He was often seen after hours in bermudas, dress slacks, or underpants, but always with an ascot. When the commanding general finally decided his hair was too long, he shaved his head completely but continued to sport a mustache. His locker was so full of delicious goodies sent by his mother that he could go for days without going to the chow hall.

Prince had trained a small group of older corpsmen so well that they could handle almost any psychiatric emergency, and he was, therefore, seldom busy after 4 P.M. Each day he spent six or seven hours interviewing psychiatric casualties. Usually they were single interviews to decide disposition. Patients were then returned to their units, to rear elements, or back to the USA. Those few he found most interesting and/or treatable he could keep for intensive short-term psychotherapy.

Only the more seriously disturbed marines got to the Division Psychiatrist; most were treated in the field or in battalion aid stations by the general medical officers. Besides acute battle fatigue or anxiety reactions, Prince saw boys accused of homosexuality or drug use, young men caught with hard-core pornography by a righteous superior, and victims of alcoholism. Many of his cases, however, were discipline problems, borderline psychopaths and sociopaths who had trouble relating to authority figures long before entering the service. Prince enjoyed his work and seemed to be a good psychiatrist. His position demanded respect because a statement from him could make you crazy by definition. That was very, very bad if it marred your service record, or very, very good if it sent you home.

"You're a doctor, and hopefully, a rational, mature, and responsible person," Prince Edwards said to me on our first meeting. "If ever you've had more than you can take, if the stress is going to break you, just tell me that you want a psychiatric medevac home, and you'll get it. No interview, no questions, just fill out a few papers and you'll be on your way home within a few hours." He spoke with a half smile, but really meant it. "No need for anybody to go to the trouble of demonstrating or acting out that they're breaking, just tell me."

"Oh, I'll try it for a few days," I smiled.

"Well, if you decide to stay, your share of the refrigerator is fifteen dollars." Prince went back to reading his book. He was always reading a book.

"And there's beer in there now if you want one." Bill Bond motioned toward the small, portable refrigerator with one hand as he shook my hand with the other. He was a handsome, self-assured surgeon from the Midwest. The wife and children pictured on his dresser looked as wholesome as he did. He was always either operating at the hospital or reading in the hooch. He was pleasant, agreeable, a very good surgeon, and the most stable member of our hooch.

"You may as well meet me, too." Marine Capt. Roland Ames was polishing his boots. "Although you won't have time to get to know me. I've only got two hundred eighteen days left in country." Roland was an honor graduate of Annapolis who somehow managed to get tied up in the marines. His immediate goal was to survive a tour in Vietnam, and to keep two engagements going by mail so that in 218 days he would still be alive and have the option of either—or neither—girl His long-range goal was to be a professor of military history. He wore his dog tags outside his T-shirt just like in a World War II movie. "If you ever need a jeep, just let me know. I'm Motor Transport."

"You'll never get one." Myron Stanley, the Division Internist, was opening a letter from home. "I've been trying to get a jeep to go to the PX for three weeks now, and all I get is promises, promises." He was a slightly pudgy, slow-speaking and easy-going Southern Baptist from Memphis, Tennessee, whose only regular vices were smoking and insomnia. He kept reading his letter as he introduced himself.

"Say, fellows, my wife has stopped working because her uterus is so big. The doctor says she's doin' fine."

"Say, that's great, Myron."

"Golly gee, I'm so happy."

"Have a beer, Myron, old man."

The sarcasm was so thick that I was afraid Myron would be wounded. Instead, he gave me a knowing smile and said, "Don't mind these sinners, you'll get used to them. You may even learn to like them. They're kinda cute—you know—like puppies." He was immediately struck from different directions by three flying pillows. I felt so at home that I hit him with a pillow myself.

Myron Stanley was extremely pleased to find out that I, too, was an internist, and he quickly made me his assistant. The two of us would run sick call, read all the chest X-rays, and manage the medical wards. During the rest of the day or night I would function as a general medical officer (GMO) giving first aid to casualties and assisting in the operating room. Myron turned out to be much more of a colleague than a boss. We shared responsibility for malaria, fevers, diarrhea, and chest pains.

"Ever treat a snake bite?" Myron asked as he showed me the Quonset hut being used as a medical ward.

"No, don't think I've ever even seen one," I answered almost apologetically.

"Well, starting tomorrow you are the Third Marine Division snake expert. Starting today you can read a whole box full of books about snake bites that just arrived from Washington. From now on anybody in I Corps who is bitten by a snake will be brought to you."

"Thanks." I almost meant it.

"In the next few days we'll get a message out to the corpsmen and doctors in the field telling them what kind of immediate first aid to initiate while awaiting transportation. You figure out what to say, and I'll see that the info gets distributed."

"I'll do it." I learned to identify all kinds of snakes and treat their bites. We kept various antisera on hand. It was also necessary to learn to identify snakes by their body color and scales because marines almost always killed the snake by destroying its head with a rock or a bullet. Over the next ten months, we saw six poisonous and sixteen nonpoisonous snake bites and the only fatality was that of a marine killed by a land mine while chasing a harmless garden snake that had bitten his buddy.

On my second day in Phu Bai I began my full-time work. I was quite nervous my first day up in triage. The average medical training in the USA does not make a doctor an expert in treating severe trauma victims. One of the experienced general medical officers remained with me to assist and instruct. At the emergency rooms in the University Hospital there was always plenty of knowledge and experience available within seconds. At the University Hospital I could always punt to the surgeons when a trauma case arrived. Soon I would be seeing many trauma victims who were very young, very hurt, and I would be very much responsible for them.

Where would I start when some poor kid full of holes was placed before me? What would I do when some mud-soaked, bloody limb came off in my hands? Anxiety and that uncomfortable feeling of impending disaster made my first morning treating casualties seem very long. It was a slow morning, and I treated only five or six minor wounds. Most of the morning was spent chatting with the doctors and corpsmen. Maybe this was not going to be such a bad job.

At about noon, five badly wounded marines were rushed into the triage area. There were two other doctors in triage at the time. By quick inspection it was obvious that two of the wounded men would live until we had more time, so each of the three doctors began to work on one of the more critically injured marines.

The young man I evaluated had a head injury. His skull was broken and he was bleeding profusely. I put a pressure dressing over the vertex of his scalp, started an IV, drew blood for type and crossmatch, and examined him from head to foot.

The senior surgeon in charge of triage that day was Bill Bond, my hoochmate. He checked each litter to see the extent of injuries to decide who needed to go to the operating room. He was the final judge regarding priorities of treatment. He approached my station last. My chance to do my best to impress my new friend.

"Yes, head injury," I began. "Blood pressure still good, pulse is steady. Pupils are dilated. He has decerebrate posture at times."

Dr. Bond was not even listening. He pulled off my poorly made bandage as I continued.

"Lungs are clear, abdomen is soft——"

He grabbed a handful of scalp hair and raised the marine's head up off the litter at which time a large part of his mashed brain tissue slid like jelly out of his broken skull and onto the litter.

"No other evidence of injury," I continued. "His——"

He let the head flop back down. "Are you shitting me?" he said. He gave me a brief look as if I were crazy and then hurried off to help the other doctors as I talked on.

"His corneal reflex is absent and——"

"We usually just leave these, Sir. Not much we can do." A corpsman had been watching the whole sequence of events. There followed a silence that made me feel empty and helpless.

"I know. I know," I said finally. "I guess I'm used to a little different approach. I just——"

"We don't always have time to be nice, Sir. You'll get used to it. Do you want me to put him over in the corner, Sir?"

"Corner? To wait to die?"

"Yes, Sir."

"Sure. Sure. Corner. Anywhere. I——" I walked out of triage toward my hooch. I was soaked with sweat, felt slightly nauseated and very inadequate.

"Parrish."

I wheeled around. "Yes?"

"You want to scrub? We need help in the operating room," Bill called after me.

"Yes, I'd like to scrub." I was lying. "Show me the way."

Bill was an excellent surgeon. His competence, honesty, and friendliness made it almost pleasant even for an internist to assist in surgery. We spent about two hours in a nineteen-year-old abdomen leaving the small bowel two feet shorter but no longer leaking—and leaving me feeling more useful.

After about a week of spending several hours each day treating casualties, I began to feel more comfortable working alone. It was, however, always good to have more experienced doctors available. Men who had been in Vietnam for only a short time, and came from extremely varied training and work backgrounds, became competent in treating critically injured boys and in delivering the highest quality medical care. Under the stresses of necessity and responsibility, and with a constant volume of work, they not only became technically skilled, but also developed excellent judgment.

"The most important quality in being a good doctor in Vietnam is the same as for being a good doctor anywhere—and that is to give a shit," Bill Bond told me. "It helps to be smart, to work hard, to have technical skills, but if you have a little judgment and you really give a shit, you'll be a good doctor."

All the doctors were willing to help one another. If a colleague stabilized his patient while I was still working, he quickly moved to assist me. In a few days, my fellow doctors taught me more about trama management than I had learned in six years of training. Bill was my favorite instructor.

"Ever put in a chest tube, John?"

"No."

"Well, watch me put this one in, and then you put one in the fellow behind you in position seven."

In the next twenty-four hours I put in seven chest tubes and became pretty good at it. I even learned how to do a little side step at the time of thrust to avoid getting blood all over my pants when the tube entered the chest cavity.

The corpsmen were aggressive, motivated, and very helpful. Those who had been in triage for several weeks could anticipate the doctor's every move and always had the correct instrument, tube, or needle available. The shelves were constantly restocked. The blood bank was always fast and efficient. The X-ray technicians knew what pictures to take by looking at the entrance wounds. We were geared up to serve the wounded, and we did a damn good job.

No matter how stressful, irregular, or unpredictable the environment may be, man can establish a routine. My goal was to get up, dress, shave, go to 'Graves Registration to pronounce the dead who had accumulated during the night, and get to the chow hall before they stopped serving breakfast at seven-thirty. I got to where I could do this and still sleep until seven o'clock—but it was always close. The fellows in Graves soon caught onto my tight schedule, and at seven twenty they always had the papers ready and the bodies exposed. Sometimes they even had the cause-of-death paragraph already filled in.

After breakfast I would run back to wake up Myron. While he was trying to get out of bed, it was time to stand in line for my turn in the "shitter." Sleeping on sandy cots, existing on cold C rations, and smelling like three weeks of accumulated body grime seemed like very manly inconveniences, but somehow group defecation was damaging to one's dignity.

Side by side, all respectfully facing north by northwest, were four small wooden frames. The interior of each was done in unfinished plywood dominated by a four-hole sitting board elevated three feet above the floor. A narrow foot board ran along the base. A swinging trapdoor in the rear admitted bisected oildrums for placement beneath each hole in the sitting board. Only the bottom half of the structure was closed in with plywood so that the straining faces of those sitting above each hole could survey the camp while splashing their wastes into six inches of diesel fuel in the waiting tub. Each day an old Vietnamese man came by, removed the tubs, burned the contents, and replaced them through the trapdoor.

The commanding officer had a private one-holer, the officers a four-holer, and the enlisted men a crowded six-holer. The Vietnamese working in the area shared a four-holer partitioned so that males and females each had two holes.

Always glad to have the shitter scene behind me, I was ready to begin my day. By now, Myron, who did not eat or defecate in the morning, would be stumbling sleepily around the hooch complaining that he had not gotten to sleep until two or three or four in the morning because of the artillery H & I fire (harassment and interdiction—outgoing artillery shells fired at random into unfriendly territory to upset and confuse the enemy), insomnia, bellyache, homesickness, or whatever. While he dressed, I would take a can of water out into the yard to brush my teeth. Usually, while I was out behind the hooch, the little bargirl named Sun who worked in the "O" Club, and slept in a tiny room attached to the rear of the club, would wake up, step out in the yard, stretch in the morning air, and make her way to the Vietnamese outhouse to relieve her morning-full bladder.

She always gave a big smile and chirped a "Good morning, Bác Sĩ." I always looked forward to seeing her at toothbrush time. Occasionally, if she didn't wake up, I'd make unnecessary noise to arouse her. If no one was looking, I'd even stick my head inside her door and awaken her.

I couldn't imagine that this cute little package could live right on base and not be raped, prostituted, or at least possessed. But rumor had it that the intelligence officers who occupied the hooch immediately behind the Officers' Club were assigned the job of keeping an eye on Sun; if she were found with a visitor in her quarters, she would be without a job, and the visitor would be in big trouble with the C.O. (commanding officer). Some people thought the C.O., who had the only private hooch, occasionally "entertained" Sun. Every morning I watched her walk to the outhouse. She always turned around and smiled to me at about the same spot—right where the boards went over the irrigation ditch.

Once Sun was in the shitter, I would return to the hooch to prod Myron on toward the medical ward where a cup of coffee and a menthol cigarette would jolt him to his senses and make him nauseated. Roland Ames, the marine captain, always left for Motor Transport Headquarters while I was at breakfast. Prince Edwards slept until 9 A.M. before going to begin his psychiatric interviews over coffee and canned goods from home. Bill slept until the first casualties arrived for the operating room—helicopters could get in as early as first light (5:30–6:00 A.M.), but the first fixed-wing aircraft with casualties from farther north did not arrive until about ten thirty.

Myron and I made rounds each morning in the medical ward. The corpsmen rounding with us already had the fever charted and the nursing notes up to date. They kept us informed on white blood counts, urinalyses, malaria smears, and stool smears for ova or parasites—the only laboratory tests available. We made notes on the charts, wrote orders, and filled out medevac (medical evacuation) forms for those patients to be sent farther to the rear or to CONUS.

We kept those with illnesses that we predicted would last five days or less, and those with gastrointestinal parasites. We initiated their treatment, observed them for a day or two, and then returned them to the rear elements of their own units for further convalescence where the battalion surgeon decided when they were fit for full duty in the field. We began doing bedside sigmoidoscopy (an internal rectal examination with a long tubular instrument) on those with severe diarrhea, and, after the first few dozen, were able to anticipate the laboratory diagnosis by hours to days, and sometimes based treatment solely on our observations. Those with positive malaria smears were treated in Phu Bai for one week, and then sent to Cam Rahn Bay for two weeks of further treatment and convalescence before returning to their units. Soldiers with hepatitis, second episodes of malaria, deep thrombophlebitis, or recurrent diarrhea were sent out

of Vietnam to hospital ships, Japan, or CONUS, and did not
return to finish their tours of duty in the war zone.

After rounds, Myron and I went to the surgery ward and
the recovery unit to visit, to consult on medical problems,
and to get a second cup of coffee. We carried our coffee to X
ray where we read from twenty to forty chest films of soldiers
and civilians sent from the hospital company sick call, or from
the local military doctors. We then dropped by sick call
which had started at 9 A.M., and saw all the patients the
GMO's had selected to be seen by the internists.

After lunch we worked up new admissions and helped in
afternoon sick call. Myron usually managed to get a one-to-
two-hour nap. My schedule was interrupted several times
daily when casualties arrived and needed stabilization in
triage. Even the casualties eventually fell into a routine. Most
of them came by fixed-wing aircraft from Dong Ha—a front-
line clearing hospital farther north.

Any infantryman, (or grunt, as they preferred to be
called) wounded in the field was transported, usually within
minutes, by helicopter to D Med (D Medical Company) at
Dong Ha, a supply depot several miles from the DMZ. Here,
in a partially bunkered hospital compound within reach of the
heavy enemy artillery in the DMZ, the casualties were
stabilized, given blood and IV fluids, and even operated on if
immediate surgery was the only chance for life. Minutes to
hours later, depending on the time of day and how rapidly
casualties accumulated, they were loaded onto large, fixed-
wing aircraft and flown south to A Med, our hospital company
in Phu Bai where definitive surgery and treatment was
performed. Nonfatal brain injuries and kidney injuries were
again stabilized and flown farther to the hospital ship or to Da
Nang.

The two most reliable fixed-wing medevac flights from D
Med usually arrived at 10:30 A.M. and 2:00 P.M. Others came
scattered throughout the day or night depending on the
number of casualties to be handled, or the intensity of
incoming artillery. We were radio warned in advance as to
how many casualties to expect. Thus, we could have an
appropriate number of physicians on hand. Three numbers
were announced in triage. The first represented the number
of litter-borne wounded, the second the number of ambulatory wounded, and the third represented the number of dead.

"Six, ten, and two, Sir," a corpsman announced as I made my way through triage on my way back to the medical ward, "arriving in twenty minutes."

"Oh, that's not bad. I'll be in the medical ward. Call me if the fellows need help."

"One of them is a snake bite, Sir."

"Oh, good. Well, I'll be back in a few minutes then." Just enough time to go back to my hooch to review my snake identification chart.

None of the wounds were very bad. Three required O.R. time. The rest were minor debridements, fevers, or diarrhea.

"Here's your snake bite, John." Bill was in charge of triage again.

A very frightened marine with jet black hair and olive skin and a medevac tag labeled "Sabatino, Anthony" was hyperventilating.

"I didn't catch the snake. We were in the water—I didn't even get a good look at him. He bit me on my leg. I don't wanna die, Doc. You gotta do somethin'."

"How long ago were you bitten?" I began to unbandage his leg and remove an already loose tourniquet.

"This morning sometime, maybe three hours ago."

"Where is the bite? You mean these two scratches?"

"Yes, Sir. It doesn't hurt much yet, but I think it was a bamboo viper."

I smiled. "Mr. Sabatino, you will get a tetanus shot, a hot meal, a good night's sleep, and tomorrow you'll rejoin your unit. If I have trouble finding the site of your bite after three hours, you're going to be fine. A poisonous snake bite is swollen and hurts like hell within an hour."

Embarrassment was overshadowed by relief. "Thank you, Sir."

"And next time you get bitten by a snake, get here sooner."

"Yes, Sir. Yes, Sir. Anybody got a cigarette?"

Any number of casualties that included more than ten to fifteen litter patients was considered "mass casualties," and all doctors of the hospital company reported to triage. It was an impressive roll call: one thoracic surgeon, one oral surgeon, five general surgeons, three orthopedic surgeons, three anesthesiologists, and ten general medical officers. The only

other time we were all in one place was in the "O" Club at
four thirty on a slow day.

My afternoon goal was to finish my work in time to lift
weights or to go for a run and a shower before meeting my
hoochmates at four thirty or five in the hooch. We made it an
unwritten and unspoken rule of etiquette to wait until all
hooch members were present before going to the club. Bill
often didn't make it, because he was operating, and Myron
often didn't go, because he didn't drink and usually was
taking a nap. This left a bizarre trio of "O" Club regulars:
Prince Edwards, who was probably crazy because he was a
psychiatrist; Roland Ames, who by definition was a psycho-
path because he was a marine; and me, a skinny nut with
glasses who could be seen late in the afternoon in shorts and
boots running in the hundred degree oppressive heat.

The Officers' Club was actually just another hooch with a
bar at one end and tables and chairs instead of beds. One of
the navy chiefs acted as bartender, and Sun was the barmaid.
Sun was a small, energetic Vietnamese woman. Her breasts
were full, but slightly low set, and her hips were almost too
wide. Her smile was a tease, and she seemed to have no
frowns. She always wore a silk ao dai, the traditional Vietnamese
female dress with long silk pants and a bright colored tunic
split from floor to waist on each side.

"Kinda cute little piece." Prince smoked a cigar and
leaned back in his chair to watch Sun walk away from our
table. A large ash fell on his purple ascot and tumbled onto
his green T-shirt.

"I'm surprised you noticed," said Roland as he set down
his second empty beer can.

"Just because I don't feel obligated to discuss every
erection, mass peristalsis, and uncensored urge, doesn't mean
I don't appreciate the aesthetically appealing," retorted Prince
on the counterattack. He never seemed to get angry, but he
expressed varying degrees of friendly aggression.

"The only sex you know about comes from talking to
perverted marines. Remind me not to shower with you."
Roland spoke without looking at Prince because he was
signaling Sun for another round of beers.

"No worry, you don't shower. Just because I don't imagine every woman as a giant vagina with legs, just because I

don't analyze everything I see as to how it would feel to thrust my penis into it——"

"The last twat that stimulated you was your mother's as you left the uterus. And don't give me this 'thrust-your-penis' bullshit. I——"

"Hey, Roland, wait a minute," I interrupted. "Thrusting-your-penis bullshit? I mean, that's real nice talk. What if Myron was here and heard you talk like that."

"I am here, what's up?" Myron had just walked in.

Roland moved over to make room. "Oh, nothing, Mr. Coke, just 'thrust-your-penis bullshit.'"

"What?"

I stood. "Let's eat it."

"Let's eat it!" cried Roland, and we marched out toward the chow hall. Roland pinched Sun as we left. She thought it was me and smiled.

It took a late afternoon run, a couple of beers, and a lot of hunger to face the evening chow. Most of the dishes had no names but were some combination of C rations, hamburger, powdered potatoes, and reconstituted sauces—all tasting exactly the same, or worse. There was plenty of peanut butter and bread. If it was a particularly bad batch, or if we stayed at the "O" Club past closing of the chow hall, we always had Prince's pantry. The worst thing about chow time was the monstrous conversations—always either shop talk or small talk.

"How'd triage go this morning?"

"Kind of slow but this afternoon we had a nine, nineteen, and four from D Med and several wounded brought in by helicopter. They're all cleaned up now except a couple of amputations still in the O.R. and a couple of brain jobs waiting to cool."

"Who's doing the amps?"

"Bond's doing one. I forget who has the other. We're expecting another batch from D Med tonight. You want some more Kool-Aid?"

"How's the through 'n through of the liver?"

"Like all other liver wounds—dead."

"Did you have to remove that kidney?"

"No. Pass the sugar. We just drained it and left it. That kid is urinating already."

Hooch 75 usually sat together so we could eat our awful food in silence. Occasionally Prince would tell us about one of his best "crazies" for the day, or Roland would remind us that he had only 191 days left.

After supper, Myron and I went by the medical ward to check with the corpsmen on any problems. The corpsmen worked in shifts, so there were always at least two of them on the ward. Myron and I alternated being available at night for new admissions or for problems. Our morning rounds were slow, careful, methodical, and full of academic and theoretical discussions; while our evening rounds were fast, efficient, and practical, but not superficial.

"Who's on call tonight, Sir? Who do we wake up for three o'clock fever spike?" a corpsman might ask.

"I am on call, and, if you get a three o'clock fever spike, get a malaria smear and cool him down—you know what to do." I was trying a special type of preventative medicine designed for allowing a full night's sleep.

"Yes, Sir. I was only joking. Can Medlin go back to the field? He's been afebrile for thirty-six hours. He feels great, and he's a pain in the ass, Sir."

"We'll talk about that in the morning." I knew Myron was going to say that. "Any more problems?"

As we left, I reminded the corpsman, "I'll be at the movie and then in my hooch."

"Yes, Sir. Where else could you be?" he laughed.

He was right. Where-the-hell-else could I be?

Meals were so early and sunsets so late, that there were always at least two hours between supper and the evening movie. It was dark enough by eight o'clock to show a movie on the outdoor wooden screen. The two hour hiatus was the hardest time of the day. Business was usually slow. People's moods began to sag with the sun. The hard-core drinkers went back to the "O" Club. Others returned to their hooches to write letters, read, or just sit. Some sat on the ground, smoked, and chatted in small groups. Those who had any energy left played volleyball in front of the shitters. Those with their weekly diarrhea from the malaria pills had the best seats in the house.

This was Hooch 75's quiet period. Each of us usually stayed in his own small section of the room. Each had a small, collapsible bed, a homemade plywood desk, and a wooden, straight-backed chair. Each had a "hot box," a simple wooden box with a light bulb inside to keep the clothes from mildewing. Prince, of course, had a folding lawn chair, a velvet covered hot box, a large double desk, and his abundantly stocked food pantry. He took up more than his share of the hooch.

If we were going to drink, party, play cards, chat, wrestle, or watch the movie, we would always wait until dark to begin our group activities. The twilight hours were reserved for each man to be to himself—to think, suffer, regroup his defenses, or escape into fantasy.

Myron would take another nap or another shower. He was very fair and slightly obese. He showered frequently. He often went to the chaplain's quarters after supper to play hearts. Myron was very much like the chaplain. Jesus would have liked his sincerity, his offerings of emotional support, his attempts at being strong, but he probably wouldn't have hung around him much. Myron and the chaplain became close friends. What support God didn't offer, they supplied for each other.

Myron was constantly miserable, frightened, and homesick, but he was excellent at coping. He tolerated. He smiled, made friends, and worked hard. He encouraged others, listened to their complaints, and played supportive roles, but then would be awake all night in a nervous sweat of anxiety and homesickness.

Myron had to write his letters in the middle of the night, and read his mail for the first time out in the yard, because of tears and inability to talk. He didn't like to see his hoochmates drink, swear, or talk about sexual fantasies of R & R.

But Myron coped. He tolerated. And he was miserable.

Roland used quiet time to write letters. He wrote his two fiancées. He wrote his friends from the academy, and he wrote letters to the editors of magazines. He read books and magazines and drew up lengthy outlines, and then spent hours writing magnificent letters. He sat with a perfectly straight back on the front edge of his chair, chain smoked Marlboros and wrote. Occasionally as he leaned back to think, a prematurely balding vertex shined through the smoke in striking contrast with his adolescentlike face. Sometimes he polished his boots or his belt buckle as he thought between paragraphs or between letters. Sometimes he restarched his green hat, which already looked very crisp and

straight, and added an extra three inches to his height—just
enough to bring him up to about five feet nine inches.

Bill Bond read at his desk. He read after supper, and he
read in the morning. He always went with us when he was
invited to the "O" Club, or to the weight room, or for a run,
or to the movies, but, when left to his own devices, he was
either reading at his desk, or working in the operating room.
He never initiated any conversation, but, when addressed,
he usually had an interesting opinion. He was so all-American
looking that he had to be a football player, a movie star, or a
surgeon.

Prince spent this time cleaning up his desk, clipping his
nails, straightening his food shelves, and . . . actually, it was
never entirely clear what the hell Prince was always doing
over in his corner, but he always seemed very busy. Sometimes, when he sat and combed his Hitler mustache, he
looked at me in such a way that I felt uncomfortable. I wasn't
sure if I was being analyzed, seduced, or E.S.P.'d. Prince
often took a shower after supper, and somehow it was an hour
or two before his unmuscular body ever got dressed again.

The twilight hours were very difficult for me to handle. I
tried writing letters. I tried reading. But I couldn't concentrate. Sometimes I paced about the hooch or took a walk
outside. Twilight was my lowest time of day. It was wrong for
me to write letters, because they sounded too depressing
and bitter. It was not easy to make work for myself because I
could not bear to see another casualty, another fever, or
another homesick boy with diarrhea.

No book or story seemed relevant. I had already read all
about malaria, and snake bites, and tropical medicine. For
awhile I had read hard-core pornography, but I could tolerate
only small doses, because its arousing content served only to
make me more restless. The only novels that could hold my
interest were those in which the hero was either alone against
the elements, or hopelessly insane, or both. I even spent
evening after evening looking up words in the dictionary and
making voluminous lists of words and their meanings. I began
making notes of my thoughts and recording some of the
important events of the day.

My inability to handle the twilight hours played some
role in my decision to learn to speak Vietnamese. I used the
hours to study language booklets. A newly-made friend from

Intelligence, who had taught Vietnamese at Camp Pendleton, agreed to spend half an hour with me as a private tutor three or four times a week, and an hour or more on Sundays. I often skipped the movie and studied far into the night. I went back to the "O" Club after supper to talk with Sun in Vietnamese. She took her half-hour break with me to teach me Vietnamese, and we often spent from ten to eleven sitting on the ground in back of the hooch talking.

I grew to like Sun very much, and she always seemed happy to spend time with me. When our commanding general put a two-drink limit on all of Phu Bai, and closed all clubs at dark, most of the drinking took place in hooches. Sun had less work. She and I started going to the movies each night and whispering in Vietnamese.

Several other doctors became interested in speaking the language of the country. We had a lot of Vietnamese patients— both civilian and military—and the MEDCAP (Medical Civilian Action Program) program in the villes was growing. The Intelligence officer and I set up a course in taking a simple medical history in Vietnamese. Six doctors took the course. I began to act occasionally as interpreter in triage.

Each day Vietnamese girls came into each hooch to clean, wash clothes, polish boots, and iron. Each hooch had its own "housemouse," who spent from 9 A.M. to 3 P.M. working in the hooch. Some of these girls spoke very little English and loved to try to communicate with me in Vietnamese.

Despite studying Vietnamese, talking to Sun, working, writing letters, reading, and taking walks, it seemed that darkness would never come and bring an end to another day. At least, when darkness came, my hoochies would help me to pass the time.

"Hey, John, how about a little monopoly tonight?" Roland was polishing his boots again.

I looked up from my book but didn't answer.

Roland continued, "The movie is some kind of romantic shit. Or are you going to study that corn-ball Vietnamese again?" He walked over and popped the corner of my desk with his shoe rag. "Why do you want to chat with some ignorant cunt like Sun when you've got your hoochies right here? What's she got that we haven't got?"

"An ignorant cunt," I replied without looking up from my books.

"Chào Bác Sĩ," chided Prince. "What good is Vietnamese going to do you? Are you going to ship over and live in this paradise?"

"Right now it's keeping me out of your psychiatric ward, Shrink. And one more game of monopoly with you finks will put me in it."

"It's just that you never win." Roland was asking for it.

Bill joined in and pointed his finger at Roland. "No one wins but you or Prince, because you two homo's always join up together."

Roland started for Bill's bed, but I cut him off in the center of the room as he passed by. The two of us had a hell of a wrestling match which ended, as always, in a draw. We sat soaking wet, gasping for breath, and, after a beer, both feeling much better.

"If I hadn't run this afternoon I'd have kicked your ass," I laughed.

"If I didn't have this bad knee, I'd have broken your head." Roland made a fist and half smiled.

"Roland is just lucky that he never made it to my bed," Bill stood by his desk, stretched, and yawned.

"You could be next," warned Roland as he mashed his beer can with one hand. "Unless your delicate surgeon hands might get hurt."

"I probably wouldn't need to use but one of them on a piece of wet toilet paper like you."

"I think you're gonna be next." Roland was standing.

"I have no fear. There is nothing to fear but fear itself." Bill returned to his desk.

"You're next!" yelled Roland as he dove across the room. The chair and the two men crashed to the floor. Another flurry of arms and legs, a few more laughs, and two beers later it was movie time. Roland and Bill left for the movie. Myron was still in the chaplain's hooch playing hearts.

I undressed, wrapped a towel around my waist, put on my Ho Chi Minh rubber sandals, and headed for the showers. I had that pleasant feeling in my muscles of being very tired from vigorous exertion. I stood beneath the five hundred-gallon outdoor tank of water, and, since no one was around, I stayed under the water longer than the wet-lather-rinse rule allowed. I could hear the movie starting as I walked back to Hooch 75. I removed clean underwear, socks, and fatigues from my plywood box. Our housemouse kept me well supplied with clean clothes. I laced up my boots, sat at my desk, and began studying Vietnamese.

Vietnamese is basically a monosyllabic language. Each syllable is a noun or a verb. It expresses a distinct idea. Occasionally two separate syllables join meanings to form new words or concepts, as in names of places Sai-gon, Da-Nang, or for abstractions like "democracy," dân chu. Verbs do not have tenses, and time relationships must be interpreted from the context of the sentence. It seemed, therefore, a simple enough language to learn in the quiet of my room.

But much actual practice speaking aloud is necessary, because tone and inflection of the voice are very important. A change of tone completely changes the meaning of a word. Until the amateur linguist becomes practiced with the different tones, he is usually received with blank stares, laughter, or knowing smiles rather than with conversation or understanding.

I studied until my hoochmates returned from the movie. Then it was time to find Sun and practice my evening's new words and phrases. She would help me with pronunciation and tone. My new linguistic abilities, although weak and limited, were to markedly modify my tour.

Phu Bai was a relatively safe place compared to the areas from which we received our casualties. Occasionally, incoming mortar shells landed close by. We were sometimes on red alert and had to spend time in our small bunkers. There were enough dangers to remind us that it was possible to die at any time especially when we saw the very unsubtle reality of thirty or more partially destroyed kids every day. But even being scared, nervous, and homesick and taking care of casualties and pronouncing the dead got to be a little routine.

Eventually one gets used to rubbing elbows and bare thighs with his neighbors while listening to your feces splashing into the smelly diesel fuel of the tubs below. Pretty soon, it doesn't really matter that you don't have time to take a shower. You can get used to sleeping with boots on during red alert and working all day with vomitus matted on your pants and blood inside your boots. The smell of a marine who hasn't taken his socks off for weeks is not offensive after awhile

especially when he's in big trouble and you're in a big hurry
to help him.

One morning Captain Street, the Division Surgeon,
placed his powdered eggs, burned toast, and bacon next to
mine. "Say, Parrish, I'm glad you're here. I want to talk to
you."

He went back for coffee. On returning to the bench next
to me, he kicked the table as he sat down and spilled my
coffee and water. Without apologizing he proceeded. "The
hospital commander tells me that you are learning to speak
Vietnamese and that you are running the Vietnamese sick call."

"Yes, Sir."

"Well, starting next week, I'd like for you to take over a
MEDCAP program here. We hold several a month now, but
it's not well organized."

"What do I do?"

"Well, it's easy. The marines go in first and secure the
ville, and while they stand guard, you come in and set up a
sick call for the population—a one-day general practice. Before sundown you move out and back to Phu Bai. One
MEDCAP each Saturday. A different ville each week. Intelligence section will tell you where to go each time. You can't do
much for a ville in one day, but the commanding general wants
to tell Washington about our great efforts to help the people."

"We will win their hearts and minds as we cure their
ills." I raised my fork to the sky and put my left hand over my
heart. "And hopefully not get killed while doing it." I placed
my fork against my stomach. Captain Street failed to see any
humor in my gestures, and I tried to return my fork to the
table as nonchalantly as possible.

"If you do a good job, we may have to keep you around
here at Phu Bai for awhile."

"I'm not anxious to begin a tour in the field. The
monsoons are coming."

"You begin MEDCAP tomorrow." Captain Street got up
to leave. "Arrange transportation with Captain Ames."

"Yes, Sir. He's my hoochmate."

He kicked the table as he stepped over the bench and
spilled the rest of my coffee. I finished eating and left the
chow hall. It was so early in the morning that I had the whole
shitter to myself. That's almost worth getting up early for.

As I carried out my duties the rest of the day, I kept wondering what MEDCAP would be like—what the people would be like. The only Vietnamese I really knew were those who came to work on American military bases. Now I could meet the real Vietnamese—the villagers, the farmers, the peasants. Somebody had decided this country was worth saving. Maybe I could find out why.

"I always wondered what the hell those MEDCAP's were like." Roland was polishing his boots again. "Sure you can have a few vehicles. Take an ambulance for supplies, a jeep for yourself, a truck and a jeep for the marines."

"Thanks, old man."

"In fact, you are going to get the best, most experienced, and highest ranking driver in this outfit."

"Whodat?!" I threw up my hands and feigned amazement.

"Me, Captain Roland Ames. I'd like to see you win some hearts and minds. And I also need to get the hell out of Phu Bai for awhile."

Next morning we were on our way. The ville was reported as friendly. I felt foolish taking a squad of marines in as security, but I had heard so many stories about VC's disguised as friendlies, that I allowed the truckful of marines to disembark and walk in first. Roland and I followed.

About one hundred women and children stood between the scattered bamboo-thatched houses and watched our every move. A few of the children ran toward the marines asking for food.

"Chop-chop?"

"You give chop-chop? Marine, number one. VC, number ten. You want boom-boom?"

The sergeant in charge of the marines was yelling at his men to keep in line. "Don't give any of those little bastards candy. They'll start a goddamn riot, and we'll never get the Doc organized. Stay out of the goddamn huts. Don't proposition the women. Keep your weapon in your hands at all times. Keep your clips in, but keep your gun on safety. Only smoke American brand cigarettes, and don't all stand together.

"Drivers, stay in your vehicles, keep the keys in your pockets and your eyes open. These kids will steal you blind. Look relaxed and trusting and friendly."

I thought to myself that if any of these people speak

English, we were through right now. We had lost their minds
and hearts.

There were only six Vietnamese men in the whole
village; four young men in fatigues and boots were the PF's
(Popular Forces), the local military men assigned to protect
their own villages, and two old, bearded men who sat in front
of a hut sharing a pipe. The PF's took charge and fell over
themselves setting up an area in the largest hut for me to
hold sick call. They spoke very sternly and rapidly to the
villagers, and seemed to be urging them to come see the
American doctor.

The hut had a rear wall made of very hard-packed dirt
and sand. It felt as though it had some concrete mixed into it.
The rest of the thatched-roof hut was open except for the
tree-trunk poles which supported the roof. The marines
searched each patient as he came into the hut. Two corpsmen
remained inside with me and manned our medical supplies.
Roland sat on the ground in the corner and leaned against a
post.

At first, the villagers were reluctant to come inside.
Some were curious. They stood outside the hut and stared.
Others ignored us as if they had seen this scene many times
before. The first villager to come inside the hut was a giggly
and very pregnant girl who wanted the Bác Sĩ to check her
baby. The next two were eight- or nine-year-old boys who
weren't sure why they had come inside. I shook hands with
them, listened to them take a few breaths with a stethoscope,
and told them they were "number one."

The PF's brought a very reluctant little girl with extensive impetigo of her legs. I gave her two bars of soap and
some penicillin tablets. An old lady complained of back pain
probably from years of work in the rice paddies. I told the
corpsmen to give her a small supply of aspirin.

Then there developed a long line of women and children
with all sorts of complaints. Most of the symptoms seemed to
have been made up on the spot. Often they were the same as
those of the villager immediately preceding in line. If I
appeared to be unhappy with their complaint, they would
make up another one. Headache, weakness, back pain, chest
pain. The marines in sick call had no monopoly on these
complaints. We gave them each a few aspirin. After awhile, I
stopped examining each one as he came through. Many

villagers returned for a second time through the line. Smiling and telling about their headaches and backaches the PF's all passed by once or twice. Soon people called out their complaints as they walked into the hut, as if they were giving their name, rank, or serial number. They marched through, picked up their aspirin, and left.

"It's really a good thing that someone with lots of medical training is here," Roland smirked. "I'd never be able to give out aspirin like that. You're wonderful, Doc."

"Will you shut up. I didn't plan this circus." I stepped back and let the line continue by without me. Roland and I had a cigarette. I smiled and nodded to each villager as he announced his complaint. Then I pointed to the corpsman with the giant aspirin bottle.

"We're just about out of aspirin, Sir." The corpsman looked through our metal boxes.

"Give them Darvon or APC's or Isoniazid."

"Or candy," said Roland.

The corpsmen combed through the boxes and haphazardly handed out pills and soaps and bandages. The line increased in length. Villagers appeared from everywhere to march through the hut. Occasionally someone with a cough or a skin infection was taken out of the line for me to examine before he was given his soap and pills.

One little girl was wasted and pale. She had a tachycardia and an enlarged liver and spleen. She may have had chronic malaria, leukemia, or another potentially fatal disorder. I asked her mother to bring her to the provincial hospital, but she insisted on pills and soap instead. I could not persuade her otherwise.

After several hours, we ran out of gear and began to close up shop. Some of the villagers were involved in a heated debate with two of the PF's. Finally one of the PF's reluctantly approached me to ask if I would go into one of the huts to see an old lady who was too sick to come to me. I agreed to go. My corpsmen and the villagers followed as we moved across the village. The villagers fell back as we approached the last hut in a long, straight row of thatched roofs.

"Wait, Doc, don't go in any of the hooches." The marine sergeant broke into a half-run as he approached. "It may be a booby trap."

"I would like to go in and examine one old lady," I insisted.

"She might have hand grenades under each arm and be lying on a Claymore mine."

"I doubt that."

The sergeant stepped in front of the door to prevent my entry. "The VC would gladly sacrifice an old woman to kill an American officer and teach these people not to deal with Americans. I'm under orders to keep you alive, Sir, and I intend to do just that."

"Then go inside and make sure that woman is safe for me to examine." I spoke very sternly. The villagers were watching, and I had agreed to see if I could help the woman.

The sergeant stood there in silence for what seemed a long time. Then he turned to one of his men. "Go get a litter from the ambulance." He turned back to me. "I hope one of my men doesn't get killed because you agreed to see some old bag. Please stand back." He motioned for the PF's and villagers to stand back as two of his men came running up with an empty litter.

"Frisk her thoroughly, put her on this litter, and bring her out here."

"Yes, Sir."

"And be careful, goddamn it."

"Yes, Sir."

"And be gentle. She might be for real."

"Yes, Sir."

The first marine lay on his stomach. He pushed the litter into the hut ahead of him as he slowly crawled into the hut on his belly. When he was inside, the second marine entered. An old woman's voice moaned with fear, surprise, and pain. The marine had probably pinned her arms to carefully search for explosives before she could move. Several minutes passed in silence.

"She really is sick, Sergeant."

"No signs of explosives, Sarge."

"You still want her outside?"

"Yes!"

The marines carried the litter with ease—as if it were still empty. The wasted, wrinkled, and ill-appearing old woman had to close her eyes as she left the hut. It was probably the first sunlight she had seen in months. The marines placed the stretcher at my feet, and I knelt beside it.

She had a small, firm, fixed mass just under the inner third of her left clavicle. Although she appeared short of breath, her lungs were relatively clear. Inspiratory efforts were weak. She had signs of severe weight loss. I felt a hard, baseball-sized mass in her lower abdomen. It seemed to be fixed to her anterior and posterior abdominal walls. Her upper abdomen was hypertympanic and distended. Her hair was matted with vomitus, and her smell betrayed her incontinence of stool and urine.

One of my corpsmen knelt down next to me. "We have a few pills left, Sir. Some Isoniazid, APC's, and some chloraquine-primaquine tabs."

"This lady doesn't need pills—except for pain pills. She has end-stage cancer of the gut. The villagers won't be too impressed with the outcome of our pills on her."

"Is there anything we can do?"

"I'd like to give her a big slug of morphine intravenously, but we can't do that." I knew the old lady was in pain, and things were only going to get worse. She would not survive a trip to the provincial hospital. It was too late for any form of treatment anyway.

I tried to explain the situation to a PF. I could not tell if he understood me or not, but he kept saying that her family would be hurt if we gave her no pills and soap.

"Are you winning the hearts and minds of the people?" Roland was standing at the foot of the litter. "Everyone is waiting for you to do something for the old lady."

The old lady smiled, exposing her black teeth and dry, cracked tongue. She knew her war was almost over.

I squeezed her hand and then stood up. "Give her some pain pills—any kind." I tried to explain the prognosis to the family. They nodded, smiled, and pointed to the medicine supply box.

I walked back toward the center of the ville. The marines were relaxed. The tension had subsided and they were sitting about in the sun bartering with the villagers. Children gathered around them to play, beg, and tease. Finally, we opened a box of candy, passed it out to the children, and left amid many waves, nods, smiles, and goodbyes.

Roland and I rode a long way without speaking. I finally broke the silence. "That was a waste. I didn't see one significant problem I could really help. I didn't have the gear or the medicine to tackle the real medical problems."

"Most of those pills will be sold, given to the VC, or wrapped in a cloth and kept forever," Roland said.

"Or taken all at once, and they'll all get sick." I shook my head.

Roland lit a cigarette. "These people don't give their minds and hearts because we come in under guard and pass out pills, candy, and soap. We just provide a little entertainment."

"And support our superiority complex," I added.

"And increase the income of some of the women," Roland gave an evil smile. "They were getting five hundred piasters a trick from the marines."

"I didn't see that." I was really surprised.

"One of the huts was really busy with two customers at a time. We were there so long that some GI's went back for seconds."

"At least they didn't rape anybody."

"Only because the women agreed to do it for money, and because this happens to be a very straight sergeant we were with today." Roland spoke with authority.

"Those guys with us today would not have raped anybody. I don't think."

"That's only because they've been in the rear for awhile now. They get laid in the villes, get enough sleep, and haven't seen a Vietnamese kill one of their buddies for some time now."

We turned onto a bigger road, and our ride was much smoother. I could hear Roland better as he continued. "You put those same kids in the jungle for awhile, get them real scared, deprive them of sleep, and let a few incidents change some of their fear to hate. Give them a sergeant who has seen too many of his men killed by booby traps and by lack of distrust, and who feels that Vietnamese are dumb, dirty, and weak, because they are not like him. Add a little mob pressure, and those nice kids who accompanied us today would rape like champions. Kill, rape, and steal is the name of the game."

Roland was getting all worked up. He lit another cigarette and continued. "You could have accomplished the same thing today by dropping a crate of soap from a helicopter."

"That may be true, but——"

Roland interrupted me. He was all talk and no listen.

"And another thing, before I forget, you can't say those women today weren't forced to screw. They made more money in one day today than their soldier husbands make in a couple of months—that is, if their husbands are still alive, or haven't run away. And their kids are hungry."

"And their hungry kids probably stood and watched," I joined in.

"And the women can probably remember watching their mothers with the French or Japanese or Chinese. That's why that old bitch smiled at you. She was glad you were the last foreign son-of-a-bitch who would ever try to win her mind and heart. She was gonna fool us all and die still keeping her own fucking mind and heart."

"We may as well try to help them though. As long as we're over here."

Roland interrupted again. "We can help them the most by not being over here in the first place. I mean, what kind of a war is this? You have to convince the people you are fighting for to like you. You have to put on ridiculous shows to convince them that we like them, when we obviously don't. You have to frisk an old lady before you can examine her. And you can't trust a Vietnamese soldier after years of side-by-side combat. If that's the best war you can come up with, I'd just as soon forget it and wait for a better one to come along."

"I didn't make the war. I was just trying to help the—"

"Help. Shit. Doctor Albert-Schweitzer-Parrish moves into the ville followed by a mob of reverent compatriots. He moves among the people speaking their language, touching them, healing them. He comforts the dying and reassures the neurotic. He councils the leaders and plays with the children."

I joined in. "His men make friends with the natives and do business with them, and, in fact, make passionate love to the women."

Roland smiled. "The natives nod and smile and give him warm glances."

"And all the time they are thinking that Doctor Albert-

Schweitzer-Parrish should get the hell out of their village and leave them alone." I placed my hands in front of me and began nodding reverently.

"And take his bunch of crude and wealthy, fatigue-covered dorks with him," added Roland.

"Ah, the minds and hearts we have won today." I put my hand over my heart. "It makes a man feel good."

We rode another few minutes in silence. The air rushing by the open jeep was hot and dry.

"Where were the men of the village?" I asked.

"Dead, run away, playing soldier, or just hiding. They don't want your fucking pills."

I thought for a minute. "They just want to grow their rice, screw their wives, raise their kids, eat, sleep, and be left alone."

"That's not asking a hell of a lot, is it John?"

"No, but we won't permit it. The peasant must fight. He must learn to care about politics, and Saigon, and the USA, and the VC. We have to force him to be involved. That's sick."

"He has to be taught to win a war," Roland added sarcastically.

"Whatever that means. Winning means killing his neighbors." I put on my sunglasses.

"Winning to these people means staying out of this mess. It means being friendly to the Americans, to the VC, to the North Vietnamese, to whomever is in your ville at the time."

Roland was getting worked up again. "We are the ones who gave them this great concept of winning, and we don't know what the hell it means. It has something to do with body counts, and passing out pills, and overpaying for a piece of ass. It has something to do with firmly establishing a 'noncommunist government' in Saigon, no matter how unrepresentative it may be. It means crushing 'un-American' activity."

"Even if we have to blow up the whole country to do it," I added.

"That's what winning is. Destroying the whole damn place. Blow it up, defoliate it, kill the natives, pave it over, and use it for a parking lot for our next campaign."

I raised my canteen. "Next Cambodia, then Laos, then Thailand—then the world!"

"Kill the men. Make beggars of the children. Make whores of all the women," Roland joined the toast.

"We are here to win at any cost."

"Pro-American, anticommunist, or blown-the-hell up!" Roland was screaming.

"If we can't win, we'll stalemate." I toasted again.

"And stalemate only costs us a few boys a day."

Back on Highway One we slowed down in a line of traffic. I sat up on the rear spare tire of the jeep as if I were the hero of a parade. I toasted each vehicle as it passed and waved to the civilians on the side of the road. Roland's laughter encouraged me to recite poems for the masses

> "Mary had a little lamb,
> It was fed by Red.
> Instead of let it eat bad food,
> Kill it."

"More, more," screamed Roland, "Ho, ho, ho."

> "Ho, Ho, Ho, Ho
> Back Ho, Sack Ho,
> Hate Ho, Rape Ho.
> But don't try to talk to Ho."

I stood up in the back of the jeep, barely able to keep my balance as we bounced along. Canteen held high, I saluted toward the peasants working in the fields.

> "Storm and thunder, kill and plunder
> Ten long years we rip asunder.
> Hide a blunder with a blunder.
> Kill a Vietcong!"

We stopped at a bridge to await the signal of a marine directing traffic. He was crossing a convoy of troops coming from the other direction. As they passed, I raised both hands in the air and yelled toward them, although I could not be heard above the noise of their trucks.

> "Watch them scream,
> Watch them cry,

*Use your M16.*
*Watch them wiggle,*
*Watch them die,*
*You're a good marine."*


"You're magnificent," screamed Roland. "More, more."
He was making victory signals with both hands. We began to
cross the bridge. Just on the other side of the bridge were a
few Vietnamese trinket shops. Everyone knew they were
fronts for prostitution in the back rooms. Roland threw our
remaining packages of candy bars along the highway, and
children appeared from everywhere to fight for them.

"See the children begging," I screamed.

"See the women whore," added Roland.

"See the men embarrassed."

"Make them beg for more," laughed Roland.

"Make them beg for more," I repeated.

"Accept love, and understanding, and democracy, or
we'll bash your goddamn heads in." Roland was weaving
around the road as he turned toward the hospital compound.

When we arrived in Phu Bai, the corpsmen took the
gear, and one of Roland's drivers took the jeep back to the
motor pool. We walked back to the hooch where our mates
were playing hearts.

"Make them beg for more," Roland said to Prince as we
entered.

"Here comes the human relations council," said Bill.

"Doctor Nyugen and his driver!" Prince bowed respectfully.

"How was it?" Myron asked.

"Interesting," I answered.

"Awful," said Roland. "Those people don't need or want a
doctor."

"They need a doctor," I insisted, "But that's way down
the list of priorities. Soap, school teacher, sanitation engineer,
tractor——"

"And they wouldn't need a tractor if someone hadn't shot
their water buffalo," Roland interjected. "But why worry
about it. In one hundred eighty-one days my war is over.
Make them beg for more."

"The ville will belong to the villagers," said Bill. "So you
have to educate them. They need their own doctors."

"Let's teach them not to shit in the street before we send them to medical school," suggested Prince.

"Get any ass?" smiled Bill. "I hear those villes have lots of hot honies."

"They're not hot and they're not honies, but there is a lot of five hundred-piaster ass," answered Roland. "I didn't want any of the VD-ridden shit, and couldn't see waiting in line with a bunch of enlisted studs with their hands in their pockets getting ready."

"Really nice talk, you guys," protested Myron. "I'm sure John didn't have the time nor the desire for that kind of stuff."

"You're right. You fellows don't really think I would get myself physically involved with a Vietnamese woman do you?" I left to look for Sun.

When I discovered that Sun had gone to Hue for the night, I suddenly felt very lonely. I missed her. I went back to my hooch, changed into my shorts, and Bill and I went for a late afternoon run.

"So how did you like MEDCAP?" panted Bill.

"Well, one thing I can say for it, is that it took me almost a day."

"So?"

"That means I'm one day shorter. One less day until I go home."

"Good thinking."

We rounded a corner. We passed two runners moving in the other direction. They smiled and waved. The sun was far off on the horizon, but it was still very hot and bright.

Bill was sweating profusely. "Were the villagers in bad shape?"

"Not as bad a shape as you are, you fat lily." I shoved Bill's shoulder so that he stumbled to the side, and then I sprinted ahead of him down the road.

Bill regained his balance and began chasing after me as fast as he could run. "You'd better run, because, if I catch you, I'm breaking your ass and both your legs." He was grunting and cursing between breaths.

I widened the distance between us with an all-out-effort run. When I reached the junction with Highway One, I looked back to see that he was well behind me. I could see his fist raised and gesturing, but he was a good hundred

meters behind. I settled down to a slow trot along the highway. I was totally winded, and my chest hurt from the
effort. I was chuckling to myself, "Kill, rape, and steal is the
name of the game—you win if you don't become insane." I
looked back down the highway and couldn't even see Bill
now. I slowly picked up the pace and made a cadence with
my mind. "Kill, rape, steal is the name of the game—you win
if you don't become insane."

A convoy truck full of marines passed me and stopped
rather suddenly. The cabin door opened, and out jumped
Bill. He was running straight for me screaming war cries. I
was too winded to make it back to the hooch, so I took a right
turn and headed out across an open field. Bill was fresh.
Gaining rapidly on me from my left flank he was laughing,
and cursing, and making awful Indian war cries. I ran to the
top of a small hill which ended abruptly in a sandy bank like
the sand trap of a golf course. As I stepped into the sand, I
lost my footing, more from fatigue than loss of balance. Just
as I resumed my upright stance, Bill made a flying tackle
from the top of the hill, and we both tumbled over and over
in the sand.

We rolled to a stop at the foot of the slope both unable to
move. Sand was stuck to every square inch of our sweaty
bodies. We lay there panting, and laughing, and spitting
sand.

"Kill, rape, and steal," I screamed. We laughed for
awhile. Then we just lay there quietly watching the sun. We
stayed for a long time without moving—resting and thinking.
Then we got up and walked slowly back to the compound.
The sunset was beautiful. I really did miss Sun.

# FOUR

"Mass casualties. Twenty litters, thirty walking, eight dead." The corpsman ran along the walkway between the doctor's hooches shouting, "Mass casualties."

Doctors grabbed shirts and hats and buttoned up as they trotted toward triage. The number had reached thirty, forty-two, and ten by the time the first chopper was unloaded. A second was waiting to land behind it.

"Fixed wing from Dong Ha in four minutes. Twelve, eighteen, and six."

For the next two hours, triage was a flurry of activity. The operating rooms would be busy for the rest of the day.

About 3 P.M. there was a call on the wall phone set. It was from Graves Registration.

"Doctor Parrish, we were washing down the bodies, and one of them moaned. I don't know how long he'd been back here. He's got two legs and an arm missing, and he's full of holes, but he really moaned. I heard him. The guys are bringing him up to triage now."

Four excited marines rounded the corner each carrying a handle of the litter, and its light burden. As reported, both legs were missing, one at the knee, one at mid-thigh and one arm was gone below the shoulder. Several small, penetrating wounds of the abdomen and chest were no longer bleeding. The skin was pale, and there were no palpable femoral or carotid pulses. I put my hand on his chest. After two or three seconds, I felt a heartbeat...then another...then two coupled beats. The pupils were large, but they reacted sluggishly to light.

"Don't stand there staring. Put some tourniquets on his legs and arm, and get me an IV set." We started a steady

stream of Ringer's Lactate into his good arm and into a neck
vein while we waited for blood. In the time it took to put a
chest tube into his left chest, secure all the tourniquets, and
tilt the stretcher with head downhill, the blood had been
typed, crossmatched, and was ready for administration. After
two units of blood were pumped in under pressure, the
marine actually began to wake up. He had a rigid abdomen,
and was still hypotensive.

"What have you got here, John, a basket job?" Bill was
in charge of triage today, and he was walking around checking
each litter.

"Yeah, he's still with us—even after a trip to Graves.
He's got a hard belly."

"The O.R.'s are pretty booked up," Bill said looking at a
list he had made on a piece of cardboard box.

"He's got to go to the O.R. now, Bill."

Bill looked at the marine, looked at his list, looked at
me, looked at his watch, and then looked back at me. "You
scrub?"

"Yes."

"I've got to finish checking all the litters. Get me another general surgeon, an orthopod, and another GMO, and
meet me in O.R. three in five minutes. Type and cross eight
more units. Tell the anesthesiologist to stop what he's doing
and put this boy to sleep—gently."

The third and fourth units of blood were pumped in as
we walked to the operating room. Bill and I operated on the
abdomen while the others debrided and reamputated the
extremities. We had to sacrifice one kidney, and tried to
repair the other—almost hopeless odds. Four hours later this
trunk had far more tubes than extremities—two drains in his
belly, a urethral catheter into his bladder, a tube to drain his
flank, two intravenous tubes, a chest tube, and a central
venous pressure line in his subclavian vein.

"Maybe we shouldn't have wasted precious time on this
guy. He's a wheelchair job and has little chance of survival
anyway." One of the orthopods spoke up. He knew there
were still hours and hours of surgery left to be done tonight.

Bill had operated in silence until now. "If this kid wants
to die later, that's his business. If you want to play God, that's
your business. Right now, I'm in charge, and we are going to

give this kid a four-plus effort. John, you close. I'm going to start another case."

"Sure, I'll close. Maybe someday this kid will be a writer."

"Or a track star," challenged the orthopedic surgeon.

"Or he can work in a Marine Recruiting Center." Everybody in the room was going to comment, but Bill walked out of the room as if he didn't hear them continue.

"Or a presidential aide."

"Or a third baseman."

"Or a third base," the orthopedic surgeon yelled after Bill.

We finished the case and transported the trunk with its jungle of tubes into the recovery area where we assigned one GMO as special duty nurse all night long. I went to the debridement area where I did minor surgery and dressed wounds until about 2 A.M. before dragging myself to bed. Roland, Myron, and Prince were very much asleep, and Bill's bed was still empty. That poor son of a bitch was still operating. A picture of the two of us laughing in the sand flashed through my mind, and I thought of the hours together at the O.R. table and our occasional drunks. If I ever got shot up, I would hope that Bill was the surgeon in charge. I might even tell him that someday. Sleep interrupted my thoughts.

By morning Bill's rack was still empty. I looked at my watch—too late for breakfast, for Sun's trip to the head, and for an early seat on the shitter. Already dressed, I took a can of Vienna sausages from Prince's cabinet and headed for Graves and then the recovery room.

Bill was examining the marine who had come back from Graves the day before. "He talked to me awhile ago. He's still hypotensive, and he's had a total of sixteen units of blood. He hasn't made a goddamn drop of urine." Bill looked very tired.

"You go to bed. I'll take over. Wake up Myron and tell him he'll have to round by himself today."

"Push fluids. You'll have to go by his neck veins. His lungs are so full of crap from his chest wounds that they will be unreliable as signs of overhydration. We have a catheter in his superior vena cava. That should help. Good luck." Bill turned to go.

"Get some sleep, you hero," I said. He didn't look back or answer.

Careful examination of the kid proved Bill's summary to be completely accurate. His chart furnished other important data. His name was Steven Rubenstein. He was a lance corporal. He was nineteen years old.

As he was rolled onto his side so that a stethescope could be placed on his back, he opened his eyes and groaned a blurred group of unclear profanities.

"Rubenstein! Steve! Rubenstein! Can you hear me?"

He opened his eyes again. "Yeah." He raised his head for a second and then it fell back onto the bed. "Where am I? Am I dying?"

"You're okay, buddy."

"Help me." His eyes closed again. He didn't even know he was missing three extremities.

During the day I returned often to the recovery room to regulate his fluids and to help the corpsmen with his drains and wound care. He woke up again for several minutes in mid-afternoon. He did not react to the absence of his legs, but seemed concerned only with pain and death. He grunted, groaned, cursed, asked for help, and tried unsuccessfully to move. Bill returned in the late afternoon.

"How's he doing?"

"He's been awake. His brain works a little. But no urine."

"No urine!" Bill was angry.

"Not a drop. If he doesn't pee soon, we'll have to give him up as a renal failure."

"Not on your life. We'll fly him out to the hospital ship and put him on the artificial kidney. Hemodialysis. He's got one kidney. Maybe it will work later."

"Acute tubular necrosis. He may have been in shock for a long time."

"It's my case. We're gonna send him to the ship. Tell the chief to radio for a helicopter ride."

The radio set finally reached the hospital ship. The artificial kidney wasn't working. The closest hemodialysis unit was in Saigon. No planes were scheduled to fly south until eight o'clock the next day.

"I want a direct flight to Saigon—a fixed wing—right now." Bill spoke as if he could actually get one.

In the communications bunker, the chief talked to the Phu Bai, Saigon, and Da Nang airports. The same answer came from all three places. They would check with flight control and let us know.

Saigon and Da Nang called back and said they could not send craft that night. Bill paced and waited. Phu Bai air strip called.

"We've got a craft. A C-130. But no crew until tomorrow morning. We'll keep trying."

Bill grabbed the headset. "Look, you guys, we've got a marine who's going to die if he doesn't get to Saigon soon. He needs to be on the artificial kidney."

"Yes, Sir, we'll try to round up a crew. We'll have to get permission from our commanding officer. Please have your C.O. call him."

"Just get me a crew!" Bill was screaming into the headset.

"Bill, Bill," I put my hand on his shoulder. "We can send him down in the morning. It will be dark by the time we get organized."

"It's four thirty isn't it?" Bill looked at his watch.

"Yes."

"Let's go to the 'O' Club and get a beer."

"I could use a beer. We'll talk over what we're going to do for the kid." I wanted to prevent Bill's making a big fuss over being refused by the big shots.

"We haven't been to the air force 'O' Club for a long time. Let's go over there." Bill was trying not to smile.

"You old fox. I'd better go with you just to keep you honest." Bill was going to raise his own crew.

Roland gave us a jeep and a driver, and we arrived at the air force base as the club was filling. Bill walked up to the bar, tapped three times, and began his speech.

"I'm Doctor Bond from A Med. I have urgent need of a C-130 crew for a medevac trip to Saigon."

"Call medevac. Radio flight control. They'll arrange it if indicated. We're not the medevac team." A big major with blond hair spoke frankly.

"Medevac has no crew up here. They can't send a plane until tomorrow," Bill urged.

"Use a helicopter. Go to the hospital ship," the major continued.

"It has to be Saigon, because we need an artificial kidney, and it should be tonight by fixed wing." Bill knew exactly what he wanted.

"You'd better talk to the C.O. I doubt if he can spare anybody, and he hates for us to fly at night."

"Look, you guys," Bill was pleading. "We've got a marine, a real basket case with no arms and legs, who has one chance to live, and that chance is a trip to Saigon—like now. We've got a plane, but no crew."

"You've got a damn good radio man right here." A second lieutenant stepped up and pointed to himself.

"And one of the best pilots in I Corps right here." Another man set down his beer and introduced himself.

A full bird colonel wheeled around on his bar stool and stood up. The room was silent. He walked up to Bill and me, and stared at us for a minute, then turned to the volunteer pilot.

"You're not going to pilot any goddamn C-130 to Saigon tonight——"

"Yes, Sir."

"You're not going to pilot any goddamn C-130 anywhere tonight——"

"Yes, Sir."

"You're going to copilot——"

"Sir?"

"I'm going to fly it. I'll fly that bird to Saigon. Get me a crew. No cargo. No hitchhikers. Just the docs and the marine. Tell the exec I'll be back tomorrow."

"Yes, Sir."

"Well," the colonel stamped his foot. "Get moving!"

I turned to Bill. "And you've got a damn good GMO right here to go with them."

The colonel put his finger on my chest. "You keep him alive, Doc. I'll get him to Saigon."

As we drove back to A Med, Bill must have been wondering if he were doing the right thing by taking the chance of a night flight and endangering a whole C-130 and crew. He didn't say anything. Steve Rubenstein was still getting a four-plus effort.

As soon as the jeep stopped in front of triage, Bill went to sort tubes and to prepare Rubenstein for his flight. I went to the hooch to get my toothbrush, clean underwear, and socks. Roland and Prince were reading.

"Where are you going? London? Paris? Athens?" Prince threw me a can of Vienna sausage. "Don't forget your camera."

"I'm going to Saigon to take a wounded marine to the artificial kidney."

"You gonna get laid?" Roland didn't even look up from his book. "I hear those Saigon honies are really nice. There are round eyes there, too."

"I'll let you know." I was out the door and gone. Bill was waiting for me in triage. The marine was ready to be carried to the aircraft.

Bill shook my hand and smiled. "Get laid in Saigon. There are round eyes there, you know."

"If this kid makes it, I'll get laid for both of us—for all three of us."

"You'll take one corpsman. First Class Sweet here will go with you." Bill turned to the stretcher bearers. "Get going." He walked part way to the plane with me, then headed back to triage.

The whole cargo area of the C-130 was empty except for the litter strapped in place right in the center. Fifty wounded could be carried in this craft. It seemed very large and empty. I folded down a chair and strapped myself in. The corpsman and a flight crew member sat on the floor and held onto a strap as we lumbered and vibrated down the runway.

Steve Rubenstein was oblivious to the vibrations and noises. He opened his eyes and turned his head toward me. I left my seat and knelt beside the litter.

"We're going to Saigon." I had to yell above the engine noise. "We need some equipment there to make you better—to make you pee."

He nodded and closed his eyes. His carotid pulse was strong, but rapid. I was determined to keep him alive now, if I had to pump on his chest all the way to Saigon. What would we do if he cooled in mid-flight? Turn around and go back?

Ton Son Nhut Airport, the busiest airport in the world. International commercial jets. Troop transports. Helicopters of all sizes and shapes. Fighter jets screaming up and away with afterburners. Miles of runways. Trucks. Business men, military men, civilians. The executive class of war. The bureaucratic switchboard. Excitement. Professionalism. Business. Big business. Busy.

An ambulance was waiting. We drove through Saigon toward the big army hospital. The streets were a mass of motor scooters, bicycles, cars, military vehicles, pedicabs, and buses. Horn blowing substituted for traffic rules. The flow of traffic, like a sluggish mudslide, was determined by group inertia. Beautiful girls in ao dais, and buildings of concrete several stories tall made the barbed wire and sandbags less noticeable. Billboards read in English, French, and Vietnamese. Busy people raced to somewhere or from something. Importance and emptiness welled out of sheer numbers. Rhododendrons.

The ambulance backed into the emergency entrance. The emergency room was clean, modern, well-equipped, and empty. A limbless marine and a dirty doctor in fatigues and boots drew a crowd at once. The doctors wore khaki open-collar shirts, and the nurses wore white like real nurses. And they had round eyes and spoke English. Those bulges in the uniforms were breasts, and beneath their starched white skirts their white legs actually joined in a bushy mass of real pubic hair.

Staring at a beautiful blond nurse almost caused me to bump into the hospital commander who had come to the emergency room to meet us. After the C.O. listened quietly to the story of Steve Rubenstein, and to the statistics of his operation and fluid replacements, he gave a jerk of his finger and directed a GMO to examine the patient. A nod of his head sent a nurse sorting through the tubing.

Being in dirty, smelly, green fatigues in the midst of quiet, clean, khaki efficiency made me feel uncomfortable and crude. For the first time, I realized that I had changed since the days of my work in the emergency room at the University Hospital. My world had changed greatly, and it had slowly transformed me. In the midst of gleaming white, I felt base and profane. My very presence seemed impolite. It was not so embarrassing as it was frightening to realize that an emotional, survival-oriented animal can gradually replace a part of one's being without his awareness of the transitions.

I was almost apologetic. "We thought he might need hemodialysis, so we flew him here. He has had no urine output."

"What are his renal chemistries?" The doctor in charge looked at the empty urine bag.

"I don't know. We're not set up to do renal chemistries."

"How about electrolytes?"

"We can't do any chemistries."

He turned to one of his GMO's. "B.U.N., electrolytes, creatinine, and hematocrit. Stat! And get arterial gases."

He proceeded to quiz me. "Are you sure the ureter is intact?"

"No, but I think it is. We could see most of it at surgery. One kidney was removed."

"What's his ventilatory status?"

"X ray shows bibasilar fluid; his lungs sound awful. Rhonchi and dullness up to mid-chest on both sides. He's been pink since he got off the O.R. table."

"I guess you can't do blood gases either."

"No. We don't really have a hospital like this. It's sort of a clearing and stabilizing area. We——"

"Well, we'll evaluate him and see what's needed. You probably compromised his ureter at surgery." He stood back and lit his pipe. "Looks like you could tell the difference between renal failure, pulmonary insufficiency, and shock—even without lab tests." He leaned against the wall and smoked his fancy pipe. "What makes you think hemodialysis will make a difference?"

All of a sudden he's a goddamn professor, and I'm a medical student, because he's got all the labs and gear and time to think. Embarrassment gave way to anger. "No telling how long he was in shock before we got him. He hasn't urinated since we first saw him. He's only got one kidney now. He——"

"So you're going to save him with a kidney machine?" He relit his pipe.

"Look, if I didn't think there was a good chance he might need it to survive, I wouldn't have broken my ass to get here and——"

"Watch your language. There are women here," he scolded.

"Yes, that's the first thing I noticed when I arrived. Look, half the time it's so noisy up there we can't hear. We're tired, under pressure, hurried, and scared. We——"

"Please, no war stories. Why don't you go get some coffee and look around. I have lots of work to do. Tell Chief Roberts at the end of the hall to give you meal tickets and a room in the doctors' quarters." A crowd had gathered by this time, and embarrassment overtook anger again. It was time to discontinue this unrewarding conversation.

**Colt M 1911A1 Cal .45**

"Thanks," I said, and went to find the coffee pot. Two powerful smells filled my nostrils—rubbing alcohol and my own body. My boots were leaving dirty tracks on the polished floor. Everyone must have noticed my dirty fingernails on the pot handle, on the sugar spoon, and wrapped around the milk carton. I left the room to take a walk around the hospital.

The steps which entered onto the large, central, open patio provided a good place for an unclean visitor to sit and think. My .45 and flak jacket seemed pretty much out of place, and, in fact, more than a little corny now. Being so involved in my own thoughts, I hadn't noticed that my corpsman was sitting next to me.

"You should have decked him, Sir. I almost did."

I smiled. "I'm glad you didn't. You'd be in big trouble." I traded him the rest of my coffee for a cigarette. "He was right, you know. This is the way medicine should be practiced."

"Yes, Sir, but you can't take all this out into the jungle."

"We almost do." I felt better after the coffee and worse after the cigarette. "We have operating rooms within minutes of the front lines and doctors right where the action is. The grunts in this war get damn good care."

"When are we going back to Phu Bai?"

The light from the hall of the hospital provided enough light for me to see my watch. "Not tonight, big shot. Meet me here at 0800 tomorrow, and we'll talk about it."

"Thank you, Sir!" A night in Saigon is the kind of thing some soldiers dream about. This was the corpsman's big chance. No quarters. No hours. Nothing to do all night long but drink, and screw, and pretend, and forget. He left for the front gate as if he knew where he was headed.

"Stay out of trouble, big shot—and make that 0900."

A smile, a wave, and he was gone.

It was ten o'clock, and fatigue made me forget that my last meal had been at noon. I went to the "O" Club, got a can of beer, and sat in the corner. The doctors were well-groomed and rested. There were several women in the club. One of the doctors sat next to me and tried to make me feel welcome. He asked me about the I Corps, and the marines, and my job. I spoke in generalities and refused to tell any war stories.

Then the realizations began to find their way to the attention center. I was in a relatively safe place. I would not be called on all night long to receive casualties. I might go twelve hours or more without watching someone die. My arms were not available to insert tubes, cut off limbs, and handle mangled flesh. There would be no brains under my fingernails tonight. My eyes were not available for viewing any horror, and my ears might hear no cries, or moans, or grunts, or groans. For the first time in more than two

months, my brain would not have to make the decisions of
preservation of life or limb. For one night my heart was not
available for breaking.

Instead of celebrating I could hardly keep my eyes open.
The jukebox was playing some old rock. Another beer clunked
down in front of me. My eyes forced their way up to see that
it was the hospital commander's hand which was attached to
the can.

"On the house," he said.

"Thanks."

He went back to the table which he shared with a tall,
not very attractive girl with brown hair that flipped out at the
shoulders. They didn't talk much, but the knowing glances
and meaningful stares broadcast the fact that the C.O. had a
little hanky-panky going. Probably an air-conditioned rack. I
could imagine him in checkered boxer shorts leaning back
against the headboard of the bed with the ugly chick lying
nude next to him with her skinny tits sagging onto his elbow,
and her legs locked about his calf, while he sat there smoking
his ridiculous pipe and saying clever and knowledgeable
things. I'd rather have Sun on the ground in my bunker.

After finishing the free beer, I left the club and went to
look for Steve Rubenstein. He had been placed in an Intensive Care Unit. A new tube had been added to the network.
He had had a tracheotomy, and the trach tube was connected
to a respirator. He was unconscious. Another unit of blood
was running into his remaining arm.

The respirator labored through several cycles with hypnotic regularity. Blood dripped slowly into the intravenous
tubing. The urine bag contained about fifty cc of red brown
fluid. No one was paying attention to him now. Several severe
burns had just arrived from Ton Son Nhut where a phantom
jet had accidently crashed into a C-130.

A nurse saw me looking at the legless marine and came
over to his bed. It was the same blond I had seen in the
emergency room. I loved her.

"How's he doing? Did he get hemodialyzed?" I picked
up his chart and began to thumb through the pages.

"No. His renal chemistries weren't too bad, and he has
begun to have a little urine output."

"He quit breathing or something?"

"No, apparently his blood gases were terrible. He's

hypoxic even on pure oxygen. The doctor said it must be some kind of blast injury to the lungs."

"Looks grim."

"Do you want to be called if he dies?"

"No."

The officers' quarters were on the third floor of the oldest building, but they were plush compared to Hooch 75. I walked into the shower fully dressed and stood under the water for a long time before I slowly undressed to wash my clothes and body. Would the blond have gone to bed with me if I had made a real try? Did she know I was in love with her? Tomorrow I would find out her name.

Right now, sleep would come in relative safety in a clean bed in a concrete building in an army hospital in Saigon in Vietnam. Without the blond. Without anyone. Without noise. Without sand.

The next morning it was the privacy and convenience of a real flush toilet in an indoor bathroom that made me decide to stay in Saigon one more day. Steve Rubenstein was unchanged. I left a message for my corpsman and decided to tour Saigon on foot.

The guard at the gate stopped me. "Do you have a vehicle, Sir? It's not a good idea to walk the streets alone."

"It's all right. I'm a guest in this country," I said, and passed quickly through the gate while the guard looked puzzled.

The people looked like the Vietnamese in Hue, in the villes, and in the fields, except that they were better dressed and groomed, and seemed busier. They ignored the jeeps and military trucks which further crowded their already jammed streets. They especially ignored the Vietnamese policemen who directed traffic with a lack of enthusiasm that seemed a confession to absence of any real authority. Honda motorbikes carried teen-age couples, businessmen, and Vietnamese soldiers. These soldiers who had walked the streets as French enlisted men now rode as Vietnamese officers.

An American officer cannot walk more than a few feet without a pedicab driver wheeling along beside him offering his services. The cyclists are eager salesmen, and many do not accept polite rejection. I tried to engage the most insistent drivers in conversation in Vietnamese, but when they realized I wasn't going to be a riding, paying customer, they had no time for me. The peasants always had time for me although, admittedly, motivation varied from boredom to a chance for a handout, to fear of insulting the powerful American.

Tree-lined avenues with large, palacelike, concrete buildings, sidewalk cafes, and motorized vehicles were spotted with permanent and temporary shops obviously designed to sell to an American soldier market. A few minutes of fast walking led to small, crumbling shacks, where people and garbage flowed onto the streets, and children without pants begged for "chop-chop" or money. Their parents did not want to talk unless you were going to give or to buy. After awhile, it was impossible to continue to respond even verbally to each begging child, and it was necessary to walk with emotional blinders down street after street until again the atmosphere changed. Rhododendrons and uncollected garbage.

Then again bars and hotels lined both sides of the street. The trees had been cut down to expand the fronts of the buildings and permit large military vehicles to speed noisily past. More Americans were present in military and civilian clothes, and salesmen left their shops to guide them inside. Most of the businessmen dressed in western clothes, the women in bright-colored ao dais. They all spoke certain key English phrases and seemed to understand English. Americans could stop and buy American cigarettes, a coke, American beer, even a hot dog. He could be offered magazines, pornographic pictures, and trinkets, and, if he stood in one place long enough, he would be offered a radio or a TV fresh off the black market.

One man talked to me for ten minutes. I thought I had found someone who found conversation an informative, interesting, or stimulating interchange between two people. But as soon as he had satisfied himself that I was "safe," he showed me to the back of his store where he tried to sell me a weapon—Chinese, American, even French. When it became clear that I was not a customer, he offered me his daughter instead.

Whenever I slowed down my pace or stopped to look around, a woman would approach. "Give me cigarette?"

"You buy me drink?"

"You want some fun, GI?"

"You want quickie?"

Everybody has a friend, sister, mother, or daughter who

wants to "boom-boom" with an American soldier. On the main drag they run over you. Near the bars and hotels they won't leave you alone. And on the back streets they ignore you. A three-year-old boy urinated on a building while his eight-year-old sister tugged at the front of my pants. "Suckie, suckie, two hundred piasters."

Suddenly this jungle stopped again and opened onto a four-block area of patios, parks, wide streets, and large decorated buildings. Conservative Vietnamese in three-piece suits, smoking French cigarettes and carrying briefcases passed with friendly "Hello's." Cheap tin had changed to the recently repaired red tile roofs of the Pearl of the Orient.

"Shine, Sir?" A Vietnamese boy in white shirt and tie had set up his stand next to the bank.

I went into a soda shop and sat at a marble top table. The Vietnamese working in the shop and the Vietnamese customers were smartly dressed in western clothes. I studied them as I ordered a salad, hamburger steak, and ice coffee. The war was very far away. Nevertheless, it was inconvenient to have a war going on. There were always stories about some peasant-type people getting killed. But, then, the peasants are always bitching about land, or war, or something anyway. The country is full of them. Occasionally the Americans bitch about the war, too, but they keep coming with pockets full of money. At night the flares light up the outer limits of the city, and the bombs and guns occasionally overshadow the city night noises. But the war keeps business up, keeps the peasants down, and keeps the Saigon government stable—or at least holds down the number of coups. Saigon is a happy place once you get used to a few minor inconveniences.

More hours and more miles of walking, and a thousand characters repeated the same scenes all about me. The city must change to engulf the American and to create a wall against the horror in the countryside. The magic formula of the change is money—the landowners' deeds, the cash of the elite, and the American green. The citizens must learn to change with the city. It is a matter of survival. Some do it with dignity. Some sink to depravity. The pedicab driver, the waitress, the prostitute, the businessman, the politician, like the peasant in the field, does what he must to survive.

What magnitude of wealth is sufficient insurance for security? How rich and powerful must one be to survive?

Why does big sister make more in one night than father earns in two sixty-hour weeks? Is there any end to the money that grows on the GI tree? There is no time to answer these questions, because the wall around the city must be strengthened, and the money in the coffers must increase. Even the Americans cannot promise that the calm eye of the hurricane will always remain over Saigon.

On the rooftop of a stately white hotel was a large officers' club with open sides and a flat, metal roof. The long oak bar at one end was packed with men in military and civilian clothes. Tables with white cloths were filling with well-dressed officers coming for dinner. A few had American or Vietnamese women with them.

Standing at the bar after eight hours of walking caused a dull, aching fullness in my back. As I took a table near the stage, four Vietnamese men in tight black pants and fluffy red and white shirts began to assemble drums, untangle wires, and tune their electric guitars.

"Let me buy you a drink, Doc." A handsome and very young air force officer sat down uninvited at my table. "I'm celebrating tonight." He waved for a waiter (an American enlisted man in white shirt and black tie) and ordered a pitcher of beer, not thinking to ask my drinking preferences.

"I flew my first honest-to-God mission today." He looked at me, but as soon as our eyes met, he looked down at the table, and his voice softened slightly. "I got up at five o'clock this morning, was briefed with a bunch of patriotic bullshit, got in my sweet jet, and took off." He held the saltshaker in one hand and the sugar in the other and began to simulate flying an airplane.

The imaginary takeoff was interrupted by the arrival of the waiter. The pilot left the saltshaker control stick. Hurried, jerky movements suggested that he had been drinking for some time now. His words were, in fact, beginning to slur as he poured the beer into the glasses and onto the tablecloth as well. He resumed the controls.

"So, anyway, Doc, I headed north to this Somewheresville marked on my map with a red X—way the hell up in North Vietnam. I made three passes at a bridge which wasn't even there. I could see the whole river, the X-ville, and everything, but there was no bridge. Looked like some pilings where there used to be a bridge or something. But no bridge."

"Well, that——" This was the first time my mouth had chanced an opening since the pilot arrived, and he put up both hands in a gesture to silence me.

"I passed by three times to make sure. But no goddamn bridge." He paused to gulp down a whole glass of beer and to light a Salem, but hurried to prevent my attempting to speak again.

"So, what do I do?" He grabbed the saltshaker again and pushed it forward like a throttle. "I dropped all my bombs on this one sandpan I saw on the river." He slammed the table with his fist. "My first mission—one fucking sandpan. And I probably missed it. And even if I did hit it, the gooks have already made another one."

He leaned back in his chair, waved for the waiter, and forced a laugh which almost sounded like the preliminary chokings of a good cry. "All my training, a million dollar machine, thousands of dollars worth of bombs, and I probably killed one poor innocent bastard and blew up the family boat."

He leaned over and put his hand on my shoulder. "Doc, I'm an air ace. I'm a hero; a fucking war hero; a superstar. Like the ads on TV, I'm tough as hell. I mean, you put me, and all that gear, and money, and know-how up against a fucking unarmed sandpan, and I'm tough as hell."

The waiter was patient. He had heard this story many times before. Finally, after noticing my signal for another pitcher, he left.

"Who knows, tomorrow I may actually find a bridge. Or maybe I'll see a big red X. Wow."

"Maybe you'll really score big and hit a bicycle trail, or even tear the shit out of a rice paddy." I held my glass up as if to toast.

He held his glass to mine. "Or a church or a schoolhouse."

I leaned over and half-whispered, "You don't have to worry about hitting a supermarket or a bank or a theater."

"Why is that, Doc?"

"They don't have any."

He roared. "I like that, Doc. Can I buy you a drink?"

"You already have."

He was still laughing. "Or a hospital, or a grave yard, or a whore house, or a——"

A loud electric cord erupted from the Vietnamese band. The drum rolled while two bikini-dressed Vietnamese girls ran out onto the stage and began to dance go-go style in perfect unison as the combo broke into some hard-core rock. There was no more conversation. Music and beer floated toward us through a meal, and coffee, and cigarettes.

By drowning out the noises of the city below, the rooftop club seemed suspended and separated from the rest of the world. The city of hot, wide, motor-filled streets and narrow, dirty, human-filled alleys was making its own noises to separate it from the silent darkness of the countryside, a terrible darkness which never failed to return no matter how many explosions and noises men used to extinguish it.

A few feet from me were two young and sexy girls whose clothing and gyrations left little to be imagined in mentally undressing them and enjoying the sensual warmth of their sweat-wet bodies. Behind them, in the distance, flares spasmodically lit the sky as they drifted slowly toward the ground. On occasion, quick pop-flashes of bombs snaked fleetingly across the ground, their sounds muffled by the city and the drummer. The lights of the city never wavered or flickered or flared. Somewhere in those lights Steve Rubenstein and his tubes and his machines were fighting for survival. Somewhere beyond those flares there were black and white and yellow boys killing one another.

My new friend was now asleep at the saltshaker controls. I left to return to the still crowded, but somewhat less hyperactive streets below. No one, civilian or military, Vietnamese or American, seemed to know exactly where the army hospital was. There were no buses or streetcars or taxis. No telephones. A pedicab driver picked me up and nodded affirmatively that he knew exactly where the army hospital was. We rode for miles up and down streets. Each time I pointed at something, he turned in that direction. It soon became evident that he had no idea where he was going and cared less. He continued to shake his head politely as I got out and paid him for his efforts.

Someone was tugging at my arm. "You buy me drink?" A moderately ugly, but smartly dressed, Vietnamese girl motioned toward a bar. She stood very close to me so that her pubic bone pressed against my thigh. Maybe someone in the bar could tell me how to get back to the hospital. She led me to the bar where the Vietnamese bartender, who obviously knew her, placed a drink of colored water before her, and took my order for a beer.

The place was dark and full of moderately intoxicated enlisted men who were fondling and being fondled by several Vietnamese girls and women. None of them knew exactly where the hospital was.

"It's way over in another section of town. You'll never get there without a vehicle. And you won't get a vehicle this late at night."

"Is there a place I can sleep tonight?" My question brought all kinds of laughs and glances.

"Yes, Sir. This place has lots of back rooms. Small but well equipped." He grabbed the ass of the girl with him and his buddies laughed. I returned to the bar to finish my beer.

My hostess began her list of memorized, appropriate questions and statements.

"You lonely? How long you are in Vietnam? You like Saigon? You buy me 'nuther drink?"

She was a little surprised when I answered her in Vietnamese, but she continued with her practiced approach.

"You number one soldier. I like." She placed her hand on my thigh. "I think maybe you like boom-boom?" She felt for my genitals as she spoke. "You like?"

"Not tonight, sweetheart. I've been trying to quit." My exit did not go unnoticed, because a flying beer glass just missed my left shoulder and crashed into the doorway as I passed through it back into the street.

The only places remaining open and lighted were bars. Many of the signs were in English. I was on Sunset Strip, USA. We had made parts of Saigon, like our God, in our image. I tried another bar. This time my hostess was very attractive, less aggressive, and, therefore, more seductive.

"Dai úy Bác Sĩ," she interpreted my collar insignia. "Come in." I sat at a table and bought her a glass of colored water to go with my beer. This place was clean, much less noisy, and less crowded. A tape recorder behind the bar played popular American music.

"You are lonely? How long have you been in Vietnam?" When I answered in Vietnamese she smiled and corrected my pronunciation. We talked for some time. Her English was much better than my Vietnamese, and her French was better than my French. She was extremely pretty and pleasant, more so with each beer. I explained my predicament to her. She, of course, suggested that I sleep with her, and, with that cue, let her hand fall into my lap where it found much more than her predecessor had found. I looked at her for a long time. And then, for reasons unclear to me, I got up and left.

Tired, lonely, depressed, moderately high, lost. I actually wished I was back with my own outfit. At least there was a place for me to sleep, and I knew the rules. There were very few vehicles on the roads. I couldn't walk the streets all night.

A jeep driven by an MP pulled up beside me. "You shouldn't be on the streets in this neighborhood without a vehicle, Sir. Either stay inside or—do you have a vehicle?"

He listened impatiently to my story. "I get off duty at midnight. I'll drive you back to the army hospital then. Hop in."

"You saved me from having an exhausting evening or from getting VD." I accepted his kind offer of a Marlboro as I spoke.

"And probably saved you from getting rolled."

"By Vietnamese bandits?"

"No, by broke American GI's who need a fix, or a piece of ass, or a drink. Or by a soul brother who's out to even a score."

"No kidding?"

"It happens every night."

We rode around for an hour. Most of the time was spent keeping drunk soldiers off the streets. The MP didn't care where or with whom they went, just so they were off the streets.

"Would you believe I have been keeping drunk Americans off the streets of Saigon for eleven months? I go home soon, a big fucking war hero. I've never seen a VC or an NVA."

"You probably pass them on the street everyday. Who knows who is enemy?"

"Well, you're right." He wasn't bitter or emotional. He didn't care anymore. His war was almost over. "Most of the enemy's supplies come through Saigon. Nightclub operators get rich. Politicians get powerful. And those with money and power want to keep the war going indefinitely to get more of the same. The people in other parts of the city don't have enough to eat, but what the hell can they do?"

"They are just like the Vietnamese peasants up where I am. They're not concerned with politics, social change, land reform, or anything but actual physical survival. That's their full-time job."

"This war won't end, 'cause it's too profitable for the Saigon elite. America will help them continue it. But I don't give a good goddamn. My war is over in twenty-six days. Twenty-six more nights of talking GI's into staying off the streets. Twenty-six more nights of watching these crooked, slimey bastards get rich while their cousins three blocks down the street starve."

"I'll bet a lot of those bargirls and pedicab men and businessmen take their earnings home to support those poor crowded families."

"I don't give a rat's ass where they take it. I'm sick of this. I'm going home and forget it. If I never see a slanty-eyed bastard again, it's too soon for me."

We rode in silence for a few minutes. "There's your army hospital, Doc."

"Thanks very much for the ride. I'm glad your tour is almost over. Take care."

Steve Rubenstein died during the night. He was just as dead as if he had stayed in Graves two days ago. Steve Rubenstein's folks would find out by telegram sometime in the next day or two. They would not know what a hell of a try was made to save him. They would not know that one navy doctor was heartbroken when he died. They would not understand just why he had died.

Neither did I.

# FIVE

Sun had lots of questions about life in the United States. The material abundance seemed like a fairy tale to her. She wanted to understand how Americans thought and how their interests in Vietnam differed from those of the French. She never expected to see the United States but assumed she would be meeting Americans for many years to come. I supplied as many answers as I could. In return, Sun spent hours telling me about Vietnam and the Vietnamese people. She considered herself more realistic and pragmatic than her more traditional thinking friends. Her friends thought Sun to be westernized, egocentric, and selfish. She did not speak of her own life unless asked direct questions. Even then, she spoke with little emotion as if describing a mutual friend, a third party.

Sun had grown up running partly naked in the streets of Hue. Her father never returned from a march against the French. Her mother worked at anything she could find while Sun kept the house, cooked, and cleaned up after her brothers who played, went to school, and finally went to war. She did not have the time or money to join the new motorbike generation which was beginning to question authority of any kind. Her only contact with men or social life was the attention given her by her brothers' fellow soldiers when they visited her house. She became infatuated with one of them and married him.

About the time of the marked increase of American support to the Saigon regime, her mother and brothers fled to North Vietnam while Sun's husband became an officer in the Army of South Vietnam. Her husband became her only family, and, unfortunately, it was not a stable one.

Before her marriage, Sun had never had relations with a man. She had never even been alone with a man. Her brothers often discussed sex in front of her as if she were not present. They were far from modest. She had seen their pornographic pictures, and was aware of their group masturbation, which had at times included her husband-to-be. She understood that men were to be pleased, and she was prepared to cooperate.

The marriage was not a good one by anybody's standards. Her ambitious soldier husband was more egotistical and selfish than was acceptable even to the ever-changing Vietnamese culture. Sun was not a good candidate for tolerating such a one-man show, but she had decided that it was her role and she tried. The fact that the first baby was a boy pleased her husband considerably, and, by the end of the second year, it seemed that a more compatible relationship was developing.

The husband left for what was to be a six-month tour of duty with a moving infantry unit. He never returned. He was reported to have been killed by VC who ambushed an American advisor led mission, but rumors also circulated that he had deserted and run away to Saigon or had defected to the north.

Although she had no great affection for the absent soldier, Sun was not prepared for another sudden loss of the predominant male figure in her life. She was lonely and bitter. She had a one-year-old child, no money, no home. An old friend of the family kept her child each day while she worked washing dishes in an American MAC-V compound in downtown Hue. It was the same site previously occupied by French officials.

Because she was pretty and vivacious and because she began learning English, she was given more important jobs such as waitress or hostess or barmaid. She began to make more money and learned ways of getting larger tips. The Americans were always laughing and eating and drinking too much. They had come to help perpetuate war, but that all seemed very far away from downtown Hue and even from the MAC-V compound.

She rented her own little apartment and hired an old lady to keep her baby and prepare meals. She sensed a respect from her neighbors that was surprising to her. She was paying rent, could provide her friends with American cigarettes, and could afford the best of clothes. She was occasionally brought home in an American jeep escorted by one of those big, clumsy, white, rich, laughing, foreigners who were making lots of her neighbors wealthy also. Americans were beginning to be seen everywhere on the streets of Hue now, some of them even making very amusing attempts to speak Vietnamese. The foreigners were back and business was picking up.

Sun pulled down a number one job—bargirl at the Officers' Club. She did well. Several times daily she was propositioned by both sober and drunk officers. Her fellow bargirls told her how they could make a week's salary in one hour by spending an hour having intercourse with some sweet old "kernal." One day Sun allowed herself to be persuaded but found the whole episode unpleasant. She was surprised to realize that she did physically enjoy being possessed again but the slightly drunk young captain somehow reminded her of her husband, and he seemed to smile as if he was laughing at her. She gave the money to the old lady and decided to stick to being MAC-V's best bargirl.

Sun then became the object of the attentions of a thirty-five-year-old army captain from Texas. He became the "O" Club's most faithful customer, began to walk Sun home every night, and bought gifts for the baby and Salems for the old lady. One night the old lady fixed a late dinner for them and the captain stayed to dine. The one room apartment was then cleared and when the sleeping mats were unrolled the captain elected to stay overnight. He made several advances toward Sun during the night but each time they would move the old lady would light up a Salem, Sun would scold her, and the baby would waken.

Within a few days, the captain had acquired an off-base apartment and invited Sun and her baby to live with him. He paid her twice her present salary to be his housekeeper, cook, and woman. Sun accepted. He was very kind to her and to the child. Sun could have anything she wanted. She gladly shared his bed and, for the first time, learned to enjoy a meaningful physical relationship. It was the Texan who first called her Sun, a name she always, thereafter, insisted upon.

They both knew that the arrangement was temporary but both expected and received absolute faithfulness. When

the captain went on R & R for six days, Sun missed him very
much. He turned down a second R & R to remain with his
temporary wife and child. They lived a good life and never
talked about the future. The captain had an eight to four
thirty life and was fortunate to remain in Hue for his full
twelve-month tour. He usually remained on base for the
evening movie and would return home about nine o'clock.
He often came home for lunch and supper. On Sundays the
captain, Sun, and her young boy would shop or just bicycle
about the streets of Hue.

When his tour ended, Sun did not ask him to stay or to
take her to the USA. She knew it was time for another
goodbye. She did not even tell the army officer that she was
probably pregnant. Broken English and tears made her seem
awkward as she stood at the door holding the hand of the
little boy.

"You be good to your American wife like you be to Sun
and she make you very happy, you number one husband."

"I'll always remember you, Sun; I'll always——" He
turned and walked away.

The three-year-old boy began to realize that the big man
who threw him up in the air and held him and loved him and
who slept with his mother was leaving not to return. He
began to cry and stamp his foot.

The big Texan left in the fall of 1966. Sun went back to
work at MAC-V after she had given birth to another child.
Again she had to start in the kitchen. She did not like her
return to this position. It seemed that now the only way to
move up would be to prostitute herself to the right people.
Sun became angry and quit. In early summer of 1967 she
began as bargirl of the "O" Club for A Med at Phu Bai. She
had to spend most nights in a small room behind the club
because the highway from Hue to Phu Bai was closed after
dark and she could not return to Hue. The old lady again
kept the children in Hue and Sun returned home on weekends. Sun shared her back room with another bargirl, Coe
Van. The two of them slept in a room barely big enough to
hold a bed. They were the only two women in the Phu Bai
area at night. They worked from four to ten and spent their
days napping or chatting with the Vietnamese girls who came
to the base each day to clean the hooches and do the washing
and ironing.

She had a brief affair with two of the Americans on base. The first was terminated when the navy chief had decided that it was too dangerous to continue because if he had ever been caught with this woman, who was living on base by special permission and who was the "O" Club's only and very popular bargirl, that he would be in big trouble. Loss of job for Sun. Permanent field duty for the chief. The other affair was a brief encounter with a navy officer shortly before his tour of duty ended.

The officer promised to send for Sun to come to the States. She never heard from him. She didn't really expect to. Sun then decided that emotional involvement with the American military men in Phu Bai was unrewarding and uncomfortable and possibly even dangerous if it should mean losing her job.

Some of the MSC officers made it clear to Sun that male guests in her hooch or her presence in their hooches would be an unacceptable breach of the contract which allowed her to live on base and have her job. Other officers secretly and openly offered to make her rich for her after-hour services. Most of the doctors simply treated her as their happy bargirl and were satisfied to leave it at that. Smiles, touches, shady jokes, good service, and an occasional pat on the ass. She listened to each of them and weighed their outlooks taking into account their sincerity, rank, and number of drinks.

Nobody really knew how she was playing it. She said she was playing it straight. With MSC, Intelligence, and navy doctors all using the same "O" Club it was never clear who was checking up on whom and nobody talked about Sun outside of joking about the fact that she would be a great piece of ass. Her job required her to play a teasing and suggestive role, and she played it very well.

I had been tempted to move in on Sun myself but felt that such a move was not right for a married man. At times, however, the constant sight of casualties, impending fear of death, sounds of war, loneliness, sleep deprivation, and horniness made it seem that morals, manner, and motives were only relative and some of them even inappropriate in war. After all, my wife and I were separated—by one year and twelve thousand miles. At times when I thought like that I was just plain afraid of getting caught. Maybe I would get sent to the field myself. The practical, survival-oriented man in me had begun to rule supreme. I played it straight with Sun and we got along very well as friends.

Sun often spoke of her friends and activities in Hue. At her insistence I drove in one day to see Hue and to tour the imperial walled city, the seat of the past rulers of Vietnam. The unoccupied temples, throne rooms, and royal chambers were impressive. I studied the time-thickened metal urns and century-dulled marble floors which had been possessed, if only for a time, by a long list of kings, conquerers, colonialists, liberators, subversives, and tourists. I wasn't sure which of these categories I fitted into, if any. I didn't know then that American weapons would be the first to destroy large parts of this ancient monument.

On one of my trips to Hue I visited the Vietnamese Provincial Hospital and met some of the volunteer doctors from Germany, France, and the United States. It was the best civilian medical care available and it was not good.

Two or more patients shared each bed in the crowded but bare rooms. Family members lived in the rooms with the patients preparing meals on the floor between the beds. Some of the old patients urinated or spit on the floor. Many of the children were without clothes. The oppressive heat acted on the unwashed patients and waste materials so that the air seemed fit only for the flies which buzzed about the room, their flights interrupted only by the slow, apathetic fanning of the more energetic family members. Small groups of men and women squatted wordlessly in the corner taking turns drinking a watery rice soup from a rusty tin bowl and feeding wasted children. A black-toothed old woman ground leaves and herbs in a wooden bowl with the bottom of a coke bottle.

To the civilians illness, like war, was just another aspect of life which had to be tolerated, accepted, and passively observed. Grief was frequent, physical, and spontaneous and went almost unnoticed as transient human displays which did not change the necessary misfortune of life. To the Vietnamese, the only puzzling thing in the hospital was the presence of American military doctors who in their strange time-conscious, great white benefactor and businesslike ways actually seemed to be concerned about the health of a Vietnamese peasant. Although the white doctors seemed repulsed by the scenes they witnessed, they returned day after day and actually felt they could change the patient. Although their goals were

foolishly optimistic it was rumored that their medicines were
very powerful and maybe better than those of the French.

I also came across a tuberculosis hospital run by a small
group of Vietnamese Catholic nuns. In contrast to the provincial hospital, the wards here were spotless. The clean, stone
floors were waxed, the hallways and walls shone with cleanli-
ness. Beds in the large, open wards were clean, neat and
each contained only one patient in clean bed clothes. Family
visitors stood quietly at the foot of the beds. The smell was
the familiar disinfectant odor of a hospital. There were no
nurses, doctors, orderlies, maids, or technicians.

After a talk with the Division Surgeon, I offered my
services to the nuns to act as the doctor for the hospital. They
were extremely grateful. They had been taking care of over
two hundred in-patients by themselves with knowledge they
could gather from doctors, textbooks, and mistakes and with
French and Vietnamese medicines supplied somehow by the
church. No physician directed the patient care in the big
hospital although an adjacent building with ten or twelve
wealthy private patients was visited regularly by a Vietnamese
doctor.

I spent two or three mornings a week in Hue at the TB
hospital. One of the nuns, Maria, was a registered nurse and
spoke a little English. She was slightly heavy, very pleasant,
and extremely bright. She became my nurse, first assistant,
interpreter, and friend. She spent hours organizing and preparing for my visits, selecting those patients who most needed
my attention. She saw to it that I was extremely busy. I
usually examined twelve to fifteen patients who were new
admissions, were not improving, were very sick, or were
ready for discharge. Each week several patients needed to
have fluid drawn out of their lungs by inserting a needle into
their chests. I looked at selected X rays and then walked
quickly through all of the wards.

I saw every kind of tuberculosis, mild and severe. Tuberculosis of lungs, skin, brain, bones, kidneys, and meninges.
The Sisters questioned my every decision as eager students
and learned quickly. Their base of knowledge was impressive
and their eagerness to learn and work hard would shame a
Harvard medical student. Patient cooperation was sometimes
minimal and patients often walked out or refused to take their
medicines. What discipline there was stemmed more from

respect, or fear, of the Sisters than from any understanding or concern about their disease. The family visitors and Sisters did not wear masks. I brought my own mask from one of the Phu Bai O.R.'s and only wore it when in close contact with a patient. My tuberculosis skin test never converted to positive.

Most all of the patients were civilians. Most had been sick for some time before seeking help. All were poor and did not pay for their care. One of my patients boldly admitted to me that he was a VC. For some reason I didn't care.

I felt like some kind of missionary doctor. These people really needed me. Work made time pass and it got me away from the constant influx of casualties which was beginning to wear me down emotionally.

To be completely practical, and there is nothing like a one year personal survival test to make one completely practical, the job at Hue would help make it necessary for me to remain at Phu Bai and not go out into the field. The TB hospital job, Vietnamese sick call, MEDCAP, language class, internal medical clinic, reading chest X rays, and being a good surgical assistant were all part of my plan of being essential to A Med at Phu Bai. Self-created importance and tricks to preserve mental health were part of my plan of survival. And I was getting better at both of them.

Sun came with me on my frequent trips to Hue. We dropped her off at her house and picked her up on our return trip. Some drivers were reluctant to drive down the side streets and break the rule against carrying civilian passengers. But since Roland was in charge of Motor Transport I never worried about that. I sometimes had a quick lunch at the MAC-V compound or at Sun's little apartment before hurrying back to resume my medical battalion duties. I got to know every mile of Highway One between Phu Bai and Hue. I knew parts of Hue very well but never had time to walk the streets or visit. The only way I could continue all of my jobs was to work twelve to sixteen hours a day and, when receiving heavy casualties, to omit my TB hospital rounds.

By noon each day, a corpsman delivered the mail to each hooch onto each man's rack. This posed a very important decision: to check the mail immediately upon my return from Hue or to go to chow hall first. The variables had to be weighed carefully. If there was no mail I didn't want to know.

If there was a letter from home I might get so worked up that I couldn't eat. On the other hand, if there was a care package on my bed I might be able to avoid the chow hall altogether.

One day I felt unusually optimistic and decided to check the mail first. Just as I approached the hooch door a corpsman called to me.

"Doctor Parrish, we need help in triage. A troop transport hit a land mine on the road to Hue."

I looked on my rack. A package and two postcards. I wheeled around and ran up to triage.

"Tell the mess sergeant to save me a sandwich," I called back to the corpsman who was already at another hooch gathering more doctors. "I'm starved."

"Yes, Sir."

Before I reached triage I noticed a marine major kneeling on the ground with one shoulder pressed against a sandbag wall. He still wore his flak vest but his helmet lay beside him exposing his tan face and matted, graying hair. He was directing a stream of angry profanities at the ground while rhythmically striking the sandbags with his right fist.

When I knelt down next to him he didn't seem to see me but his cursing stopped and tears began to roll down his cheeks. The knuckles of his right hand were raw and bleeding as he continued to pound at the sandbags and stare at the ground.

I grabbed the wrist of his bleeding hand and held it firmly for a few moments until he no longer struggled to free it. When I loosened my grip, he tucked his hand against his chest, pressed his head against the sandbags, and sobbed like a baby. I left him there against the wall. It wasn't long before I knew why he was crying. Triage was a mess.

A second troop truck had brought in all of the dead and wounded in a pile without any splints, battle dressings, or first aid. The truck was backed up to the triage door and doctors and corpsmen were up in the back of the truck picking and separating the bodies and lowering them into litters. At the same time a line of litters were being carried in the other door from a fixed wing just arrived from Dong Ha.

I climbed up one side of the transport truck and lowered myself over the railing in among the horrible pile of bleeding flesh. One marine with a large wound in his neck tried to stand up and take a step toward me. He fell into my arms and we both crashed into the middle of the pile. Screams of pain came from beneath us. I pushed my hand behind me to right myself and placed it inside a gaping feces-filled tear through a marine's rectum and pelvis.

The marine next to him vomited blood and began to aspirate. I tried desperately to turn him over on his stomach so that he could breathe. I pulled at the leg that prevented me from turning him and noticed that a leg was all I had. There was no body attached to it. The marine who had vomited stopped breathing. I started to bang on his chest until I saw the brain tissue matted in his black hair.

We finally all made it into triage where I spent the next six hours giving first aid and debriding wounds. Then I scrubbed in with Bill in the O.R. where we spent three hours patching up the intestines of a big black staff sergeant.

"This case is taking me too long." Bill was upset, "We've got two more bellies and all the orthopods are busy with legs."

"You can only do the best you can, Bill." I was trying to be helpful.

"Cut." Bill was staring at my stilled hands in the wound.

"I'm sorry. I wasn't ready," I hadn't seen the tie. Bill and I had operated together enough times so that he shouldn't have to give me instructions in assisting him. I picked up the scissors and cut above the knot.

"Cut." Bill was shouting.

The scissor came in too low and cut the knot.

"Sorry."

"Goddamn it." Bill was pissed.

"Tie. Hold that retractor back will you." I couldn't move fast enough to satisfy Bill.

"Tie!" Bill paused, "Tie, goddamnit . . . here, I'll tie it myself."

"Sorry, Bill."

"That's all right, John. I'm just tired."

"I hate to be a pansy ass," I said, "but if someone doesn't get me a coke or a drink of water I'm going to pass. I haven't had a drink of water for twelve hours."

A corpsman left the room and returned with milk in a cup. He fit a straw under my mask and into my mouth.

"I dumped some sugar and salt in it, Sir."

"I noticed. It tastes shitty. Thanks. Get me some more."

"Yes, Sir."

We operated in silence. Bill started closing the belly. "You okay, John?"

"I'm ready for another belly."

"Good, put the skin ties in this one. I'll start another one next door."

We left the O.R. about midnight. I was tired all over. Even my eyeballs were tired. I smelled like a truckload of dead marines. We walked out under the naked light bulbs of triage just as a jeep pulled up and unloaded a marine missing his left foot and another marine with a stiff neck and headache. Two MP's entered the other door wrestling with a very drunk marine.

"He's running around trying to kill everybody," an MP spurted out. "He's really drunk."

"Shove it, mac. Leave me alone." The drunk stumbled and fell and took one of the MP's with him. He tried to strangle the MP. After much loud scuffling, cursing, screaming, and effort, the two MP's immobilized the intoxicated marine, face down on the deck.

Bill and I had used this time to evaluate the two casualties. Bill stopped the bleeding in the stump on the first boy and started an IV. He walked over to where I was working on the second patient.

"What's up?" he said.

"I think he's got meningitis. His neck is stiff as a board and he feels hot."

"Well, that's your bag. You take care of him. Call an orthopod for the leg. I'm going to bed." Bill turned and slowly walked out of triage rubbing the back of his neck and looking down at his feet.

I sat down on the bench and watched the struggling drunk. He was about eighteen or nineteen, big and strong, and very loud.

"It's not fair," he kept screaming between profanities. "It's not fair."

I looked over at the corpsman undressing the boy with meningitis. "Get me a spinal needle and set up an IV. Wake up the lab tech and get me a cup of coffee." I didn't think I had the energy to stand up again.

"Doc. Doc." The MP grunted between efforts, "What do we do with this drunk shit? He wants to kill somebody."

"That's what he's over here for. Give him a gun." I could not break my tired, straight-ahead stare at the floor as I spoke.

"Seriously, Sir, what do we do with him?"

"I don't really care," I said.

"I know what I'm going to do to him if he kicks me again," grumbled the other MP. "I'm going to beat the shit out of the cock sucker."

I spoke to the corpsman who was now helping subdue the big marine. "Give him fifty milligram of Thorazine IM and lock him up."

"It's not fair," screamed the drunk. "Goddamn it, it's not fucking fair."

I finished treating the boy with meningitis about 1 A.M. and walked slowly back to my hooch. I thought of my package and my two postcards. I was too tired and depressed to be hungry anymore. All the hoochies were asleep.

I picked up the postcard.

"We of the First Baptist Women's Circle are praying for you. May God be with you and bring you safely home."

Signed by someone I never heard of.

I threw it on the desk and grabbed the other card.

"The Women's Prayer Circle is sending cards to remind our church members overseas that God is Love. His will be done. We prayed for you tonight."

I threw the card on the floor and ripped the package open. Inside were thirty hand-printed letters from a third grade class in Winter Park, Florida. I threw my hat on the desk, sat down on the side of my bed, and holding my forehead in one hand began to read the letters.

"I am sorry that you are in a war. Did you kill anybody?"

"I hope you will be home for Christmas."

"My name is Robby. My dad has a new boat. He takes me for rides. Do you have boats in Vietnam?"

"Are there children in Vietnam? Do they get hurt in a war? Are they afraid?"

"Would you send me a picture of you with your gun? Do you shoot good?"

"I hope your war is short. I just had a baby brother."

"How is the weather in Vietnam? Does it snow at Christmas?"

"I hope you are a good soldier. My teacher says you are brave."

"My name is Sally. I draw good pictures. Here is a picture of you and a dead communist."

"I hope you don't get sad. I hope you will have Christmas in Vietnam. I like you."

"My sister's boyfriend is a soldier. Do you know Eddie Kullen?"

"I hope this war is over soon so that you can come home. You could see our school carnival."

"I saw your war on TV. I saw lots of helicopters. I saw one man get hurt."

"I hope you come home. My name is Roberta. You could ride on my pony."

"I wish that the war was not so far away so you would not be so lonely."

"I hope in the war nobody gets hurt. I . . ."

I fell back onto the bed now filled with letters. "It's not fair," I thought, "it's not fucking fair." I fell asleep.

Several hours must have passed because it was light when my burning eyes tried to open. A mellow baritone on the tape recorder was just clinging to the old "Rugged Cross." I didn't want to move. I sensed that all my hoochies were up and moving. I somehow knew, without looking at my watch, that I had missed chow and Sun's trip to the head. Graves marines were wondering where I was and there was probably already a line at the shitter.

Mornings were bad enough when I was on top of things but to start late, out of step, tired and with the crowd was more than I could face. I did not want to begin again. Everyday led eventually to the same place—triage—where the same kids had the same wounds and made the same noises.

A hillbilly tenor and a country alto were now singing, "Amazing Grace." Their nasal voices were not quite one third apart and they slid onto each note so that you couldn't be quite sure when they found it. The music, the prone position, and vague awareness of my body all seemed good. Everything else seemed not only unnecessary, but also threatening. I was totally engrossed in a battle between attempting to open my eyes again and yielding to the escape of sleep. Parts of the conversation in the hooch began to make it to my brain.

"Say Myron, will you get that shit off the recorder. It's not even Sunday." It was Roland's voice.

"Do you some good," came from Myron's corner.

"I don't want to be as good as you," barked Roland between early morning cigarette coughs, "you miserable creep."

Carefully spoken words in early morning bass voice from Prince's corner, "Myron, I know you need your religion, but we don't need that music at eight o'clock in the morning."

"Do you some good."

I forced my eyes to open and there was Bill fully dressed combing his hair. "Speaking of religion," he said, "today's my birthday. You guys make sure and gather up some presents today."

"I got your present right here hanging down," coughed Roland as he lit up a Marlboro.

"Happy Birthday," said Myron.

"Well I guess tonight is party time," smiled Prince. "We'll have our own little party right here in the hooch."

By now I was sitting on the side of my bed. "Happy Birthday," was all I could manage until I was more awake.

Myron walked over to my bed, "See you in the medical ward. We'll start rounds whenever you get there."

I shook my head and Myron left. Bill and Prince were right behind him. I heard them clomping away down the wooden walkway toward the hospital.

A tenor began to sing, "I Come to the Garden Alone." His voice was clear and true and somehow relayed a lack of effort on his part. I stretched to bring life back to my limbs. My bed was filled with children's letters and my boots hurt my feet from their all night tightness.

"You look like shit," accused Roland, "and you smell worse. You'd better start your day in the shower." He headed for the door. "Come to think of it, chief said the shower's not working now." He left.

I was alone except for the tenor on the tape recorder. I stretched again and sat back down on the side of the bed. The background music stopped and the tenor carried on unaccompanied so high and true that I got goose bumps.

"And he walks with me and he talks with me . . ."

My eyes were filling with tears.

"And he tells me I am his own."

My defenses weren't ready. I felt so sad and alone.

"And the joy we share as we tarry there..."

In my mind I could see my dad in the pulpit telling people about his God and his Jesus. He had tears in his eyes too but he was smiling.

"None other has ever known." The tenor ended and there was silence. I began to unbutton my rotten shirt.

I closed my eyes and could see a very real image of my dad telling the congregation about God. In my mind I could hear him telling how God had taken his oldest boy from him, his firstborn child when he was only ten years old. My mother in the tenth pew had tears rolling down her cheek. My dad's voice was trembling as he tried to carry on his sermon. His boy had died and gone to be with God. But it was okay because somehow God was still love. I thought how the death of my older brother had irreversibly shaken my very religious parents, warped my early childhood and how all those boys in Graves everyday were doing the same thing to peoples' minds at home.

The music returned to the hooch and the tenor sang again.

"The love of God is greater far than tongue or pen can ever tell..."

I pulled the foul-smelling green T-shirt over my head, balled it up, and wiped the tears from my face.

"It goes beyond the highest star and reaches to the lowest hell..."

I closed my eyes again.

"Oh the love of God how rich and pure..."

I was crying.

"How measureless and strong."

For the first time since I had come to Vietnam, for the first time I could remember, I was crying.

"It shall forever more endure—The saints and angels song."

I buried my face in the T-shirt. The tenor kept singing. I kept crying. I knelt on the floor by my bed with my face on my sandy blanket. My body odor mixed with blood and shit and vomit filled my head. "God, help me," I said to myself and maybe to God Himself, "help me."

Myron had already started rounds when I joined him.

He was standing at the side of one of the cots where a marine with malaria lay. The marine seemed to feel fine.

"Good morning, John."

"Good morning." Our eyes met for what seemed to be a long time. "Join me for coffee?"

"Sure." We headed for the big urn back in our private corner of the ward. We fixed our coffee in silence.

"Myron," I paused because I wasn't sure what I was going to say. "Are we going to make it?"

"Sure, John. Sure we are. We are going to make it like champs."

"What are we doing here?"

"We're taking care of sick marines. Sick kids." Myron studied my face. "It's our job right now."

We drank coffee in silence. Myron sat at his desk and held his cup in both hands. I sat in the chair where the patient usually sits. I took off my glasses and began to rub my eyes.

"Myron."

"Yeah, John."

"Nothing."

"What's up?"

"Nothing. Let's get to work."

We made rounds, read X rays, drank more coffee, and then I wandered up to triage. The Dong Ha special was just arriving with eight, six, and two. I spent the rest of the day in sick call or triage whichever was busiest. I seemed to be slower and less efficient than usual that day.

About five o'clock things suddenly slowed down and I went for a run. It felt so good to sweat and hurt that I ran to the point of exhaustion.

The shower had been fixed. I felt a little more at peace with the world after I was clean and had finished two cans of Prince's Vienna sausages and a beer. I sat at my desk to create an answer to the letter from the third graders. I read all the letters again. I thought of my own kids and since my hoochies were not home I put on the most recent tape from home. I had heard it twice already.

"John, you should see Lynn. She's really grown and she looks like you. I've tried to teach her to say Daddy but it always come out 'Da Da.'"

I was getting choked up again, damnit. What was happening to me?

"When are you coming home, Daddy?"

I didn't want to cry again. I gripped the sides of my desk and wished my hoochies would come back.

"We are really all fine. I miss you very much and think about you all the time."

Goddamn tears again.

"The kids talk about you. They won't forget you. Susan tells her friends that you are taking care of children in 'Veet-Nam' and that you will come back some day."

Pansy-ass bastard, I was crying again, twice in one day.

"Daddy, would you please come home just for Christmas? You could go back after that."

I had only been in this fucking mess for two months. It seemed like two years. And I had five that long to go. I could not possibly last one more day.

"When are you coming home, Daddy?"

I heard Prince and Roland coming down the walk. I cut off the tape recorder and removed the tape. I barely got The Mamas and Papas tape in place when they walked in the hooch.

"It's about time you farts got here. Where the hell have you been?" I spoke loudly because The Mamas and Papas had already started singing, "This is dedicated to the one I love."

"We were just securing a little booze for the party." Prince smiled, "Tonight is Bill's birthday party, you know."

With minimal effort, I carried on a conversation with my hoochies. I acted like I was reading something at my desk but I was really concentrating on every word The Mamas and Papas were singing—just for me.

That song, that very song was playing the night my wife and I danced until 2 A.M. two days after I got my orders to go to Vietnam. We looked right into each other's eyes and a million unspoken messages were firing at rapid rate, said for us by the record. It was almost as if we knew how bad things were going to be, how long a year was going to be, and how we would both change. After that night, we didn't have to say much. It had all been said. All the rest was a big empty show of strength to help the other.

We had played it again in the jukeboxes of San Francisco on our last weekend together over a hundred years ago. Would that be our last weekend together forever?

Roland turned the music up and began to dance around

the hooch. Prince watched. Bill came in from the O.R. and stood next to my desk.

"You not dancing, John? You having a downer today?"

"I'm earning my family separation allowance today. Happy birthday."

"Big party right after the movie," Prince announced. They left for the movies.

I began to try to write a letter to the third graders.

Dear Third Grade Class:
Thank you for your letters, I was glad to hear from you.

I thought for a minute. I had nothing else to say. I put the letter aside.

Dear Women's Prayer Circle,
Thank you for your cards. It's good to know that someone is praying for us. I was glad . . .

I had nothing to say. I tore up the letter. I tried to imagine the prayer circle. Silent prayers. Verbal prayers. Some were probably sincere.

I had nothing to say to the third graders or prayer circle. I wrote a letter to my wife. It was a lonely, mushy letter. So mushy it was almost pornographic. So pornographic it was almost beautiful. Would I reach the point where I had nothing to say to my family? My own wife? The thought was frightening.

Myron walked in with the chaplain.

"Hi, John."

"Hi, John."

"Hi, fellows."

"Little hearts tonight?" asked the chaplain. "Myron is getting too good for me."

"No thanks," I apologized. "Letter writing time."

The chaplain sat down on my bunk, "John, would you lead the prayer at services Sunday?"

"I don't pray out loud very well, Chaplain. I'll read the scriptures or something if you want."

We both knew it was just a ploy to get me to Sunday services. I hadn't been for weeks. Myron and the chaplain knew I grew up in a Baptist church and worried about my soul. So did I. And my body. And my mind.

The whole crew returned from the movies. We sang Happy Birthday to Bill and gave him our presents. A book. A pair of Ho Chi Minh shoes made from an old tire. A big bar of soap on a rope. A big green towel.

"Well, thank you all very much. I'll always remember this as the shittiest birthday I've ever had."

"I'll drink to that," Prince broke out a bottle of scotch and several goodies from his pantry. Over the next four hours he and Roland finished the scotch, Bill drank most of the beer we had in the ice box, and Myron left to visit the chaplain. I had to leave twice to see fever patients in triage, but after midnight I helped Bill knock off the beer.

I sat in the corner of my bed with my knees drawn up and my bare feet on the sandy blanket. I leaned against a two-by-four that held the screen wall in place and watched Bill and Prince and Roland dance arm in arm about the center of the room, stumbling, laughing, spilling their drinks, and trying not to care. Forget. Escape. Drown.

Myron was tolerant. He was sleepy. He understood. He looked over at me and smiled. I shot him a thumbs up and he smiled again.

Roland turned the tape recorder up and his dancing grew louder as he stomped about the hooch.

The hospital C.O. appeared at the door. No one saw him until he spoke.

"Will you assholes quiet down. Turn that music down and get the hell to bed. You're not supposed to drink too much. You're not supposed to make so much noise. You're not supposed to have your goddamn lights on. I could hang your ass."

"It's Bill's birthday," said Prince as if to explain away his activities.

"I don't care if it's Christ's birthday. Keep the noise down."

Myron shrugged toward the C.O. apologetically and turned the tape recorder down. I looked down at the floor and the three dancers quietly retreated. The C.O. stormed out.

"Asshole," said Bill loudly.

The C.O. stormed back into the room. "I don't know who said that but this time I'll pretend I didn't hear it."

"I'll pretend I didn't say it," Bill belched. The C.O. left again.

"Asshole," whispered Bill. He got up and turned off the light.

Bill, Prince, and Roland pulled chairs up into a tight circle and talked like buddies in a bar. I threw in my comments from my bed. I wished I were drunk. I wished I didn't care. I wished I had temporarily escaped. I opened another beer.

"Asshole will probably close the club for a week now," Bill said.

"Or bar us from going in it," added Roland. "Fart head."

"Or enforce the two-beer limit," laughed Prince.

"Or make it a dry compound."

"And lights out at ten o'clock."

"Sorry we can't take casualties tonight. It's after taps."

"The doctors can't come to triage. They are being punished."

"General, General, my doctors are drinking. One of them called me an asshole."

"Well, you are an asshole, Commander."

A round of laughter and a few coughs.

"So once a year we get a little loaded and the military minded C.O. turd pulls a big scold job."

"Scold job. Scold job."

I had been thinking quietly and I was ready for the presentation of my theory.

"Are you ready for the Law of Standard Military Reaction?" I called.

"Yes." They all silenced and waited.

"Quiet," whispered Myron.

"One, assume the worst."

Cheers from the trio of drunks.

"Two, overreact."

More cheers. "Yes. Yes."

"Three, make a hard fast rule."

Cheers grew louder. Roland fell out of his chair.

"Four, create a new job."

Applause. Roland pulled on the arm of Prince's chair to

get up and Prince turned over on top of Roland. Neither tried to get up. Loud laughter.

The door swung open again. The C.O. came in red-faced. "Okay okay now you've done it. You doctors cannot be trusted with alcohol. I just might get you all sent away. Tomorrow the two-beer limit is in strict effect. No exceptions. The chief will be in charge of keeping strict records. You guys have pushed me into this. Now get the hell to sleep." He said it all so fast and so loud that nobody moved. I pretended to be asleep. Prince lay on top of Roland on the floor and Bill stared at the C.O. from his chair as Myron quaked in the corner.

The C.O. stormed out.

"Asshole," whispered Bill.


"It's not so much the fear of when they're charging your perimeter. I mean that's just a scared-shitless quick burst and its over." The Pfc. couldn't have been older than seventeen or eighteen. He was sitting across the desk from Prince in his hospital office.

"Yes, go on," Prince was holding his head in his hand and drinking black coffee. I had come by to see how Prince was surviving his hangover.

The kid was sweating. He held his hat in his hands and looked at the floor. "It's not so much thinking about them shells hitting you when they're falling all around you. I mean the one's you see fall and the ones you hear obviously ain't gonna get you. Right?"

"Right," said Prince. I put two aspirin and a Darvon next to Prince's coffee. He smiled and nodded. I didn't speak and sat down in the corner.

"It's not even the killing. I mean I got twelve or thirteen confirmed kills. I saw one poor sucker die ten feet from me. I made so many holes in him that he splattered blood all over me. His face looked like a boy. But it was him or me. Right?"

"Right."

"I killed an old lady. I thought she had a gun. I was so pissed off when my buddy got it that I blew up two kids riding a water buffalo." The kid was talking faster now and really sweating.

"It's not all that. It's something else. It's not the quick and awful things. It's that scarey, lonely feeling I have all the time that wears me down. I can't sleep. I can't eat. I can't think. I can't even shit anymore. Sir."

Prince looked down at his desk. There was a long silent period.

"It's like a fucking Chinese torture. Drip. Drip. Drip. It's always there. I'm so alone. I'm so scared I can't stand it. Right now I feel like screaming—or fucking crying—or running—or something."

Silence.

"I just can't take it, Sir. Don't you see. I'm afraid I might kill my gunny or some kid—or—or myself."

"Do you really think you might kill yourself buddy?" Prince spoke like a sympathetic father.

"I can't think at all." The kid was yelling. "I don't want this on my record. I'm no chicken shit. I just need some nerve pills or something. Just give me some fucking pills, Doc, and I'll get back to work. Tell the gunny I'm okay. He thinks I've flipped."

"Relax."

"Fucking gunny thinks I'm crazy." The boy was fighting tears. "Fucking gunny took me off my watch. I can stand my own fucking watch, I just need some nerve pills or something. I can stand two watches for every one the fucking gunny wants me to."

"I think you could use some rest. We'll talk again later."

"Fucking gunny. I could kill that son-of-a-bitch. Toughest gunny in the corps. I love the bastard. If he wants me to stand watch, I'll stand watch all night every night."

"I know, buddy."

"It gets so fucking black at night. Everything moves. My eyes play tricks. I get so worked up that my breathing is louder than the crickets and I hear voices. I shot at the fucking voices. That's why the gunny sent me here. If they'd been VC I'd be a fucking hero. Now, I'm crazy. It's not fair."

"We'll talk again." Prince called for a corpsman who stood by the desk while Prince wrote something on the chart. Prince handed the chart to the corpsman, "Snow him. The usual. Thorazine. Phenobarb later. I want to talk to him tomorrow."

"Is he crazy?" I asked.

"Don't know, John. We'll find out tomorrow when he's rested. They're all crazy when they first come in."

"I guess his gunny realized he needed some rest."
"He shot his gunny in the head."

The three mornings in Hue returned some structure to
the week. For the first time in months, I was again always
aware of what day of the week it was. At least the misery in
the TB hospital was a different kind of misery in different
kinds of people. That too quickly became routine.

The work at Phu Bai continued without change. The
steady inflow of sick and wounded marines was only interrupted
by occasional mass casualties, a snake bite, an unusually big
day at Graves, or handfuls of civilian casualties. The long
evenings and nights were all the same except for occasional
red alert, a third-rate USO show, or a drunk by some of the
Hooch 75 crew.

We began to entertain ourselves at night with pornographic movies obtained from marines sent to the Division
Psychiatrist. We saw every possible sex act with every possible combination of man, woman, or animal. It soon became
boring in such large doses.

I was getting too busy to continue my Vietnamese classes
and studied and read less. For the sake of my mental health,
I was faithful to my runs and my chats with Sun. Time
crawled. Making myself busier and busier did not seem to
help.

One night Prince told me that he had been offered an R
& R to Bangkok. He could not go because he had a meeting
in Da Nang. He offered me his R & R billet. Prince was
wearing plaid bermudas and a purple ascot tucked into a
green T-shirt. As always, he was occupied at his desk.

"Let me think about it, Prince."

Roland had been listening. He joined in. "Don't do it,
John. Half the fun of R and R is anticipating it. Counting
days. Waiting. It breaks up your tour. You haven't been here
long enough yet. Wait. Don't use your only R and R after
only three months in country."

Myron agreed with Roland. "I'm saving my R and R to
meet my wife in Hawaii after she recovers from having the
baby. It'll be wonderful."

Everyone had to give his advice. Bill was almost shouting,
"Do it! If he offered me his R and R, I'd be packing right
now. Your chances of a Hawaii billet are zero. Tomorrow you

may die. Go. Get laid. Get drunk. Get VD. Get the hell out of here."

I couldn't decide. "I'll let you know in an hour, Prince. I'm going for a walk."

It was almost sunset. I was walking in order to think and to get away from my opinionated hoochmates. Out of habit, I wandered toward triage. Three doctors were busy treating several casualties. I watched for a moment and walked out toward the helicopter pad.

A helicopter approached from the west at rapid speed. It slowed, hovered briefly . . .

# SIX

The Da Nang airport was packed wall to wall with green fatigues and tropical khakis on sitting, lying, standing, walking, sleeping, waiting bodies. One of the waiting faces was familiar and his collar revealed that he was a navy doctor.

"Hi, I'm John Parrish. I think we were in the same group at Camp Pendleton."

"Yeah, how are you? I'm Jim Veesar. We came to Vietnam on the same bird." His smile was so complete that he looked a little insane.

"How could I forget? Where have you been working?"

"I've been out in the field with the infantry. Near Con Thien."

His dirty, grungy fatigues fit with his permanent five o'clock shadow, narrow beaked nose, and maloccluded teeth. Add a Lucky Strike, a helmet with dangling chin strap, three inches, and forty pounds, and you would have the cartoon GI of World War II.

"Well, I've been with the hospital company in Phu Bai. Busy as hell. Thirty or more casualties a day plus sick call and MEDCAP and Graves and all. Plus assisting in the operating room." I didn't want him to think I had just been skating. "How is it out in the field?"

"Boring." Jim Veesar was sweating like everybody else in the big, tin-roofed building. "Mostly just boring. Sometimes I'm tired. Sometimes I'm very dirty and smelly. Sometimes I'm scared shitless, but usually just bored. If you're moving, you've got too much to do, and you're too scared to do it. When you're sitting, you're fuckin' bored stiff."

"Sounds bad. Many casualties?"

"No, they all fly right over my head. The choppers take

them back to you guys at the hospital company." His eyes were so penetrating that you would think he might be evil if his mouth didn't keep that silly grin all the time.

Nervousness or guilt made me ask, "Do you get shot at? I mean, is it really dangerous?"

"Hell, yes. Our second lieutenant got it ten feet from me in the woods one day. My tent was blown away one day, and two days ago my dirty laundry took a direct hit. It was in a bunker which took a hit with a dud rocket shell that came right through the fucking sand bags and tore one guy's shoulder off. But I only have eleven days left in the field, and I'm going to spend five of them in Bangkok on R and R."

"Hey, I'm going to Bangkok, too."

"When?"

"This afternoon," I said. "That's why I'm here in Da Nang."

"Me too. We must be on the same fucking flight." He stood up next to me, sized me from toe to head, looked at my suitcase, and proceeded. "You don't have any extra civilian clothes do you? Every piece of clothing I brought to this goddamn country got blown away."

"Sure, you can use my stuff. I may be too tall and skinny for you, but you're welcome to try. I always take too much stuff anyway."

"Just till I can get to a store in Bangkok and buy some clothes. That's great. Thanks." He sat down again. "I'm gonna screw till I can't walk, and then get drunk and screw some more."

"It will be nice to get away." Such an inappropriately conservative statement was unusual for me, but Jim didn't notice. He was still talking.

"Five days. Can you imagine? Honies for five days." That full face grin again.

"Then if I get held up in Da Nang on the way back, I'll be almost through in the field. Then a simple nine months in the rear, and I'll be home. It's all downhill from here. Whoopee!" Jim let out a yell which caused several people to glance our way. He didn't seem to care. "I need a drink."

"None around here," I said. "We'll make up for it tonight in Bangkok." We sat on the floor and told Camp Pendleton stories and war stories for two hours.

Jim sat next to me on the big commercial jet that took us

into Thailand, and the big, friendly airport in Bangkok. The only time he stopped talking about getting laid in Bangkok was when he was talking about how he would like to put it to the stewardess with the black hair and big hips. Or the thin redhead.

Just a change of environment would have been enough. But Bangkok was clean, friendly, and pretty. From the airport we took a bus downtown to the R & R center. There we had some corny welcome speeches (you are a guest here, be nice), a lecture on VD (to avoid VD, don't get laid, but if you do, stay with the approved bars and government-inspected girls) and all kinds of advice (watch your wallet, don't drive, stay away from drugs). We were especially warned that PDA (public display of affection) was very offensive to the Thai people. In your hotel room you can touch anything they've got with anything you've got, but at other times, no PDA in view of the Thais. Don't touch. Not in a cab, not in a car, not on a dance floor, not in a bar. Even though everybody you pass knows that this Thai chick is going to do it to you for cash, don't insult her or offend her people with a hug or a kiss (you physical bastards).

We had all our American money changed to Thai currency. All our MPC (military payment currency) and Vietnamese money had to be changed to American green before we could leave Vietnam. Now all of our green would be changed to Thai money.

Then the Thai businessmen welcomed us, and some pretty Thai girls sold us four tickets to see "all there is to see in Bangkok." R & R business was big business, and these businessmen, who were allowed to get to the American cash first, were obviously getting rich. Some connections somewhere made them an "official" part of the R & R program.

It was obvious, however, that some American government control was necessary even if it did appear to create monopolies. Two hundred eat-drink-and-be-merry kids with a month's pay in each pocket, a time limit of five days, a language barrier, sexual starvation, total ignorance of the city and its people, and too much alcohol need to be protected from civilians. And the civilians need protection from them. The R & R staff created an adequate buffer.

By late afternoon the troops were getting restless. But the talks continued. Enough talk. Enough briefing. Enough warnings. Let's get at it. Let's eat it. Drink it. Spend it. Smoke it. Screw it. We've only got five days. Every minute counts.

One of the "approved" touring agencies began showing slides of all the beautiful sites available on tours A through F in the mornings, and tours G through R in the afternoon. The price of each tour was posted, and ticket girls moved about the room collecting money. It was getting dark outside. The troopers were going crazy.

Outside that room were women, beer, lights, bars, music, laughs. They had been in mud and blood for months without bathing or without eating a hot meal. When they weren't having nightmares about their buddy's death, they were dreaming of R & R and a soft woman and safety. They had been scared to death, curled up in a ball waiting and hoping that the next shell would not be sudden death. Urinating in their pants as they waded through the stream because there was no time to stop. Crapping in their shallow foxhole. Stumbling up a hot, sandy hill with parched lips and dry tongue and a thousand-pound pack. Placing their helmets just right so that when they did pass out in the mud they wouldn't drown. Listening to those endless machine gun bursts, the long, searing crunch of artillery shells and the loud piercing whistle of rockets. Watching the truck just behind them or just ahead of them hit the land mine. Surrounded by people they do not trust and killing those people because of hate, fear, or just confusion. Sleepless nights. Hate. Fear. Heartbreak.

And now a one quarter-inch plate of glass, a wall, and a few doors were all that stood between them and heaven. One hand grenade, even one rifle butt, could break that window, and they could be out there on the streets. Instead they were watching slides of temples and gardens and floating markets and elephants.

But I had already stopped being amazed at these kids. They tolerated it like they tolerated everything. They waited, still dreaming, and finally it was over.

We went back to the buses and headed for the hotels. Each time we stopped at a hotel, names were called out, and several soldiers quickly got off of the bus. The Thai people at each stop would sell us Thai beer by the quart through the windows of the bus. R & R was starting. Jim and I were booked at the last hotel and had time to drink a considerable amount of beer by the time we checked into our big single rooms.

As late as check-in time, I still had not decided if I was going to participate in the fornication of foreigners (being a moralist at times). As best I could remember, I was married in my pre-Vietnam life. The bellboy asked me if I wanted a girl to come up to "give me my bath." My first reaction was polite refusal, but, after reconsidering, it seemed appropriate that the Dai úy Bác Sĩ should be given a bath.

The bellboy explained that he was to receive a fee for obtaining the services of the girl (seven dollars), and that her fee was separate (also seven dollars). He brought the girl, introduced her, and left. The girl feigned appropriate embarrassment. I had already stripped to my shorts and T-shirt when my Thai guest arrived. I acted as if I were busy unpacking while I chatted with the pleasant little Thai girl.

"I am Jan," she said bravely in moderately good English. Nice American name. I wasn't sure if I was Lieutenant Parrish, Dr. Parrish, GI Joe, or Mr. Lonely, but I decided that in my shorts, in my bedroom, in Thailand, on vacation that I was John.

"I'm very hot and dirty," I hinted.

Her perfect little Asian face broke into a smile and she went into the bathroom to prepare the tub. She wore a light blue dress that looked like a beauty-parlor outfit or a nurse's uniform. While the water was running, I smoked a cigarette. She refused one, and we made the kind of small talk that American servicemen have been making with women of many nations for the past three or four wars.

When Jan announced that my bath was ready, I tried to act very nonchalant as I took off my T-shirt and shorts and proceeded into the bathroom. A quick downward glance confirmed my feeling that my Caucasoid dork was still flaccid.

I stepped into the tub. The water was so damn hot that my left foot received a certain first degree burn before I could redistribute my weight and hop out of the tub. When Jan tried to assist me as I screeched and limped about the bathroom, a flying elbow hit her in the eye and almost decked her. She was very apologetic as she readjusted the temperature of the water.

When the tub was again ready (this time I tested it with

my finger), I stepped in and sat down. The extra water needed to lower the water temperature flooded over the side and wet Jan's skirt en route to the floor. She quickly mopped up with towels and slipped off her thin blue dress. She had on a small flowered strapless bra and a half slip.

Her breasts were moderately large for her tiny frame, with a cleavage that needed little help from the bra. Her belly was flat. She smiled when she noticed that I was studying her body, and I immediately liked her.

Jan knelt beside the tub and carefully washed my face with soap and a dark green washcloth. As she rinsed my face, I suddenly realized that when my eyes opened again I would be in a real bathtub being bathed by a beautiful woman. No. Impossible. Not a bathtub. Not a beautiful girl smiling at me. Never.

I opened my eyes. Incredible, what a picture! There I was in a real bathtub being bathed by a beautiful girl. That flaccid penis carried upward by flotation was mine, and those tan and dirty arms being bathed were both still attached to my body. This bathroom was as safe as if it had a thousand layers of sand bags around it. There was no noise, no sand.

Jan rubbed my belly with the soapy cloth. That toilet over there actually flushes and those towels are clean, I thought to myself. She rinsed my chest and abdomen. That door leads to a clean, soft, safe, big bed. She began to soap my pubic hairs. Right here is a real woman with two real tits. She dropped the washcloth and began to soap my genitals with both hands. And beneath that slip she probably has a real beaver, a real cunt. That all sounded so impossible. Could it be true?

I could actually see the tits. I could not resist reaching inside the bra and lifting out one of the firm young "breasts." Jan began soaping my enlarging penis with a half closed fist. And right there you have it folks—another American erection in Bangkok.

"You like?" she asked.

"I like."

She proceeded to wash my legs and feet, and then motioned for me to follow her out of the bath. She spread several towels on the bed and told me to lie down on them.

I lay face down. She stood at the foot of the bed and began to pull on my toes. Can you imagine that? She pulled my toes until they popped, and then she moved them in all directions. It hurt, but I didn't stop her. Then she started bending and kneading and twisting my feet. The pain was pleasurable, and I began to relax all over. She leaned over and put all her weight onto my calves and pressed and struck at my lower legs.

Then Jan got up and stood on the back of my thighs. She had to hike up her slip in order to walk in the right places. I could see her in the mirror. Finally, when she began to walk on my buttocks and back, she removed the slip altogether.

She slapped my butt as a signal to turn over. Again she started on my feet and worked her way up, massaging every muscle until it was totally relaxed. She knelt in the bed beside me and both hands massaged my pectorals and neck. I slid my hand between her thighs. She parted her legs slightly to permit my hand. I was surprised to find that the entire darkness at the crotch of her bikini underwear was moist, actually soaking wet. Immediate erection.

"You want?" She smiled.

"I want."

"You pay more?"

I nodded. I did not want money to destroy the "relationship" at this point. She quickly hopped up, undressed, and was on her back beside me before I could make another move. The South Pole was in her Thai box within seconds, and my R & R was off to a start. I had finally made up my mind. I would get laid in Bangkok.

My navy semen scarcely had honorable discharge when Jan was up and in the bathroom. I heard the water running

**AK 47**

and imagined her very womanly but unladylike pose as she washed her Thai box. Wrapped in another of the endless supply of towels, she returned and led me quickly into the running shower where she soaped and rinsed my then more manageable organ.

She got completely dressed and gave me another rub down as I lay against the headboard in my shorts and smoked a cigarette. I was hungry and happy. I liked Jan and was temporarily at biological equilibrium. I was lonely as hell.

"Give me money?" said Jan in a way I could not understand.

"Okay, Sweetheart, see you Monday." (It was Saturday.)

"No, no, you give me money," she laughed.

We repeated our lines two more times before I realized it was cash she wanted. She was not madly in love with me. Her actions were not even for physical pleasure. Well, I had at least made her beaver all wet (I had forgotten at the time that the tub had flooded her lap). She left slightly richer.

As the door closed behind her, I realized that my timing was poor. My blood pool had just redistributed enough so that my penis was bouncing with each heartbeat.

I was suddenly overcome by a fantastic sense of safety, freedom, and privacy and alcohol. I was very impressed that I had two arms, two legs, hands, feet, a head, and a penis. They were all intact and would probably remain so for the next five days. I was extremely glad that I had decided to get laid in Bangkok. Why be moral? Next week I could be blown away. The reward of a good life might be an AK-47 round in the chest or a mortar fragment in the head. Right now I was safe, intact, and functioning. I was going to function some more.

I was so happy that I masturbated with only a tiny trace of irrational teen-age guilt. I rationalized that I would get all the Jan germs out when I fired. Even a clean, private place to masturbate was a circumstance that couldn't be passed up. I smoked as I fired to add a little more evil, devil-may-care to the atmosphere.

I took a tetracycline (antibiotic to prevent VD) tablet, dressed, and went down to the hotel lobby. I had a cheeseburger, French fries, a milk shake, and coffee. By the time I finished eating, I was horny again. How had I survived three months without it?

I decided that it was time to take a long walk to see Bangkok and to find another honey. I soon found that a young American male walking the streets of Bangkok is constantly harassed by friendly natives in search of cash, kids selling trinkets, men selling pornography, women selling their bodies, and all combinations thereof. I stopped at a small bar and immediately gained a female companion.

The system was the same as in all busy R & R neighborhoods in several big cities of the world. In order to take a girl to your hotel room, it was necessary to pay the bartender a fee (anywhere from five to twenty dollars). The girl's fee was separate and was usually about the same as the bartender's. The hotel then charged extra for your overnight guest, and the bellboy stationed on your floor expected a little tip to usher you both to the room, to get ice, and to see that you were not disturbed. As many people as possible got a cut of the action; most taxi drivers got a cut from the bar if they brought you there. None of it was taxed.

Certain bars were "approved" by the R & R people. The girls who acted as "hostesses" carried cards which showed they had their monthly VD check and were clean at least at the time of their examination.

The small talk was also standard. It didn't vary from country to country, from R & R to R & R, from generation to generation, from war to war. The music was up-to-date, American rock and roll. The lighting was dim. Big business.

I wasn't choosy that first night. I bought the first girl who approached and took her home with me. I screwed her rather mechanically and was suddenly very tired. She didn't talk much. She seemed tired, too. And young. Sixteen or seventeen. I screwed her again and seemed to hurt her. She stopped moving and started complaining in broken English of back pain.

I was drunk.

Despite her discomfort, my typical, American male orgasm worship kept me driving to culminate my second conquest. Every stimulation must end with orgasm. Who was she to complain? I had paid for her. She was mine. She was a fuck machine. She was nothing but a 110 pound twat. She was a big fist for masturbation. Our goal was my orgasm. A business arrangement for me to come.

I finally managed to force out another ejaculation and became weak jelly-putty ready for sleep. And ready for closeness. Ready for embracing and sleep. But there was no one to embrace.

The girl sat on the side of the bed. Her back was hurting. I rubbed her back. I wanted to sleep. I wanted her to get the hell out of my room. I had never been quite so lonely. And I had no one, not even myself. John Parrish had left me to go in search of pleasure. Of orgasm. Of escape.

I was in Travis Air Force Base. I was in a bunker waiting to be hit with an artillery shell. I was in triage overrun by casualties. I was in a foxhole with VC running toward me. I was in my bed in Phu Bai crying with homesickness. I was in Bangkok with some goddamn whore with back pain. I was in hell.

My clean sheets had been soiled. My privacy had been invaded by a stranger. My morals had been raped by a high sperm count and a boggy prostate gland. I had violated a sacred oath made to my important woman five years earlier. The war had now taken away another part of me. One of war's dirtiest tricks is to leave you physically intact and systematically take away little pieces of your very self. A hotel room and a thousand miles could not protect me.

I gave the girl cab fare and more, and told her to go. Take away my pleasures, my sperm, my guilt. Just go.

I had a safe place to sleep. I had physical fatigue. I had biological equilibrium. I had terrible nightmares.

The front desk rang at seven o'clock the next morning. My first tour of Bangkok began at eight o'clock. Floating markets, jewelry stores, Thai silk, snake trainers, temples, souvenirs, and beer. Tiger Paw beer, called Tiger Piss by the servicemen. It was good beer. Folk dances, more Tiger Piss. Shopping, ordering bronzeware, silver jewels, and silk to be sent home. More Tiger Piss. Thai boxing.

The boxing was exciting. The boxers were allowed to use their feet. They could kick and knee the opponent legally. Their lightweight, good physical conditioning, and quick defensive moves offset the powerful kicks to the head and body. Thai boxing and Tiger Piss beer. More shopping. Tours.

The tours were not over until four o'clock. The bus let us

off at our hotel. Too much beer. Too many cigarettes. I
needed a nap. The privacy of my room would be welcome.

The sun was still very bright. Several soldiers were
swimming, diving, and sunning in the large pool in front of
the hotel. As I walked up the front walk, I noticed someone
leaning out of a sixth-floor window. Shading my eyes, I
stopped and looked up. I squinted. I couldn't believe my
eyes.

Jim Veesar was screwing a chick on the window sill. And
with a drink in one hand and a cigarette in his mouth. They
were both completely nude. Each had one leg hanging out
the window as they straddled the window sill: The girl lay
back against the side of the window, and Jim leaned forward
on top of her. They were going at it full force right in the
damn window.

An appreciative crowd gathered on the front walk and
cheered. Jim waved and held his drink high. He must have
really been smashed. He would kill himself. I bolted up six
flights to his room. The door was unlocked.

"Jim, you crazy bastard. You could have killed yourself."

"John, you want my chick. This is Ti." Jim stood up. He
was not erect, just a little swollen from overuse.

"You crazy bastard——"

"John, you take her. I've had it. Screw her once. She's
not bad."

"Jim, do you realize——"

"Have a drink, John. It's on the dresser there. Have a
drink. Have a screw. Have a cigarette."

"You go to bed, Jim. You're in bad shape. You——"

"Fuck the chick, John." He paused. "Fuck me. Fuck the
world."

The girl stood up and put one leg up on the bed. She
held a towel between her legs and strained to push the juices
out of her Thai box. She strained so, I was afraid she was also
going to shit in the towel. She stared at me the whole time I
was in the room. She was short and very well built, almost
stocky. Her pubic hair was a jet black tuft, and her scalp hair
was long, straight, and equally black. Her breasts sagged
slightly from their great weight, but maintained a ski-jump
shape and did not bounce much when she walked. Her belly
protruded slightly, and her buttocks had one or two folds on
each side. She sat on the edge of the dresser, spread her legs,

and slowly rubbed her clitoris up and down with two fingers
as she stared at me without smiling.

"Yeah, Jim, fuck the world." I started to leave.

"John." I had never seen Jim without his grin. "John,
you can't save the world, so save yourself."

"I'm not even sure I can save myself."

"If you can't save yourself, why not experience all you
can?"

"Fuck the whole world?"

"Fuck the whole world, Big John. You can start with Ti."

I put my hand on Jim's shoulder and smiled. "Eat it, Big
Jim. Eat it. Drink it. Suck it. Smoke it. Screw it. Have a
good time."

That wonderful ridiculous grin returned. "Fuck the whole
world."

I left to return to my room for a nap.

It was eight o'clock when I awoke refreshed, hungry, and
horny. I dressed and took a taxi to Club 21, a "must" for
officers on R & R in Bangkok. It was a long ride, and for some
reason I was very nervous during the trip. I felt like a
teen-ager going on his first date.

Club 21 was an elegant place. The music was jazz, and
the lighting was low. The prostitution was subtle. The ar-
rangements were made by a pleasant obese hostess.

"You want to meet nice girl?"

"Just a drink, now, Mamason."

"I find you nice girl to talk to while you drink."

"Not now, Mamason. Later."

"Okay, soldier. You let me know."

The bar was near the front close to the live combo. The
tall bar stools were filled with American men. The back of the
large room was filled with tables and booths where the
American soldiers and their "hostesses" drank and talked.
The hardwood dance floor in the center of the room was filled
with couples rubbing bodies and dancing. The girls were well
dressed in western clothes.

By the time I had finished a beer, the combo switched to
rock and roll, and the fat, overdressed, friendly woman
approached again. She sat on the stool next to me.

"You want to dance with nice girl now? I find you
special, number one, girl."

"Okay, Mamason."

Second later the pudgy hostess returned leading a beautiful girl by the hand. I couldn't believe my eyes. She was taller than the other Thai girls. She had a fantastic hourglass figure poured into a tight black dress. Her face was oriental, but her skin was light. Her hair was long and black. Her face was perfect. Some western blood in there somewhere.

"This is Suzie. She likes to dance."

"Hello, I'm Doctor Parrish."

"Hello, pleased to see you."

"Would you care to dance?" I said. Mamason nodded agreement, and Suzie and I headed for the slippery, hardwood dance floor.

Before we had finished a few gyrations testing for each other's style, the rock stopped and a slow waltz ensued. Suzie danced very close and overlooked my clumsy style. She smelled wonderful.

After two dances, we found a table in the corner and ordered drinks. I was surprised that she did not begin any of the corny, worn and trite phrases of welcome and questioning. This left us with nothing much to say.

"I'm a doctor. I work with the marines in Vietnam."

"Your work must be very sad. Are you frightened as well?"

She spoke perfect English. She was self-confident and bright. I was taken back by this unexpected find. Especially after my experience with the dumb machine with back pain.

"I'm often frightened and often very sad. But I'm very happy now and not afraid anymore. I'm not even afraid to try dancing again."

"Your wishes are mine."

Where had she learned to speak English like that?

We danced several rock and roll numbers. I really enjoyed dancing with Suzie. I was in no hurry to "buy her out of the bar." Between dances we were content to just sit and listen to the music. For some reason the conversation lag was not uncomfortable; she could say a lot with her smile. We stayed at the club for about two hours.

"Would you go home with me?" Again that silly nervousness.

"Yes, I like you. Excuse me just a minute." After another warm smile, she left the table.

Mamason approached and sat next to me. She lit a

cigarette and put both elbows on the table. Her giant breasts rested on her left forearm as she leaned toward me to speak confidentially.

"You want take Suzie to your hotel? She nice girl, Number one girl."

"Yes, I——"

"Well, you are very smart and very lucky. Number one girl."

"Thank you, Mamason. How much money?"

"Well, that's up to you."

"Well, I——"

"You want short time or all night?"

"All night."

"You want good time, or very good, number one time."

"Well, number one, I guess. I——"

"Suzie is very good girl. Your give her twelve dollars and she go with you."

"Good. I'll——"

"You give her fifteen dollars and she will make you very happy."

"Okay, that sounds good. If——"

"You give her twenty dollars, and that will make Suzie very happy. She will think she is special. She will love you very much. Very special night. Number one night."

Silence.

"You will not be sorry." Mamason winked and squeezed my arm pressing a big tit into my elbow.

"Okay, Mamason. Twenty dollars. All night."

"You tell her later how much. She will love you. Number one. You very good boy."

"Thanks, Mamason. You're number one, too."

"Thank you. You're sweet."

Mamason left and Suzie returned to the table as if she had just been to the powder room. She acted as if she were unaware of Mamason's visit.

"Let's leave and go to my hotel."

"I'll get my coat. I will be right back."

Suzie was gone for about ten minutes. She returned in different clothes, a pants suit and matching lightweight, full-length coat. She carried a large purse. She reached for my hand as I stood and guided me across the dance floor, past the bar, and out onto the street.

She sat very close to me in the taxi and rested her hand on my thigh. Again we were without conversation, but the silence was a warm one. As I watched the lighted streets of Bangkok, I imagined making love to beautiful, warm Suzie. It was a pleasant fantasy and about to come true.

The desk clerk collected an "additional guest fee," and the bellboy showed us to my room and brought ice. He conversed with Suzie in Thai. She did not seem to appreciate his comments. I tipped him. Suzie spoke to him again, and he quickly left the room as if being thrown out.

I took off my coat and tie while Suzie went into the bathroom. She came out wearing panties and a see-through frock that was very complimentary to her young, firm body. I was not sure of my next move, so I lit a cigarette and sat in the bedside chair.

Suzie sat in my lap and began unbuttoning my shirt. She untied and removed my government-issued shoes and took my hand to pull me to my feet. I undressed as she pulled back the bedspread and the sheets. We got into the bed.

I tried to kiss her cheek, but she turned toward me, and, after a prolonged openmouthed kiss, I mounted her. If her movements were forced or feigned, she was a perfect actress, for the clutching and deep breathing were very convincing.

Suzie broke all the rules. She didn't dash off to the bathroom. She continued to kiss and to fondle me until her hands told her I was ready again. She seemed even more ready. It was not until after our second, heated sexual interchange that there was any conversation at all.

"You are very good," she said. Still no trip to the bathroom. No towel wrap. No embarrassment. No awkwardness.

I smiled and got up to get a cigarette.

"Let's go it once more." She lifted my spent penis gently as I lay on my back propped up against the headboard.

"You'll have to wait a minute, Sweetheart. I'm out of shape."

"I want one more," she smiled. She lay on her back next to me.

I finished my cigarette. Then, beginning at her ears, I slowly ran my hands over her fine body. I moved my finger over the bridge of her nose and around the rim of her nostrils. She closed her eyes, and I gently massaged her eyeballs through her closed lids. I rubbed her lips, and she moved her tongue around and around my finger.

I grasped her throat and gently squeezed. Suzie was completely relaxed. I firmly massaged her upper chest making her breasts move slightly as they were tugged by the movements of the skin.

Her breasts were firm, and the dark brown nipples were erect. She had two long black hairs just lateral to one nipple, the other had three. Her belly was flat and pliable. Her pubic bone moved upward to increase the pressure of my fingertips which tangled and combed through her short, black, straight pubic hair.

She parted her legs making her moist inner lips barely visible. Still with eyes closed, she breathed deeper and faster. By then, half of the movements of massage were provided by her own pelvic muscles. Her bent knees separated widely to completely submit her slippery crotch, which now smelled of woman and semen. The muscles of her upper trunk and arms stiffened as she opened her mouth and turned her head away from me. She made a fist with her left hand and began to slowly, gently, and rhythmically pound the side of my chest.

Suzie grabbed the wrist of my exploring hand and pulled my arm up and across her guiding my body to turn toward her. She twisted and snaked her way underneath me. Her readiness was contagious and I entered her again. She elevated her pelvis so that the angle was a little uncomfortable for me. I tried to use the weight of my body to force the warm wet box back to a more natural position, but it was locked in its upward thrust and would only move side to side and with amazing speed.

Although the ride was very pleasing, I didn't feel as if I could manage another ejaculation. I placed my elbows over Suzie's shoulders to force her down toward the foot of the bed. I buried my head in the pillow and banged for all I was worth.

Suzie grunted and gyrated faster than I could thrust. Consequently, there was a minimum of in and out movement. Still I continued to push and drive my hips against her uplifted pelvis. Suddenly Suzie threw her arms around my trunk and squeezed very tightly. Her pelvis climbed even higher into the air and then stopped moving. Her legs stiffened. I could feel the involuntary contractions of her inner pelvic muscles as they rhythmically squeezed me—milking, clamping, releasing, clamping. The fixed position of her frozen, elevated pelvis allowed me to make several long, full thrusts, and I followed her orgasm with one of my own.

As Suzie relaxed, the grip of her arms and legs loosened while that of her Thai box tightened. Our limbs and bodies slid effortlessly with our own sweat as we separated. I rolled off onto my back, raised my arms in the air, threw my head back, and moaned. "Well, Sweetheart, there's your one more."

This time Suzie did head for the bathroom. She seemed to be in there for a long time. I had to urinate. I went to investigate. Suzie was fully dressed and putting on makeup. She looked at me in the mirror and smiled.

"You leaving?" I said.

"Yes."

"But I thought this was an all night affair."

"You said 'one more.' I have to go. I have to go see my family."

"Okay, Suzie. You go." I kissed her lightly and returned to my bed.

I heard the door close. Suzie was gone. I urinated, took another tetracycline, lit a cigarette, returned to bed, and leaned against the headboard to think.

Fantastic. What a screw. Suzie and I were on the same wavelength. A woman. A real woman. I was in a clean bed with a woman. No one was shooting at me. No one was trying to kill me tonight. And I was getting laid in style.

Wait a minute! Suzie just made me a "short-timer." She's going back to Club 21 to pick up her "all-nighter." She fucked my brains out on purpose. I've just been taken for a ride—so to speak.

No. Not sweet Suzie.

It doesn't matter.

Who cares.

We did our thing and I loved it. She thinks I'm a fish. But I'm very happy. I'll get some sleep. Fuck Suzie. Fuck me. Fuck the whole world.

I had probably just gotten to sleep when the phone began to ring. When I answered, I still wasn't sure where I was.

"Big John, come on up. I've got two chicks."

"Hello."

"John, it's me, Jim Veesar. Come on up. I've got these two fantastic honies. I can't keep them both going. They're killing me. Come up. Let's have a party."

"Hello."

"John! You're not asleep are you? Where is your honey? Bring her up, too. We'll have a party."

"She's gone."

"Good. Come on up, John. We can get laid together. Fantastic chicks."

"What time is it?"

"One thirty. I told the girls you were coming up. I told them you had a two-foot dork and a nineteen-inch tongue. Try to live up to *that*, Big John."

"Well, I think I'll pass. I——"

"Pass? What is this pass shit? We're having a fucking party."

"Maybe tomorrow, Jim. I'm not in the mood right now. I——"

"Mood, smood. You must be insane. You must be some kind of goddamn nut or something."

"Yeah, well I'm not up to it right now."

"Well, just come up for a drink. We'll put on a goddamn show for you. A live skin flick."

"Jim! I just——"

"What more could you want? A free drink, a live fuck show, some free ass."

"I'll think about it, Jim. But if I don't show, please start without me."

"Well, okay."

"Goodnight, Jim."

"Fuck you, John."

"Fuck the whole world, Jim."

The next day the tours and shopping seemed important only in that they made time pass until I could go back to Club 21 and find Suzie. When I returned from my busy day, there was a note on my door from Jim.

"Meet me at 'Thai Heaven' at 6 P.M. Great place. Fantastic honies. Wild ass."

I tore it up. I did fifty sit ups, thirty-five push ups, ran in place for a few minutes, decided to never smoke again, took a shower, and lay down for twenty minutes. Another cheeseburger, this time with lettuce and tomato. No fries. Coffee. Cigarette. I felt great again. Coat and tie. Taxi. Club 21.

I sat at the bar drinking a beer and listening to the same jazz. Not much business yet. I was early. Mamason approached, winked, and stood next to me.

"You like?"

"I liked."

She left.

Seconds later Suzie was standing next to my bar stool. She had on a tight knit mini dress with a zipper all the way down the front. She didn't say a word. She looked both ways with caution, and then looked at me and smiled as she unzipped the dress down to her waist. She was braless. She zipped up, smiled, and left.

Mamason returned.

"Well, number one soldier, you want to——"

I flashed a twenty and Mamason left.

This time Suzie did not seem to be in a hurry to wipe me out or to leave. We slept most of the night. It was great to wake up next to her, and our sunrise job simulated our parting shot of the night before.

When I got dressed to go to breakfast, Suzie was still nude in bed.

"You want some breakfast, Suzie?"

"Yes."

"You want to go on a tour today?"

"Yes."

"You will stay with me for the rest of my time in Bangkok."

"Yes."

Suzie and I spent the next two and a half days together. Tours. Tiger Piss. Shopping. Sex. Usually with feeling. I gave her twenty dollars each night. She never asked for it, but I gave it to her, because I didn't want to know if she would ask for it.

On my last day in Bangkok, Suzie and I went to a late afternoon Thai boxing match. I drank beer all during the match and tried not to think that I was to leave at three the next morning. Suzie explained the ceremonies which accompanied the fights and tried very hard to keep my spirits up.

It was getting dark when we left the matches. I wasn't hungry. We stopped at a Thai restaurant so that Suzie could eat while I had another beer. Then we went back to my room.

Suzie began to undress. I just sat on the side of the bed. I was not interested in sex. I had drunk too much beer and was beginning to think about returning to Vietnam. Suzie sat nude beside me and without speaking held my left hand in both of her hands. She kissed my neck as I stared at the floor. I put my arm around her, and we sat motionless for a long time.

"I think I'll go to bed, Suzie," I said finally. "I don't feel much like going out tonight."

"I'll stay with you. I'll stay until you have to leave." She assisted my undressing. "Will you make love to me?" she asked softly.

"Sure, Suzie."

I climbed in bed and held Suzie for another long time.

"You are falling asleep." Suzie moved to arouse me.

"No, just thinking, Suzie."

"Make love to me." Suzie held tighter as she spoke.

I made love to Suzie. Hawks and doves fought in my head. Paper tigers danced about the room, and an endless line of dominoes fell in succession around and around the room. Dragon ladies glided softly in and out of the room, and the bellboy began taking money from my pockets. The tiger did not pause, and the mighty elephant was tiring.

I put my head to Suzie's warm chest. Her heartbeat sounded like marching soldiers. The soldiers were really Vietnamese women and children in uniform. They were protecting a small white man with Vietnamese features dressed in an expensive green suit. He was surrounded by cardinals and police cars and American army officers. A horde of starving peasants were attacking him with rakes and hoes. The peasants were limping and screaming and throwing charred-black babies and buffalo dung.

I tried to sleep but giant neon signs flashed in my brain. PACIFICATION. STRATEGIC HAMLETS. PRIVILEGED SANCTUARIES. INTERDICTION. SEARCH AND DESTROY.

A Frenchman was sitting in my bedside chair. He spoke

to Suzie as if he knew her, and she answered in French. Then they both began to laugh. They seemed to be laughing at me.

"Search and destroy." The commander in chief was standing next to my bed with a megaphone. "Search and destroy. Search and destroy." He would not let me sleep.

"Search and destroy."

Destroy! Body counts. Parts of humans and water buffalo exploded upward into the air and glided toward the ground. "Honor our commitment," screamed the megaphone. "A just peace."

I put the pillow over my head. "Bombing pause." I held Suzie very tightly. "Free fire zone. Kill anything that moves." I clenched both fists and began to tremble.

"American casualties were light to moderate." No, No. Stop it! One casualty is all it takes to break your heart. "American casualties were light to moderate." Restore one limb, and I'll never take another R & R. Restore one life, and I'll never screw again. "American casualties were light to moderate."

Please, stop it. Stop!

"We must save face. We have commitments." A sixteen-year-old boy stood to throw a hand grenade. When he heard the megaphone, he stopped, still erect with the grenade in his hand. It exploded and tore him into a hundred thousand light-to-moderate pieces. Shrapnel flew all over the room. Suzie was killed. I died with her.

The phone woke me at 3 A.M. Suzie raised up as I dressed.

"Goodbye, Suzie. If I ever get back to Bangkok, I'll look for you."

"Yes."

"I enjoyed being with you."

She didn't answer, but stared into my eyes. She smiled. "You made my R and R very wonderful, Suzie."

"You're number one," she said. I thought I saw a tear in her eye. I hoped so. She was still in my bed when I left.

The bus picked us up at the front door of the hotel. Most of the soldiers were drunk. They were saying very physical goodbyes to their Thai girls in the lobby. I wanted to go back and stay with Suzie.

The bus pulled out. I began to think about Vietnam. About my poor hoochmates. About Jim Veesar.

Jim! Where the hell was Jim Veesar? He had missed the bus. That crazy bastard was really going to get into trouble now. Probably drunk. Maybe rolled. Maybe passed out. Unconscious.

I went to the front of the bus.

"One of the officers is missing. He didn't get on the bus."

"Sorry, we can't go back. We have to be at the R and R center at 0400. The plane leaves at five thirty.",

We spent one hour being processed at the R & R center. Changing currency. More lectures. The soldiers were asleep. Drunk. Hung over. Sad. Where the hell was Jim Veesar?

Another bus took us to the airport. We waited. The sun was rising. We waited. Why the hell had they gotten us up at 3 A.M.?

Finally we lined up to get on our flight. A taxi came speeding right out onto the air strip. Jim Veesar stepped out in a very wrinkled set of khakis and a two-day beard. That same big, insane grin.

"John, you weren't going to leave without me?" The grin changed to an openmouthed smile.

"Jim, you crazy bastard, where have you been?"

"I fell asleep at some bitch's pad. She took me home with her."

"You could have——"

"Jesus Christ! I almost missed my fucking flight. Wow! Close. Let me tell you about this fantastic chick. You have a flask with you?"

"No. You don't need a drink, you crazy bastard."

"I fucked this chick right in her own house."

"You could have been rolled. Killed. Kidnapped."

"Who gives a shit. Fuck the whole world."

As we talked, an unbelievable scene unfolded. It was the most amazing thing I had seen thus far in my tour of war. Sixty-three American men, who knew what war was all about, who had been in Vietnam, and who knew the score, began to file onto an airplane to return to Vietnam. They had gotten on a plane at Travis Air Force Base, and now they were getting on again.

But now they knew better. They knew what was going

on. They had heard the small arms fire and the mortars and the rockets. They had killed. They had seen their buddies fall. They had been scared. They had cried and vomited. They were going to cry and vomit again. Some of them were going to die.

# SEVEN

I put my canvass suitcase in the corner and began to make some order out of a mud brown, blood red, shaggy mass which used to be the left foot of a nineteen-year-old boy.

As usual, Bill was walking around with a clipboard keeping score, lining up cases for the O.R., and helping where needed.

"John!" He stopped in his tracks. "You old son-of-a-bitch! Welcome back. How was your R and R?"

"Good. I enjoyed it. How are you? How's Hooch 75?"

"Same. Same as ever. What you got?"

"Amputation. Probably at the ankle. Maybe mid-foot, though. He's okay otherwise. Stable. Typed. Ready for the O.R."

"Okay. It'll be a little while. We've got three bellies so far. Do the hoochies know you're back?"

"No. I just walked in. Haven't been to the hooch yet."

"Well, tonight it'll be beer and R and R stories."

"Good." I spoke as I finished up a hasty pressure dressing.

Bill passed on to the next litter as my marine patient was carried to X ray. I looked around for untreated wounded.

A lone soldier sat on the bench against the wall of triage. He leaned forward with his elbows on his knees and his face in his dirty hands. He still had on a flak jacket and helmet, and was covered with yellow red dust. As I sat down beside him, I noticed from his collar device that he was a navy doctor.

"Hi! What's up?" I said quietly.

His distant stare was directed at the floor just in front of his dust brown boots. Beneath the dust and a three-day beard was a frightened, pale, and very tired face. I remembered him from Camp Pendleton, but did not know his name.

Shrugging his shoulders slowly, he said, "I just got on the chopper, that's all. I just got on the fucking chopper."

"Are you okay? Are you hurt?"

"I'm not hurt. I just got on the goddamn chopper." He stared at the floor and spoke with blunted affect.

"You can take your flak gear off." I lifted off his helmet and laid it on the bench beside him.

He slowly reached for the snaps on his flak vest. "I just jumped on the goddamn chopper."

His .45 was loaded. I took the gun from his belt, removed the clip, cleared the chamber, and then replaced the weapon. He began mumbling in a barely audible, broken monotone. "For six days and six nights I've been in there. For six fucking days I've been in the same bunker without seeing the outdoors, without sleeping. My outfit has been getting the shit shelled out of it. Constant shelling, all day, all night. It never stops. And they keep bringing these blown up kids into my bunker." His lips trembled a little. He stopped talking for a minute. A single tear turned some of the dust into a small circle of mud.

"We couldn't get enough choppers to take them all out. I had no blood, no fluids, no sterile gear. I couldn't do much but stop bleeding, give morphine, and talk to the poor kids.

"When a chopper did get in, we'd usually lose another kid trying to get the wounded from the bunker to the craft.

"It smelled like hell. We had to shit in a sandbag and throw it out. One of my corpsmen stuck his head out to look around, and a frag took his head off with such force that it jerked him right out of the bunker like some fucking skyhook had lifted him away.

"When this chopper came in, I was helping them load the casualties, and I just fucking jumped on the chopper. That's all. I just jumped on." He buried his face in his hands again.

I put my hand on his shoulder without speaking. I didn't know what to say.

He turned and looked at me. "Am I a deserter? A hero? A psychiatric casualty? A coward?"

"You're just a tired son-of-a-bitch, that's all. You'll be okay." I took a cigarette from his shirt, lit it, and handed it to him.

Bill walked up with his clipboard. "What you got, Jim?"

"Nothing. Just a friend visiting me from the field." I motioned Bill to leave us alone, and then turned to the doctor who had now closed his eyes and was almost asleep. "Let's go get you a shower, a beer, and a rack." I helped him to his feet and led him away. Shuffling like a robot, he followed behind me like a well-disciplined puppy.

"I just got on the fucking chopper," he kept saying. He drank a whole canteen of water and fell asleep twice while we undressed him for bed.

"We'll talk to you in the morning. Don't worry. You'll be okay."

"I just got on the goddamn chopper," he mumbled. He was asleep again.

"Look, Doctor John Parrish, we know you've been on R and R, so you can get out of those goddamn stateside khakis now." It was Roland's voice booming behind me.

"What the hell are you doing in the hospital? Why don't you go drive a truck or something?" I extended a handshake as I spoke.

"How was the R and R?" Roland knocked the flexor surface of his crossed wrists together in the modern marines' gesture of sexual intercourse. "Get a lot of ass?" he smiled.

I guided him away from the sleeping doctor. "I'll tell you all about it, and you'll eat your heart out."

"Come on, tell me now. I won't tell Myron," Roland laughed. "But first get those goddamn khakis off."

Myron was napping as usual. My entrance woke him. "Well, welcome home. How was it? Lots of great dinners and shopping, I'll bet."

"Yes, Myron, lots of great dinners and shopping," I said. "How's the medicine service? Were you very busy?"

"Well, let's put it this way, I'm glad you're back."

It wasn't clear to me how to tell Myron how awful it was to be back. Before I could arrange an answer, Prince returned from a shower wrapped in a long violet towel with matching slippers, back scrubber, and soap dish. "Well, Doctor Parrish, so nice to see you. I want a full report on *my* R and R."

"You'll get one," I said. "I have a patient I'd like for you to talk to—a doctor who rode a medevac chopper here to get away from his outfit because they were receiving heavy incoming fire."

"He doesn't need to talk to me. That sounds like a pretty sane thing to do. If someone were shelling at me, I'd run too. I only talk to crazies."

While talking, Prince removed his decorative paraphernalia and sat nude on the side of his lawn chair. "I see sex-starved kids who get caught with pornographic pictures and trained killers who get drunk and take a swing at obsessive-compulsive second lieutenants. I see black kids who are paranoid enough to get the ridiculous notion that they are being discriminated against in the service—and now you want me to see someone who runs when someone is trying to blow him up."

"Prince, settle down. This guy could be in trouble. He left his outfit without being authorized."

"What do you mean, without being authorized?" Prince was being socratic. He was not angry. "As a doctor he authorizes evacuations all the time. The corpsmen authorize medevacs. Some lance corporal in the field can call for a chopper to extract a sick or wounded man."

"I know that, Prince, but you know his colonel will be pissed off about the way he just took off without notifying anyone, without being wounded or sick or——"

"He was probably scared and exhausted and disgusted," Prince interrupted. "People are allowed to be overcome by these feelings. That doesn't mean they're crazy."

"I know, Prince, but——"

"It doesn't even mean they are sick."

"Will you stop it, Prince. I never said this guy was crazy." I didn't need to hear all this now. "I just want you to talk to him tomorrow, because he is physically and emotionally exhausted, and because he may be in trouble. Maybe you can help him."

Still nude, Prince lit a long, thin cigar and leaned back in his lounge chair. "Maybe for one brief moment he was totally sane. With all of his awareness he saw where he was and what was going on. All his defense mechanisms, denial, sublimation, and repression were exhausted. His religion deserted him. His talents disappointed him."

This was too much. I had to take one of Roland's cigarettes. I joined in Prince Edward's drama. "For one brief moment he saw the truth, and he had to get out."

Prince looked past me in deep thought. "For a moment his sanity survived when all else had deserted him."

"Bravo! Bravo!" clapped Roland. He had entered during Prince's last lines.

I stood up and placed my hand on my forehead. "Man's rational nature will prevail."

Prince jumped up on his bed and placed both hands over his heart. "Man's inherent emotions tell him what to do." He leaped back to the floor and began to do a soft shoe about the hooch.

Myron stood by his bed and raised a coke to the sky. "Man's soul is good. God will show us the way!"

Roland was still clapping and stomping his foot. "The crazies have prevailed disguised as those who say what must be done. Those that know the truth are called crazies."

"Ye shall know the truth, and the truth shall make you free," shouted Myron with his Bible in hand.

"Truth! Freedom!" Roland and Prince, with arms about each other's shoulders, were doing a cancan. Standing in front of them on a small wooden box, Myron was preaching the word.

I told Roland's M16 and slowly circled around them. "Kill! Rape! Steal! plunder!" I yelled. "What is this truth shit? What is this freedom bullcrap?"

We all joined in the chorus line—I in my khakis, Myron in his shorts, Roland in his green fatigues, and Prince in his purple ascot with penis and flabby chest bouncing with each kick. "Kill, rape, steal. Kill, rape steal. Kill, rape, steal."

"Don't forget 'plunder,'" screamed Roland, as he accidently stepped on Prince's toe.

"Ow! Plunder. Goddamnit. You crushed my foot, you military turd. Plunder your ass! You clumsy, antagonistic, militant, Nazi-Gestapo boot polisher!" Prince limped back to his bed.

Roland carried on with a high-kicking Russian dance. Myron preached louder, Prince lay nude on his bed screaming in pain. And I put on my helmet and belly-crawled on the floor with Roland's M16.

I don't know how long the corpsman had been standing at the door, but he finally made himself heard. "Doctor Parrish, Doctor Parrish. There's a bad insect bite we'd like you to see up in triage."

"Kill, rape, steal," I yelled.

"Doctor Parrish!"

"Okay. Okay. I'll be right there."


While taking a nap, a marine major was awakened by a burning pain on his upper lip. He found a four-inch centipede firmly attached to his skin. Because pain and swelling continued to increase after the insect was removed, the major had come to the hospital area.

The chief called me aside as I approached triage. "This guy is important. He's the aide to General Hochmuth. Take good care of him."

"I take good care of everybody, Chief," I said. "His lips are like anybody else's, even if they've kissed a general's ass."

"Yes, Sir."

The major was waiting on a bench in triage. His upper lip was markedly swollen, and he had hives on his trunk and upper extremities. He was intelligent, polite, and clean-cut. He did not object to my suggestion that he spend the night in the medical ward for observation and treatment. He was given a large dose of Benadryl and put to bed.

I returned to the hooch where I spent the evening telling R & R stories to my hoochmates. Not wanting to hear my stories, Myron left to play cards with the chaplain. Prince was amused, Bill didn't believe me, and Roland vicariously enjoyed every scene, always asking for more detail. Because of Roland's prurient fantasies, I could not resist exaggerating the stories of sexual conquests.

We laughed, drank, and talked far into the night. I was lying in my rack still talking when I realized that everyone but Roland was asleep. I began substituting totally inappropriate descriptive detail in order to test his level of receptivity. When his responses stopped, I slipped into a verbal fantasy of free flight of ideas. Soon I feel asleep mumbling, "Kill, rape, steal."


Tuesday, November, 14, started like any other day. As I entered Graves the dead looked the same. Had I really been on R & R? Nothing had changed.

It was good to see Sun at toothbrush time. I gave her a small bottle of her favorite perfume which I had bought in Bangkok. She was especially appreciative.

Myron and I made rounds on the medical ward. The major's lip was much less swollen. However, he was very nervous, preoccupied, and irritable—not at all the same man I had met the night before.

"I have to leave. I've got to go." He paced about as he buttoned his shirt. "Just got some serious news. I've got to go check on something."

"Sure, Major, sure," I assured him. "You can go. What's up?"

"Can't say. But it's serious. I have to go. I must go check on something." He looked frightened as he hurried out.

Angry and out of breath, the hospital commander approached. "Where is Bill Bond? Where the hell is Bond?"

"He was in his rack asleep when we left. What's up?"

"Just go get him and tell him to stand by in triage." He left in a rush.

"What's going on, Myron?" I said.

"I don't know. Let's finish rounds. Send a corpsman to wake up Bill."

Three men from Intelligence came into the medical ward, asked the whereabouts of the major, and left with the same frightened haste.

After rounds I noticed a big crowd gathering outside Graves. I saw the major among them.

"What's going on, Major?"

"It's General Hochmuth. His chopper went down. He's dead, I think."

I went inside the Graves hooch. Several doctors and Intelligence officers were going through the papers and I.D. tags of a group of badly mangled bodies. The Graves marines stood by waiting for them to leave so that they could go about their routine. One man entered with a camera, set his flash and meters, and checked his settings. As he focused for the first picture, he paused. A sense of revulsion crossed his face. He lowered his camera and left without a picture. The others followed, and the room was quiet. The usually talkative Graves marines were silent. I followed the crowd out of the room.

"Doctor Parrish, Sir, we need somebody to fill out the forms."

"Sure, you get them ready," I said softly.

The marines began to undress and clean the bodies. An

ugly black typewriter clicked away in the corner as a lance corporal prepared the death forms.

The bodies were terribly broken and mangled—heads elongated, misshapen, burst. Limbs bent at places where there were no joints. Faces were torn away. Various internal organs were exposed.

I knelt beside one of the bodies. The skin was that of an older man. The scalp was bald. There were two stars on each of his collars.

I sat on the floor next to the body and waited for the forms. The typewriter clicked on. The freezer motor hummed as it kept privates and lance corporals cold in their green bags. Water splashed from the hoses as the marines washed down another body. Bones and joints cracked as the corpse was lifted into a green bag. A full-length zipper sealed away the vestiges of another wasted life. The bag dropped into the freezer.

I looked outside through the green wall. With hat in hand and head bowed, the major stood motionless in the morning sun. He was still standing there when I left.

"I'm sorry," I said as I passed him. He shook his head in silence. I was sorry.

Roland passed by as I returned to the hospital compound.

"Well, that ends the two-beer limit," he said with a smile. "See you at the club tonight."

The rest of the day was like every other day in Phu Bai. Fevers, diarrhea, casualties. It was as if I had never left. Back pain, sore feet, headaches. Had I really ever gone on R & R? Chest films, chest pain, rash of unknown origin. Had I been in Phu Bai all my life? Amputations, head injuries, rigid abdomens. Would I be in Phu Bai the rest of my life? Chest tubes, IV's, blood. Some of these kids would end their lives in Phu Bai. In triage. In the operating room. In Graves.

My late afternoon run was particularly painful after my week of self-abuse and debauchery. The sweat seemed to cleanse my skin, and the deep breaths and grunts were a toilet to my lungs. Rich blood was forced through my lazy muscles which only cried for more.

Prince and Roland were already drinking scotch when I returned from the shower.

"It's about time you got here, Big John. We're ready to

go to the club." Roland was repolishing his boots. "The two-drink limit should be over since the general is dead."

"Go ahead. I'll meet you there. I have to sit for a minute."

Combing his mustache, Prince looked over the top of his mirror. He winked at Roland. "John probably wants the two-drink limit to stay so Sun can spend more time with him."

"By running in this god-awful hot sun, John wants to prove to you that he's insane," accused Roland.

"John wants you two farts to get the hell out of here," I said, "so he doesn't have to listen to a bunch of crap."

Roland put The Mamas and Papas on the tape recorder and began to teeny-bop around the center of the room. Prince stretched out on his lawn chair and watched Roland's every move. Roland danced over to the fridge, removed a beer, and danced it over to me as I sat on the side of my bed.

"Thanks, farthead."

"You're welcome, you skinny shit."

By the time I finished the beer, I was up and dancing, too. The three of us went to the "O" Club.

The club was full. We rolled to see who would buy drinks and Prince lost.

"Two scotches and a beer," he said to Sun as he patted her well-padded ass. She winked at me and said something in Vietnamese which I didn't catch. I smiled and she left.

"I'd really like to poke her," said Roland.

"You'd like to poke anything," remarked Prince.

"You fellows need an R and R," I said proudly, "to return to biological equilibrium."

"We should get Roland a water buffalo," said Prince. "We could keep it tied to his bed."

"You'd be jealous," returned Roland. "Where's Wild Bill?"

"Still in the O.R., I guess," I answered. "He'd be here or in the hooch if he weren't still operating. Where the hell else could he be?"

Roland looked at his calendar watch. "This time last week Big John was probably pumping some Thai bitch in an air-conditioned hotel room."

I smiled.

"Is that all you can talk about?" Prince shook his head. "Tell us about one of your jeeps, or one of your trucks. How's your carburetor?"

"Any good crazies today?" I asked Prince.

"Mostly the same old stuff. Had one marine who got caught blowing his buddy in his foxhole."

"You're a doctor," laughed Roland. "Tell me, where is your foxhole? Is that close to your asshole?"

"Quiet, guys. Here comes Myron."

Myron sat next to me and lit a cigarette. "Hate to disturb you, John, but they've got a couple of fevers up in triage, and it's your turn."

"Okay, I'll look after them. Think I'll get some chow first. Anybody want to eat it?"

"Let's eat it," shouted Roland, and we were off for the chow hall, for liquid hamburger and green Kool-Aid and baked beans.


A nineteen-year-old with malaria and a chief with diarrhea waited for me in triage. Within a few minutes I had heard their stories and examined them and I was writing their history and orders when I heard a helicopter landing. It was a little unusual for choppers to come in at night and this one cut its engines and didn't take off again.

Still in flak vests and helmets the frightened helicopter crew came running in with one of the crew members on a litter.

"He got it just a couple of minutes ago, Doc. We were just flying over Highway One and took one round, so we set right down."

The corpsmen set up the metal stand to hold the litter and began to remove the gear and clothes. The excited crew tried to help but their inexperience and nervousness made them more of a hindrance. The boy on the litter had a hole in his right groin and was white and lifeless. His pupils were reactive but there was no palpable carotid pulse.

"Get the vest off." I yelled. "Get it off." I reached underneath to feel his heart as a corpsman cut the straps and peeled back the vests.

No heartbeat.

"Put your finger in that hole." I directed one of the corpsmen as I began to give external cardiac resuscitation.

"Mouth-to-mouth him and get a tourniquet on his arm," I barked to another corpsman. "Get me an endotracheal tube and an intracath. Get me another doctor, too. Quick. Cut down set!"

A corpsman took over the cardiac massage. I poured a half bottle of iodine over his arm and with a scalpel blade laid open an area of his inner arm, picked up a big vein, and inserted a tube with fluids running wide open into the arm. I put another tube into his subclavian vein by inserting a needle through the skin just beneath the clavicle.

By the time another doctor arrived I had also placed an endotracheal tube. A weak spontaneous heartbeat had returned.

"What's up, John?" One of our new GMO's was out of breath.

"Cardiac arrest. We got two lines in now and he's started up again. Bag him while I get some blood for type and cross."

I turned again to the corpsman. "Tilt him head down and don't take your fingers out of that hole."

His pupils still reacted. His wound started to bleed again. I felt his carotid pulse. Several rapid weak beats. Then coupled beats. Then it stopped again.

"Get me a surgeon. Hook him up to the EKG machine." I started rhythmically massaging his chest again, banging down with considerable force. The other doctor gave him some epinephrine and continued bag breathing.

The corpsman hooked up the EKG. By now wires and tubes were everywhere. The helicopter crew looked on with amazement and concern. I looked at the EKG. "He's fibrillating. Let's shock him."

I placed the big electrode paddles on his chest. "Stand back. Hands off!"

Everyone stood back.

"Now!"

The corpsman hit the switch and the wounded marine suddenly stiffened as the electricity jolted through his body.

Nothing.

"Turn it up. Hit it again. Stand back. Hands off."

Again the marine bounced with muscle contraction. I looked at the EKG tracing.

"He's going. Normal sinus rhythm. Fantastic."

"He's got a pulse now," the GMO said. "Let's get him to the O.R."

Bill Bond rounded the corner just as the blood bank tech brought the blood.

"Femoral artery, Bill. He's arrested twice already."

"Let's go," said Bill as he led the way to the O.R.

Ninety minutes later I left the O.R. One of the crew members, the pilot, was still standing in exactly the same spot in triage as when I went to the O.R.

"How is he, Sir? Did he make it?"

"So far, so good. They're still repairing his artery, but he looks good so far."

"Thank you, Sir."

I didn't answer. I walked on by him.

"Doc."

"Yes."

"I mean it. Thank you. You saved my buddy's life and I——"

"You want some coffee or something to eat? A beer?"

"No, Sir," he paused. "I mean, yes. I could use a beer."

I motioned for him to follow me. I got two beers from our hooch and we sat on the ground leaning against a bunker.

"I'm Lieutenant D. J. Ragan, Sir and I really..."

"I'm Doctor Parrish, or John. I'm not 'sir.'" I smiled.

D.J. smiled. He was a tough-looking kid of average build with a big scar on his right forehead. He had finished his beer before I had even gotten comfortable. I returned to the hooch and got him another one and we talked for a few minutes before I left him to return to my hooch.

Next morning I saw D.J. standing in the hall outside the Surgical Intensive Care section. As I walked by I was in the middle of a conversation with Myron so I just shook his hand without speaking as I passed. His friend, the copilot, recovered and was returned to the States.

Two weeks later I saw D.J. again in triage. This time he was a patient. He was missing the fifth finger of his left hand and had several minor shrapnel wounds of his flank. We treated him and kept him in Phu Bai for ten days. I saw him often in the "O" Club at night.

D.J. requested transfer to Phu Bai and often dropped by triage to see me and help the corpsmen on his time off. He said he was going to go to medical school when he got home.

D.J. was there the day the chopper brought three pris-

**C-34**

oners to our landing pad. It was late afternoon. The C-34 had come in too close and almost hit the low wall next to the landing pad. The three Vietnamese were stripped to the waists and bare footed and had their hands tightly tied behind their backs. The two marine escorts had clips in their M16 rifles and one of them had a knife stuck in his belt.

Two of the prisoners were guided by one escort to a clear area just in front of triage where they squatted on the ground. The other was brought to me in triage. He was about twenty-five years old, very muscular, and well fed. He seemed to ignore the long gaping wound on his left shoulder. I spoke to him in Vietnamese but was not able to interrupt his silent, stoic stare of fear and hate.

Since the wound appeared clean and very recent I instructed one of my corpsmen, who was eager for the practice, to debride and primarily suture the wound closed. The corpsman, the prisoner, and a marine escort left to go to the debridement area.

A truck pulled up front of triage to pick up the other two prisoners. The marine kicked one of the Vietnamese in the rib as a signal to get up. I walked over to them. As they moved away from me toward the truck the escort pushed the prisoners forward. One of them fell on his face and stumbled forward as he tried to regain his feet. The angry marine drew back his rifle butt and was about to strike the Vietnamese when he saw me standing next to him.

The three of us held our stance for a moment. The prisoner on his knees turning his head away to ward off a blow. The marine with weapon lifted. He looked at my collar devices and then directly into my eyes. I stared at him without speaking.

"He was trying to escape." He lowered his rifle. "Cock sucker was trying to get away." Anger gave way to nervousness.

The driver of the truck and the passenger, a marine second lieutenant came around to the rear of the truck and helped both prisoners aboard. The escort backed away a step or two, turned, and boarded the truck. They drove away.

D.J. and I sat on the ground in front of triage.

"I think I kept that marine from really beating his prisoner," I said.

"No you didn't, Doc. You just delayed it."

"Really?"

"Right, Doc, a roughed-up scared prisoner talks. Besides if the slope had the gun he'd beat shit out of the marine. Probably torture and kill him."

I didn't answer.

D.J. continued. "That's nothing, Doc. In the bush they give them water torture. Cut them and really beat hell out of them."

"No."

"But even that's better than turning them over to the Koreans or the Arvans or PFs, their own people."

"Why is that?"

"They put their heads into urns of water, cut their balls off, break their fingers, cut their tongues, shoot their feet, and all kinds of things."

"For information or just for hate?"

"I don't know. Maybe for kicks."

"That's terrible, D.J."

"I guess they figure they gotta make 'em talk 'cause it might save their own ass if they find out the right things."

I had no comment.

It was almost dark. We sat for another few minutes. Then I took a walk and headed back to my hooch. The hoochies had gone to the movies. I sat at my desk trying to understand D.J. and marines, and this war. It was all so confusing. After all these weeks I certainly didn't have any answers. So many things seemed wrong. Somebody must see a good or a reason or at least a goal somewhere in the mess because we sure as hell were in it. I sure as hell was in it. And I hated it.

The hooch door opened behind me. I could tell from the quiet, shuffling steps that it was Sun. She stood beside me and without speaking put her hand on my neck as I continued to stare at my desk. Without thinking I put my arm around her hips, and she stood closer to me. She massaged my neck and it made me start to forget. Without effort my hand slid to her inner thigh. Her stance widened and my fingers almost mechanically pushed the two layers of silk into the groove between her legs.

Sun stopped me and motioned to follow her to her quarters behind the "O" Club. I tripped as I stepped through the doorway of her bedroom and knocked her onto the bed. She ignored my clumsiness and stood on the low bed, making her height the same as mine. We embraced and kissed. Keeping one eye on the door, I began to mechanically undress her as quickly as I could. She pulled herself away, put a latch on the door, and stripped completely. I was nervous and fumbled for a cigarette, but hadn't brought any. I wanted to get out of the room. Sun lay on the bed. I thought for a second and then, without further foreplay and fully dressed, boots and all, I quickly mounted her. I fired as quickly as possible, not so much out of overwhelming desire, as out of fear that someone would discover us. When I tried to get up, Sun held me very tightly. She wanted more. She began talking in Vietnamese so rapidly that I could not understand her. Her voice was filled with emotion. I told her in English that I had to go, and after a quick goodbye kiss, I did so.

I went back to my hooch and stole one of Roland's Marlboros. I sat on my bed and leaned against a two-by-four in the wall. "Quick and easy," I thought. Now I was really confused. I smoked the cigarette down to the filter.

I had just gotten laid by one of the only two women on

this whole damn base, and she loved it—and probably loves me. I smoked another Marlboro, put one in my shirt pocket, and went to the movies.

In my mind's eye I imagined Myron walking in and finding me screwing Sun on the floor of the hooch. I began to laugh. Some asshole on the screen was giving a very sincere graduation speech. I tried to imagine Myron's face seeing bare-ass bodies going at it on the hooch floor. I laughed out loud. I laughed so that I had to leave the movie. It was an idiot's laugh. In the darkness I tripped over someone's foot and fell into a blanketful of corpsmen and spilled their hidden beers. Then I went back to the hooch, got a beer, and took a long walk. I felt better.

Later, back in the hooch, I put on a tape and began to dance around the room to "Sgt. Pepper's Lonely Hearts Club Band." For a person who had never danced much before, I was getting pretty good at dancing by myself. My hoochmates returned, and Roland and Bill joined me. Roland opened a bottle of his favorite scotch and changed the music to The Mamas and Papas. We danced on. Myron sat cross-legged on his rack, smoking Salems and snapping his fingers. Prince studied us from his chair and wiped out half of Roland's scotch. We stopped dancing only to open another beer or to wait for another song. I kept thinking about my new relationship with Sun, but I decided not to tell my hoochies. I didn't really want to admit it to myself.

About 1 A.M. an up-tight MSC officer from the next hooch stormed in demanding quiet. The three drunk dancers merely added appropriate finger gestures to their motions.

"I'll get the C.O. if you fellows don't quiet down," he insisted in a sleepy voice.

"And you'll never ride in another jeep," sung Roland in time to the music.

"And I'll cut your gall bladder out," Bill danced by him.

"And I'll proclaim you insane," Prince belched without apology.

"And I'll kick your ass." I was "frugging" my head so fast he could not see my face.

He stormed out toward the C.O.'s hooch. By the time the two sets of footsteps returned, the lights were out in our totally silent hooch, which smelled like Sweet Pine air freshener. We were all fast asleep.

The next morning I had a terrible headache. I hurried. I had to make it to toothbrushing position in time to meet Sun.

As I settled onto the west hole of the shitter, the clod next to me was carrying on about the "terrific" full moon of the night before. "Fuck the moon," I thought. "I just screwed Sun." I was beginning to think like the fucking marines.

That night during movie time I visited Sun again and stayed longer. She taught me to say "I love you" in Vietnamese. I found that easy enough to say, although I would not have been able to say it in English. We began having occasional sessions during movie time, and, sometimes when I wasn't on call, I would creep back into her room after my hoochmates fell asleep. At first, this was a little awkward, because her roommate was there, too. But roommate would pretend to be asleep on the bed next to us. Once roommate held up two fingers to me at toothbrush time, indicating how many times I had scored the night before. She was nineteen, and better looking than Sun. I was tempted during my visit to reach over and grab her, but I didn't. She was doing it on occasion with the head technician of the blood bank.

Sun was a tiger. She never had enough. She arranged meetings behind the "O" Club, in the chow hall after hours, in empty hooches, and occasionally in the bunkers. She really enjoyed sex, but she was limited to a brief, almost ritualistic, foreplay and to the classic man above position. She held to very strict, unspoken, rules. When she was aroused, conversation was terse and limited to Vietnamese. I usually didn't say much, because my Vietnamese was still somewhat inadequate, her roommate was sometimes next to us, and I really didn't have much to say at 1 A.M. anyway. At times I wasn't even sure I wanted to be there.

We continued to have our long talks and private language classes during the day, and I continued to take her to Hue two or three times a week. I was not sure how long I could keep my secret. Often I worried about the consequences for me and Sun if we should be discovered. It could cost Sun her job, I thought, but it could cost me my life if I were sent to the field.

One night I told Sun that we had to discontinue our midnight meetings because of the dangers of being discovered. She told me that my reservations were only in my mind, founded in guilt and not in fact. Sun knew that my wife and my return were the things I counted days for and wanted most of all. When I bravely and righteously discontinued the physical side of our relationship, Sun patiently waited, knowing that I could not stay away from her—I couldn't.

I often wondered if anyone would really care that I had screwed Sun. Sometimes I felt that the Intelligence officers who lived behind the "O" Club must have known, but I was always afraid to confide in anyone.

Late one night after all my hoochmates were asleep—except for Myron, of course, who never slept at night—I crawled into the bunker behind our hooch and groped silently in the darkness until my hands found the waiting Sun. As I began to undress her in the darkness, I heard someone come into our hooch. I quickly returned to find a corpsman with a flashlight standing over my empty bed.

"Would you come with me, Sir? The hospital commander wants to see you. Right away."

I was used to having corpsmen waken me in the middle of the night for new casualties, for fever spikes, or to assist in surgery. But now what? What did the C.O. want with me in the middle of the night?

I put on a shirt and jogged over to the commander's lighted quarters where several officers from the medical company and from Intelligence were standing about looking concerned and sleepy. The C.O. greeted me as if I were the guest of honor. Surely all these people were not concerned with my screwing Sun.

"Hi, John. Come in." The C.O. introduced me to the Intelligence officers and to two army officers. Was this a midnight court-martial? Was I going to the field tonight?

The commander continued. "These men are army advisors, and they've got a problem. It seems that seventy to eighty Cambodian mercenaries are sick—some kind of severe vomiting and diarrhea. None of the American advisors are sick. They think it's probably cholera or typhoid fever."

I turned to the army officers. "How many men in the outfit?"

"One hundred fifty."

"You mean that one-half of your outfit are sick at once?"

"Probably more by now. They've been dropping like flies all evening."

"Did it begin today?"

"This afternoon."

I turned to the C.O. "It sounds more like food poisoning to me—everybody getting sick at once and almost everybody getting it."

"We don't know what it is," the commander answered. "Apparently some of them are very sick—prostrate, dehydrated. They may need hospitalization and IV fluids."

Now I was beginning to see why I had been sent for. I was going to take care of all those vomiting Cambodian mercenary bastards while they shit all over each other. I acted concerned. "Can we make room for them, Sir?"

"Well, we can make some room, but getting them here in the middle of the night will be a problem. They are about four miles outside our perimeter and providing their own security."

I looked at my watch. It was midnight.

"We thought the smartest, and probably the safest thing to do, would be to have a doctor go out and evaluate the situation and see what needs to be done. We could send some IV fluids, medicine, and corpsmen. While they were gone, we could rearrange things here to make some extra beds available."

It was obvious what was coming next. He was not about to risk his own ass four miles outside the perimeter protected by puking Cambodians. And he had not called me in just to meet these nice army advisors. I noticed that everyone in the room was studying me in silence. I felt like a man receiving a sentence. The C.O. finished verbalizing his plan.

"We thought we should send someone with internal medicine knowledge and with good judgment——"

"Cut the shit, commander," I thought to myself.

"——I can't order you to go because it's not Americans or even Vietnamese in trouble, and it's outside our perimeter——"

"And if I get killed it would look bad on your service record if you had ordered me to go," I continued keeping my thoughts to myself.

"But if you were to volunteer to go, Captain Saunders here has promised a few marine volunteers to go with you as security."

I looked again toward the army officer. "Any deaths, or any look like they're not going to make it?"

"None dead yet. They look pretty sick to me."

"Any spoiled or unusual foods?"

"They provide their own chow for the most part—from chickens they catch or steal, and from the land. The rest is just plain old army C rats."

"How many vehicles can I have?" I didn't bother with any dramatic acceptance speech.

"We can spare two ambulances." The commander was almost apologetic. "And Chief Tucker has promised four corpsmen."

The army officer stepped forward. "We have two jeeps with us and six men as escorts."

"Well, let's get going." I turned to Chief Tucker, but I made sure the C.O. heard me also. "I want IV fluids, Lomotil, tetracycline, penicillin, and Compazine—all in I.M. and P.O. forms." I sounded too much like Ben Casey now, or John Wayne.

I went back to my hooch to get my .45, my flak gear, my stethoscope, and to read quickly about cholera in an old textbook of medicine which stayed on my desk.

"Hey, Roland," I whispered. "I'm borrowing your M16 for a few hours."

Roland woke up. "Where the hell are you going in flak gear in the middle of the night?"

"Some Cambodian mercenaries are sick, and I'm going out to check on them."

"Where?" He raised his head.

"Four miles outside our perimeter—to the west, I think."

"Where?" Roland sat up in disbelief.

I didn't answer. Roland was standing now in a sleepy fog. "What are you doing?"

"Cambodian diarrhea," I whispered. "Cambodian diarrhea." I was laughing.

"You're crazy. You've finally flipped."

"Cambodian diarrhea." I spoke out loud and woke up the whole hooch. Before my hoochmates could gather their wits, I stood at one door and screamed, "Cambodian diarrhea." And with an imaginary fixed bayonet, I charged the entire length of the hooch, out the other door, and into the night.

Our convoy had to wait forty minutes at the outer checkpoint while some dumb lance corporal tried to get clearance for us to go outside our perimeter. It took him so long that I assumed that phone calls were being passed up through the chain of command all the way to the new commanding general. I almost hoped the general would not let us go.

"Okay, go ahead." The lance corporal signaled us through. "I'll pass the word so none of the friendlies will shoot at you."

"Thanks a lot. You're a thoughtful man," I said with a nervous crack in my voice.

Using only our parking lights for illumination, we traveled slowly over a narrow dirt road on flat sandy land. Lights flicked to our right and to our rear, but ahead there was only darkness. I was in the second vehicle. I hoped that if the head vehicle ran over a mine we would be spared. Four miles seemed a long way, especially when I kept imagining myself running all the way back with NVA and VC shooting from behind, and marines shooting from the front, and Cambodians shooting in all directions. I imagined myself throwing IV bottles and handfuls of pills at the enemy and swinging my stethoscope around my head like a lariat. I was getting so nervous that I thought I might have a little diarrhea of my own before the night was through.

We arrived at the Cambodian compound; more sandy land with four large tents in poor repair. No bunkers, no hooches, no shitters. The largest of the four tents had its flaps rolled up. It was filled with men lying side by side. The sea of men extended beyond the confines of the tent in all four directions.

Except for a few scattered figures waddling quickly back and forth to the latrine, all of about one hundred Cambodians were lying on the ground. Covered only by their shirts, most were nude from the waist down. A low, monotonal, continuous moaning was interrupted by sharp outcries of pain, despair, and vomiting. Liquid feces and vomitus were everywhere. The smell was enough to make the unaffected ill.

I was treated like some kind of great white father. The interpreter bowed many times, and the Cambodian officers nodded continuously like some kind of dime store toys. The interpreter hurried me into the tent. The moaning increased in intensity. I selected one of the ill who seemed to be delirious. I felt his skin. His temperature was normal. He was not even dehydrated. I turned to speak to the interpreter, but he was vomiting on the ground behind me. I examined several others. The findings were the same. Normal temperature, normal state of hydration, and soft, nontender abdomen. None would stop moaning long enough for an adequate cardiopulmonary exam, but the pulse rate was only slightly elevated.

The interpreter returned to my side, and we questioned one of the ill. A simple question requiring a one word answer stimulated a long question and a longer, emotion-packed answer.

"Does his stomach hurt?" I asked, pointing to my stomach. "Does his belly hurt?"

The interpreter began talking to the ill man. Three or four minutes, several hundred syllables, and several heated interchanges later, the interpreter said, "Yes."

"Does he hurt anywhere else? Pain, anywhere?" I was pointing to my head, my chest, my rectum, my neck. "Pain? Hurt? Ow?"

The interpreter and the ill man began another heated interchange. After another debate he said, "Yes."

"Where?" I questioned, and again pointed to various body sites. "Where?"

Another debate followed, during which the interpreter seemed to get very angry with the soldier. After the soldier moaned and groaned another soliloquy of despair, the interpreter looked up at me and pointed to his stomach.

"Oh, never mind." The interpreter gave me a questioning look. "Never mind," I said. This precipitated another debate between the two men, and I walked on to examine thirty to forty more soldiers.

I realized that the most consistent finding, other than the obvious diarrhea and vomiting, was overwhelming anxiety. A contagious, mass hysteria was sweeping through the soldiers. Men were embracing and crying. Some were chanting as they moaned. A mob psychosis was magnifying a real illness. I called the interpreter. "What do these men think is wrong with them?" He didn't understand. "Why do they think they are sick?" Silence. "Are they afraid?" He began another debate with a nearby soldier.

It was time for some magic. I selected nine men who were slightly dehydrated and told my corpsmen to start IV fluids on them. Then, depending on what orifice was least active, we gave all the men some form of medicine—Compazine or Lomotil; orally, rectally, or intramuscularly. At first the approach was organized, but shortly the mass of vomit- and feces-smeared men began to crowd and shove toward us.

"Just make sure every man gets some kind of medicine. I don't care what it is. Each man gets one pill or shot of something—just one." I went back to question the army advisor.

A truckload of grapes left over from a big Officers' Club party in Da Nang had been driven up to Phu Bai in the hot sun. The next day it was given to the Cambodians. The grapes were the most likely source of a staphylococcal food poisoning. I told the army advisors and the interpreter that everyone would survive. Combined with group pity and American-reinforced hysteria, the major problem was fear of "plague" or "poisoning," or impending death. The fact that a medicine had been given led to immediate improvement in many—long before any medicine had time to be effective. I instructed the army medics concerning the use of further drugs and IV fluids.

We returned empty-handed to the compound. I was surprised to find that several people were still waiting for us and that a ward had been prepared for any returning sick.

"Food poisoning," I said. "No problems. If you're interested, send someone out tomorrow to check on them again and to culture a couple of stools. A truckload of rotten grapes did it."

I sat on the side of my bunk. It was 4 A.M. I was exhausted. All was quiet at Phu Bai.

"A bunch of grapes," I thought to myself. "A bunch of fucking grapes."

It was only two or three hours before time to pronounce the dead. I fell asleep with my boots on.

I was tired when I awakened the next day, but I knew that by this time I could do my work almost automatically. After the first few hundred fever patients, the investigation, diagnosis, and treatment of such cases became routine. Even the wounded began to look very similar to one another as days and weeks changed to months. Every day—all day—we saw wounded American boys who had been intact and healthy earlier in the day and who now were mangled, bleeding, torn, and dying. Some days were busier than others, but it never stopped happening. We saw the price tags of war—the cost in bodies, the debt in minds.

We never saw victories or defeats or liberations or massacres; no glimpse of what it was we were buying, just the price we were paying. The price of a freedom, the barter of a stalemate, or the cost of saving face. This is the part of war that soldiers fear, generals accept, heroes ignore, and some politicians pretend does not exist. I was not sure what it was we were buying, but we were paying one hell of a price. Even after a full night's sleep, often it was tough to get out of bed to face another day.

I missed toothbrush time and Sun. While I was still at Graves, the day's casualties began to arrive. My usual schedule was interrupted so many times that day by large groups of casualties, that I essentially spent the whole day in triage and left Myron with most of my other responsibilities.

During my early days in triage, I had carefully studied each wound to determine the exact extent of nerve, vessel, and muscle damage, and to estimate the viability of tissue and extremities and the physiological changes induced by trauma. But all of the wounds began to look similar. There were no clear limits to nerve or vessel damage, and the soft tissues were smashed and unrecognizable.

Definitive extent of damage made little difference in the emergency treatment anyway. All of the changes were gross, and most decisions to be made were obvious. Any seriously injured man needed IV fluids; hypotensive patients needed blood. The decision between local debridement or surgery in the operating room was usually obvious immediately, and a period of observation was seldom necessary. A penetrating wound and a rigid abdomen required laparotomy; a chest wound with signs of fluid in the lung needed a chest tube. A blown-off leg was a blown-off leg.

After I became comfortable in making decisions and felt confident with and accustomed to severe trauma in the living and the dead, I began to wonder just who these wounded kids were. I used to ask them their names and hometowns. I encouraged them to tell me all about themselves.

Usually the marines were quiet. They just lay there thinking, waiting their turn to be treated. If time allowed, I usually attempted to initiate a conversation as I worked over them.

"Who are you, buddy? What is your rank, your job, your outfit? How long have you been in country? What are you doing in the marines? Are you scared? Are you a killer? How many confirmed kills do you have? What makes you tick, kid? What's up, kid? How're you doing, buddy? What's the trouble, son? Hi."

Most of them were low-ranking enlisted men who looked like the kid down the block and who had been in Vietnam several months. They weren't particularly angry or bitter— yet. The bitterness, anger, and paranoia would come later back in the States when they saw people with two arms and two legs. When they were ignored by a society which had sent them to war. Right now, they were glad to be alive. They had just seen a buddy on the left and a friend on the right get killed, and they were still alive. They weren't particularly afraid, at least not nearly as scared as they had been in the fire fight from which they had just escaped. Their pain tolerance and stoicism was very impressive, and would put any obstetrics ward to shame.

Usually without emotion, most of the claimed, admitted, or stated that they had killed a certain number of enemy. The only time they showed any emotion was in asking about their buddies.

"Is Sergeant Barrall going to be okay, Sir? We couldn't have gotten back without him. He's a tough son-of-a-bitch."

"How's Daniels, Sir? The guy two stretchers over. Is he going to make it?"

"Not me next, Doc. Miller is pretty bad off."

"Please don't move my leg. It hurts like hell."

"Am I going to lose that arm, Sir?"

"It's my leg, Doc; some fuckin' gook put a round through my leg."

"Hey, Doc, will this get me home?"

"My goddamn leg is blown to shit. It hurts like hell, Doc. Please give me a shot or something."

"Do you take incoming here, Doc? Am I safe?"

"Is my pecker okay? Can I use it again?"

"My fuckin' belly is ripped open. That's what's the trouble."

"Just a scratch, my calf."

"Oh, I'm a commanding general disguised as a private. I'm here to inspect the hospital facilities. I figured the best way to slip in unnoticed was to blow off my foot."

"A land mine, Sir. It blew my buddy away—just knocked me out for awhile. I'm okay."

"I don't know. I was walking down the road and next thing I knew I was in a helicopter with my legs all bandaged up. Are they gone, Doc? Where are my legs? Let me look. I gotta sit up, Doc."

"That goddamn hill. That goddamn mud. Those goddamn gooks. I ain't never going back there. No one can make me."

"You better save that finger, Doc. I'm the best fucking 'geetar' man in South Memphis."

"Hey, Doc, our gunny got it. Right through the neck. The best fuckin' gunny in the marine corps. Toughest mother in the valley. He was like our dad. Hey, Doc, the gunny got it—right through the neck—hey, Doc . . ."

"Rod Queen, Dallas, Third Battalion, Third Marines, grunt, nineteen years old."

"Billie Foster, Albany, Georgia; could I have a drink of water?"

After a few weeks of asking "who" I began to wonder "how." How did each marine get wounded? I tried to picture each battle scene and to reconstruct the moment of impact. I imagined the nearness of the enemy, figured the angle of fire, and estimated the size of the piece of shrapnel.

"How'd you get it, buddy? Did you see the guy who shot you? Where were you when it hit? Did you hear the round that got you? Did you have your helmet on? Did it knock you down? Did it hurt right away? How long ago did you get hit? What time was it when you got wounded?"

"Fifteen hundred, Sir," said a marine lance corporal.

"About three o'clock," said a navy corpsman.

"How the hell would I know what time it was," argued an army enlisted man.

By now, however, I was concerned with a different, more basic question. Although I continued to make talk with the troopers, I was constantly asking myself, "Why?"

"Why are you bleeding, kid? Why did you lose your leg? Why are you dying, buddy? Why are you dead, Sam Gallagher of Boston? Why are you crippled, Joseph DeLito of New York

City? Why will you always be scarred and ugly, Mike Garner of Los Angeles?

"Why do you wait for me in groups of three or four or five or ten or fifteen in Graves each morning? What's in it for you, kid? What makes you come over here in groups and die in clusters?"

When a boy first realized he had lost an arm or a leg, his face looked like he was going to ask why. Why me? Why my buddy? Why anybody?

"Don't worry your ass about questions you can't answer," Roland tried to rest my mind. "You can't figure out why. Just do your job, stay alive, and go home when your tour is over."

Sun told me that war was just a part of life like illness, storms, and death. War was present when she was born. War would be present when she died. Her feeling was that peace is not possible in the present world, because men are impatient for material wealth and power. As long as any foreign power is invading, manipulating, or "helping" Vietnamese, there will be a war. But the Vietnamese will be self-governed, even if they must wait several hundred more years. Impatience will not force them to accept less. War helped create some nations, and it is an important part of the existence of others. Why else would a nation which was powerful and safe from invasion by its neighbors travel half-way around the world to look for a war? Sun never read a newspaper or magazine. She never watched television. She just observed the world around her.

Myron told me that this war must be God's will. "All things work together for the good of those who love the Lord. He works in strange and mysterious ways. A God-fearing nation or a God-fearing person is the final victor."

"Then I'll be a winner, because I'm scared shitless of a God that uses this war for anything." Bill slammed his book closed. "I have enough trouble explaining why nationalism, exaggerated fear of communism, power struggles, and crooked politicians have anything to gain from this sick, stalemate murder. But if this nation-turned-butchershop is working for good, it is in a strange and mysterious way, indeed." He walked over and took one of Roland's Marlboros. "I'd give you the whole fucking rice paddy for the return of just one of those blown-off legs we see every day. The lives of the gang that come through Graves on any one day are worth more than the whole damn Saigon government. We're paying blood money to put on a puppet show that the audience doesn't even like."

Bill was pacing up and down the hooch. He pointed his finger at Myron. "If this war is working for anybody's good, I can't see who it is; unless it's the bunch of two-faced, ass-kissing dictators in Saigon."

Prince interrupted with his usual calm, considered insight. "The Saigon government is being kept alive by the war as it is today and some businessmen in this country and at home are made wealthier by war economy. But Myron is right in a way. People don't allow wars unless they see a good in it. They often use a god or a moral good to rationalize the horrors they subject one another to."

Bill was still pacing. "Man must want war. He has the ultimate stalemate with nuclear power—a chance for peace through fear which is better than no peace at all. But what does he do? He agrees to back up and fight a 'limited war.' It's crazy?"

I also took one of Roland's cigarettes. "People must believe that the consequences of war, as terrible as they are, are less terrible than the consequence of not fighting a war. You know, freedoms and all that bit."

"Being able and willing to fight is the only way a nation can protect its interests." Roland took a cigarette himself. "Our job is to be able; the government decides if we're willing." Roland was always refusing responsibility for the war.

Prince could stand the sophomorism no longer. "You nit-wits talk as if this were an original discussion. War is a basic part of human society like religion, law, and organized economy. It has been a useful and creative economic booster. Occasionally, it has fairly redistributed land and wealth. Most importantly, it has served as the final judge in major unsettled disputes. The winner of a war is right by definition, and society can proceed from there without unresolved problems."

"Spoken like a true psychiatrist," Myron joined in again. "And, if you'll look at history, the nation that sided with God was the just decider, the victor."

"That's because they survived to give us our image of God." Bill was on his feet again. "The God of the winner survives. When two countries want a piece of land all of the rights and wrongs and gods and goals are just trumped up anyway. They both want the same goddamn piece of land, and the most powerful one gets it and comes out 'right.'"

I interrupted to get Myron off the hook—I don't know why. "But today, wars are basically 'inside jobs' unless some big powers feel like taking advantage of internal struggles to play a little monopoly. Therefore, the stakes are higher; it's your own home, and the price is higher; the people dying on both sides are your own people. With those stakes and that price people should be quick to accept settlements without war. Maybe that's a good . . ."

"Unless some outsider mothers encourage them to keep it going," Bill interrupted. "Supplying 'moral support' in the form of cash, arms, and men."

"And the arms are too good," added Roland. "An ignorant peasant with an AK-47, or a satchel charge, or a land mine is a powerful man."

"Still it remains a limited war," Bill added. "And this one can last forever, because the fucking VC guerrillas have the three essential elements for their continued survival. They have popular support because they directly descend from Ho and his boys who liberated this country from the French. Secondly, all the things they say about the Saigon government are probably true. And, finally, they promise the people possession of their own goddamn land. Sure they need some outside assistance, but the NVA and China and Russia provide that. They need someone to hate, and we do our little part to provide that role. We also have lots of money and young men to keep things going indefinitely."

"This kind of war cannot be won," Roland volunteered. "We're not always sure who the hell we're fighting, much less if we're defeating them. We can get a lot of confirmed kills, but so can a crazy man in a supermarket. This is the only war we've got, but it's a pretty shitty one."

"Gee, I'm sorry it's not a very good war for you, Roland," Bill said with as much sarcasm as possible.

"We're trying to make it better." I didn't allow Roland to answer. "We bomb and escalate little by little, and search and destroy new areas all the time. We try to improve things so you marines will make the war more."

"Don't give me that marine shit." Roland was on his feet. He pointed his finger at me. "You goddamn self-righteous doctors make me sick. You're just as much responsible for this bloody rice paddy as the marines. And so is every American who sits back and lets this go on. I'm sick of this marine, marine shit—you're as guilty as——"

"Nobody is innocent," Bill agreed loudly. "We're not only supporting this goddamn mess, we're carrying the brunt of the whole stinking thing. South Vietnam hasn't even mobilized for war. The totally inadequate Arvans couldn't fight even if they did want to, but they don't. They avoid contact. They cry for help when they get a scratch. You've seen them in triage. They avoid responsibility. They don't give a shit. They——"

"They're like any soldiers in the world," Roland added. "They fight if they have a reason to fight and if they have good leaders to respect. The Arvans don't have either."

"The Army of South Vietnam is representative of the whole society it pretends to defend." Prince was his usual calm, academic self. "Nepotism, corruption, inefficiency, factionalism, and thievery are a way of life."

"The rape of life and property we're offering is no better," Bill suggested.

Prince ignored Bill and continued. He tried to summarize our floundering comments. "Maybe war is no longer as useful a social tool as it once was. The questions are more complicated than simple territorial acquisitions. The tools of war are too good. The most important role of war is to make the final judgment or the ultimate decision, so that differences that cannot be resolved by reason are finally resolved by force. Mankind moves on from there. But a war which ends in stalemate, or doesn't end at all, cannot serve this purpose."

"God is the final judge. War is just one of the tools he uses." Myron was trying to agree. "It's just that man in his stupidity——"

"I agree; man is stupid," snapped Bill. "But you're not helping him with all your irrational Sunday school shit. 'Play it cool in this world, and you'll get yours in heaven.' Right now, in this world, I want to know what good this ridiculous war is doing for anybody."

"The wisdom of the overall good is not available to us now. Only in retrospect can it be seen, such as in the Bible." Myron could not be stopped. But neither could Bill.

"Yeah, all we have to do is find out what God's will is and do it. Sounds simple. How do we find out? I don't think we can, because I don't think it will be decided what God's will was until the winner looks back and decides what it was. And this war is not going to have a winner."

Prince looked at Myron. "Let's say the problem of a Vietnam was presented to Solomon and all his wisdom. What would he do? Vietnam is the disputed infant presented to Solomon."

Roland added, "Except this infant is a young man and can probably look out for himself."

Bill did not allow Myron to answer. "We didn't wait for an answer," he said. "Our country took the role of Solomon and got so insanely involved that we're busy sawing the baby in half right now."

"That's just it," responded Myron. "We can't set ourselves up as judge, if war is not a good judge anymore. We may be no better judges. What we are using is war and not——"

"You're not making sense," challenged Bill. "The question is, 'What good is this war?'"

"I guess the real question is like John said. Are the consequences of not fighting a war worse than fighting one," Prince added. He was putting on a fresh ascot, a signal that it was time to go to the "O" Club.

"Trouble with that is the people who decide to fight wars know the least about what they are really all about." Roland began putting a rag to his boots.

"Somebody will have to tell them," I said. "Someone has to tell them what this war is all about."

I did not join my friends in their escape to the "O" Club. A noontime run in the hundred degree heat and a busy day in triage had left me exhausted. I was even too tired to go to chow. The heat and overexertion had made me nauseated anyway.

I lay back in bed in the empty hooch. Within minutes I felt a strange, almost voluntary, weakness extend peripherally over my body. I was paralyzed, transfixed, depressed, and empty. My eyes were open, but the tin roof was blurred. The naked lightbulb pierced my retina, tiring the rods and cones as flesh and bones became sticks and stones. My sclerae and conjunctivae burned. The act of closing my eyes seemed all that I could manage. The movement of an extremity, a finger, a muscle, could not even be considered. Phu Bai gradually became very quiet, as it had never been quiet before.

My bed became more comfortable and actually changed shape to fit my body. It was made of cotton and air. It gently and gradually lifted and shifted me to an upright position, though I was still supported by the air and cotton and clouds. I could not tell if I was floating or walking, because my travel was so effortless.

I approached a green valley where the flowers and insects and tiny birds told me that it was spring. Young men lay about in the grass in groups. Some were sitting, but most were sprawled loosely on the grass. They were talking, smoking, drinking beer, and laughing a quiet, relaxing laughter. Each young man wore a dark, three-piece suit, a dark tie, white gloves, and black shoes. They did not notice my approach. Their pupils were widely dilated. Their eyes were unseeing and uncomprehending. Some had missing arms or legs. One had a missing head. Most had small holes in their bodies.

"Excuse me, son," I said to the young man closest to me. "Your leg is missing."

"Why?" he said.

I turned to another. "You cannot see me because your eyes are missing."

"Why?" he said.

I proceeded further into the valley and talked to each of the boys.

"You can't hear me; you have no ears." He stared at me with fixed, dilated pupils, and I had to look away.

"Excuse me, you have no head." He only shrugged his shoulders.

"Your arm seems to be missing."

"Why?" he said.

I hurried farther into the valley, because I did not want to talk with these inquisitive people. But I encountered another group of boys in white dinner jackets. Their bodies had great holes in them, and their black pants were torn. Each boy had blood on his chest and shoulders.

"You boys are all badly hurt!" I blurted out.

They looked at me as if I had told them some surprising news.

"Why?" they said.

I turned to run back, but the path had become an eight-lane superhighway. It was filled with elderly women—thousands of them. Each lovingly cradled a small bundle covered with a flowered baby blanket. Filing past me, each carefully exposed her burden—an arm, a leg, a foot, a hand, or a head. Some carried torn Vietnamese babies.

They showed me their precious packages with smiles of pride. They were surprised and hurt if I showed any disgust or shock. Each pointed to her beloved object and said, "Why?"

I ran toward the mountain range in the east, but a battle was raging there. I turned toward the mountains in the west, but bombs fell and the ground shook as pieces of homes and water buffalo filled the air. The boys in the valley did not notice the bombs or the battle. The women did not see the boys. The boys did not see the women.

I ran farther into the valley. Helicopters came from all directions bringing hundreds of casualties. I was alone. There were no corpsmen. There were no doctors. There were no stretcher bearers. I had no tools. I had no blood. I had no fluids. I had no chest tubes. I had no drugs, no medicines, no magic. I ran to each boy explaining that I could not help. Each called me to his side, raised up, and whispered into my ear so that his buddies could not hear: "Why?"

I began to scream. "Mass casualties. Mass casualties." A small piper cub flew by and dropped a piece of paper which floated to the ground. I ran over, picked it up, and read aloud. "We have received your message."

The number of wounded increased. I was sweating and trembling. All of the casualties were naked except for an M16, green jockey shorts, and dog tags. I began tearing my clothes off to make tourniquets for bleeding arms and legs.

"Mass casualties," I screamed. The call echoed into the valley. Another piper cub flew over.

"Message received and being acted upon through the proper channels."

I used my last bit of clothing. I was naked except for government-issued glasses, dog tags, and stateside boots without socks or laces. The piper cub returned.

"Please verify your last message through proper channels. Message received by us was as follows: 'Mass casualties.'"

I sat down in the middle of the dying boys and began to cry. The seabees moved in around me and built a giant outdoor triage. A supersonic jet landed next to it on a new prefabricated runway, and two thousand corpsmen got off bringing equipment and fluids. Forty-three doctors arrived by hovercraft in the brand new port, and one hundred twenty-two medical students with short white coats and little black bags began walking among the wounded, stroking their chins, looking interested and sincere, and asking, "Why?" A nurse with giant tits and an awful face handed me a megaphone and said, "You'll have to write it all down. We can't take verbal orders."

A USO troop set up a live combo in one corner and began to play 1957–1960 rock-and-roll music. Philippino dancing girls danced around and among the casualties as the doctors and corpsmen began the mechanical work of saving lives. I tried not to notice that all of the doctors were robots, and the corpsmen were prepubertal school boys.

Picking up the megaphone, I screamed in time with the rock-and-roll music. "Work, work, work!" The music grew louder.

"Tell me why, oh why, oh why, oh why," I sang into the megaphone.

I moved along behind the dancing girls. I tried not to notice that they were Vietnamese men dressed up like Philippino girls.

"Why are you bleeding, son? Why did you lose your leg? Why are you dying, buddy? Why are you dead? What's in it for you, kid?

"Hey, flash, without the legs, your legs bought us eighteen seconds on Hill 661. We'll give it up tomorrow, but we have it now. Thanks."

The more I talked the faster the people worked. I tried to ignore that the nurse with the big tits was now topless except for tassled pasties on her nipples.

"Hey, you, with the brains on your chest, while you're waiting there in the corner to die, let me explain a few things to you. You've got a few minutes. You see, kid, there are these dominoes and if one goes, we lose the whole game. You see, buddy, there are these rich friendlies in Saigon who may, without our help, get hurt, or replaced, or even go down the tubes. We can't let that happen. Their successors might not like us."

I put down my megaphone and sat next to the head injury. I spoke quietly—just to him. "You see, kid, there's this complex political situation which you can't understand, especially with your brains on your chest, and it's important that we don't embarrass ourselves—as a nation, that is.

"I mean, shit, kid, you don't want us to be embarrassed do you?" I was fighting tears. "Please try to understand, buddy."

As I was speaking a casualty was carried past me on a litter. He was completely nude. His M16 hung over the stretcher handle and his boots rode between his legs. He was so black that the mud on his skin was light by comparison. He was long and muscular and his spidery fingers curled tightly around the sides of the bouncing litter. His whole body was glistening with sweat which reflected highlights of the bright morning sun. The sweat on his forehead did not drip, instead it remained like tiny drops of oil and glue fastened tightly to his skin.

His eyelids were forced widely apart and his stare was straight ahead into nowhere, seeing nothing, having seen too much. He threw back his head and his white teeth parted as if he were trying to speak, to curse, to cry. A spasm of intolerable pain wrenched the muscles of his face into a mask which hid a grinning skeleton beneath. His chest heaved rapidly. The muscles of his black steel arms bulged as he grasped the muddy stretcher. A small hole in his abdomen permitted a steady snake of red and brown to spill onto the litter. His left knee was flexed and his long uncircumsized penis lay over his right upper thigh. His left foot arched as his toes grasped for the litter.

As he passed by he raised his head almost involuntarily. It seemed as if the contracting straps of his neck muscles would tear off his jaw should his head not rise. His neck veins swelled in protest. His mouth began to open, at first for air but then as a silent plea for help. He extended a dirty hand directly toward me and I rose to follow him. The others did not notice him. Walking faster and faster, the litter bearers passed right on through the triage area. I chased after them.

I followed the litter out into an open, sandy area. Several giant helicopters hovered overhead and the wind and sand

**CH-53**

and noise were overwhelming. A CH-46 touched down and a mound of bodies tumbled out of the open tailgate. A CH-53 lowered a net full of bodies right in front of me. I tried to skirt around the bodies.

The black marine on the litter was half sitting now as he got farther from me. That round may have slipped underneath his liver. He could be saved if I hurried. But with each step, the wash of the CH-53 swept me farther and farther from the purple brown and red green litter. I shouted but no one could hear above the helicopter's roar.

"I'm coming, you innocent, hurting bastard. Why should you die?"

Captain Street walked by. I slowed to salute. He made some comment about my boots needing polish. The marines lining up for sick call blocked my way, and I couldn't get through all the backaches and sore feet. As I skirted around the long line, a large, wire gate swung closed in front of me. A giant clock behind the gate read 1630. The gate was guarded by closely-shaven, cleanly-pressed soldiers in dress uniforms covered with metals, ribbons, rank and name tags. I begged one of them to open the gate, but he shook his head and pointed to the clock.

I ran along the compound fence. The litter was almost out of sight. I begged for a jeep ride, but one driver was waiting for a general, and the other wasn't authorized to go around the compound. I was afraid I would not get to the litter in time.

A crowd of long-haired, young people marched toward me with banners. We were on the campus.

"Stop the war. Peace."

I couldn't get through them. I shouted. "Let me through, you verbal, overeducated, overexperienced, uninformed, self-proclaimed bastards. That boy needs help." They couldn't hear me because electric acid music drowned out my cries. Some were too stoned to care.

I tripped over two sweet ladies who stopped in the street to pray for "our boys overseas." A thousand sports fans pushed me against the wall as the mob surged like cattle to the ticket windows. I was crushed, exhausted. A beautiful Thai girl took me to her room, but I ran back into the street. The litter was out of sight. A rich and pleasant Saigon businessman would not give me a ride in his new Chevrolet. He was late to dinner with the ambassador.

I stumbled forward. Moms and dads rushed toward me. Sweethearts embraced me. Wives and children and friends greeted me with happy tears. Their strong embraces held me so tightly that I could not break loose to follow the litter. My commanding officer made me stand at attention to receive medals and praise. I approached the microphone to give my speech.

"That poor black kid needs help. He's hit. He's got a goddamn hole in his belly."

Trying to get to him, I pushed my way through the crowd, but the people shaking my hand blocked the way. They asked my opinions of the war, but did not want to hear the truth.

They forced me to sit down at a debate and talk about stalemates and victories and politics and freedoms and saving face and grace. I couldn't think. I didn't have time. He was bleeding. I kept trying to fight my way through the sea of concerned people. I kept trying to get to that poor kid on the litter.

He was gone.

I sat down on a long green bench in triage and stared at the asphalt floor. There was a steady flow of tears but I was making no noise.

"Lose a buddy, Sir?" I looked up to see a boy of fifteen or sixteen sitting next to me. His left foot was missing, and the stump was wrapped in a bloody battle dressing. He was wearing fatigues and flak gear and the rank insignia of sergeant.

"Yes, every few minutes I do," I answered.

"I know how you feel, Sir. I just lost my two best friends. Our troop carrier hit a land mine. I was lucky. I just lost my foot. Everybody else in the vehicle was killed. My lucky day, I guess."

"You are fortunate, my son. You are only wounded, crippled. Your will is shaken. Big dreams and schemes and hearts are broken. People will feel sad. They will like you—briefly. You are very fortunate to be a victim, man—ruined—not to have to be one of us who carry Cause."

"Will I be going home, Sir?"

"Yes, you may go. There will be others coming to take your place."

I noticed for the first time that one whole wall of the new triage was a giant, fifty-yard TV screen. The picture on the screen was a giant living room in which a twenty-foot high, middle-aged man and woman sat staring straight at us. Their faces were blank and expressionless. The woman was wearing a nightgown and smoking a recessed-filter cigarette. Her hair was in curlers. She yawned frequently. The man was fat. He wore only a pair of boxer shorts. He was drinking beer, belching, and looking very bored and sleepy. The woman got up and walked out of the room. The man looked at his watch, belched again, and walked toward us. His giant hand reached out toward the bottom of the picture, and with a loud snap the whole world became black and quiet.

"Somebody will have to tell them," I said. "Someone has to tell them what this war is all about."

# EIGHT

"I have a plan," said Myron. "A plan by which we can escape."

"Escape?" I opened one eye.

"Yep. Leave Phu Bai and fevers. Forget diarrhea."

I sat up in bed. "Get away from casualties and Graves and the shitter?"

"I have a plan of temporary escape." Myron was sitting cross-legged on his bunk. His fat-supported nipples pushed out against his white T-shirt.

Roland stopped his letter writing. "Will you shut up? You and your goddamn fantasy life of escape. You're here for a year, Baby."

Prince walked to the center of the room. He was nude again. "Let him use fantasy life if he needs it. He obviously can't handle sex or heroism, all he has left is escape. Right, Myron, old boy?"

"This isn't fantasy. This is a real good plan."

"Let's have it." I was wide awake now and ready to listen, fantasy or not.

"I have a plan by which we can go to Da Nang for a weekend." Pleased that he now should have everyone's attention, Myron paused to straighten the open fly of his green underpants and to light up a Salem. "We can escape to the big city of Da Nang and spend a long weekend in safety and comfort. We can——"

"You're so full of shit that you have bad breath." Roland stopped his letter writing again. "Nobody goes to Da Nang unless he's dead, wounded, leaving Vietnam, or a big shot."

"Well, my plan is to——"

"Captain Street goes to Da Nang," added Prince.

"Reporters and USO entertainers can return to Da Nang the same day they come up here," I said. "But how the hell are you going to get to Da Nang?"

Myron sat on the edge of his bed. His face was growing red. "Each month the doctors in the Da Nang area have a luncheon meeting to discuss mutual medical problems and to set policy of treatment. We could——"

"Those meetings are just an excuse to take a day off and drink." Prince turned around to face Myron. "The guys in the rear know how to live."

"We could get orders to go to the meeting if Captain Street were approached in the right way. They even call it the 'I Corps Medical Society,' and that sounds impressive enough."

"Captain Street knows all about that," challenged Prince. "He goes himself every month."

"But we could talk him into letting some of us go with him. It's worth a try for a weekend off."

"Our own C.O. won't even let you go to the PX, Myron," I said. "And you expect Captain Street to let you go to Da Nang. Your plan is fantasy. Roland was right."

"I'm going to talk to him. I think it will work."

"Good luck, Dreamer."

Myron spent the next two days talking to the hospital commander and to Captain Street. He was more successful than we anticipated. He returned to the hooch after supper one night and broke the sacred rule of the quiet hours.

"I did it, you doubters, I did it!"

"Did what, you dumb shit?" Roland never looked up from his letter writing.

"Not only will Captain Street permit John and me to go to Da Nang, but he's also going with us."

"Fantastic!" I leaped up and shook Myron's hand.

"Not only that," he continued, "but he has also arranged transportation. Our own chopper. There'll be five doctors going all together."

"You lucky shit," rebelled Roland.

"I didn't want to go anyway," said Prince.

"Wait 'till Bill gets back from the O.R. He'll be pissed off," squawked Roland. "Why can't he go?"

"Maybe next month," said Myron. "We can't all go."

"A whole weekend of quiet, rest, safety, and booze!" I was pacing back and forth. "Fantastic, fantastic."

"And when we get back," smiled Myron, "we'll——"

"I know, I know," I laughed. "We'll be three days shorter."

"Hooray!"

"Thank the C.O. for small favors," frowned Prince. "Congratulations."

"When do we leave?"

"Tomorrow, Big John, tomorrow morning."

"Fantastic!"

The flight crew was amused by the sight of five doctors with overnight bags and .45's acting like excited kids going to camp. The doctors sat in the two rows of tiny metal seats in the center of the UH-1B army helicopter. The machine gunners sat on the floor; the pilot and copilot up front.

We rattled, shook, vibrated, and lifted like magic straight up into the air. Phu Bai grew smaller beneath us and disappeared thousands of feet below. Vietnam was a beautiful green carpet scarred only by an occasional shell crater. There seemed to be plenty of green for everyone. Why the bloodshed? Why the misery and murder?

I sat next to the open door and looked straight down to the earth below. I could not resist leaning over to get a complete panorama beneath me. Mile after mile of green passing beneath had almost hypnotic effect.

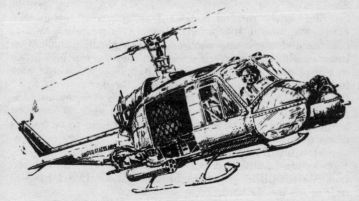

**Huey**

Without any warning a single, loud, metallic, cracking, jolting noise burst just above my head and the engines stopped. My heart exploded in my chest. Immediately our helicopter took a nose down position and began a dead-weight free fall through the air. The seat belt dug into my waist as my body tried to float upward away from my seat. The machine gunners grasped for straps and frame and seats—anything—as we increased speed in our heavy-boulder plunge toward the earth. Myron's fingers dug into my thigh. Objects on the ground rapidly zoomed larger and larger as we fell in total silence. We were headed for the earth like Newton's apple. We were crashing! No one spoke.

Basic animal fear stuck in my throat and tore into my belly, but it quickly passed away. Although I was not able to move, my thinking seemed accelerated. I didn't review my whole life as a flash before me. I didn't cry out. I was angry. I was mad.

I was pissed! Twenty-eight years old. A lot of things to do. And I was dying. Dying in some fucking country on the other side of the world. My bones and blood and skull and guts and soul would be smashed and would soak into that green carpet. The solid parts would be collected onto a green bag for return to my family.

Dying! What the hell for? Why God, why? No, I didn't want death yet. Not ready. Scared. Pissed. Really pissed off. Shit! No!

We slowly rotated backward as we raced toward the earth. We would hit bottom down. Our vertebrae would collapse and crush one another and explode like chalk. Our heads would drive into our necks and chests as our legs broke in ten places beneath our busted buttocks. We would look like General Hochmuth and his crew. Dead.

Helpless. Helpless. A number in a newspaper. Sudden death of a young man. A tragedy. No. Not me!

Not me! I wanted to go home. I didn't want to be here. I didn't even want to come to this war.

How much longer? Does it take forever to crash and die? Even anger had passed. An emptiness was left—an exhaustion of epinephrine, of thought, of emotion. Did I have to wait much longer to die?

Hold it! We were slowing. We had stopped accelerating. We were still racing toward the ground, but our speed was reducing by the second. Our pilot had the controls in his hand. He was moving sticks and levers. He was somehow keeping us bottom down and slowing our fall. Although there was no engine noise, the blades above my head were making their whirling noises again. That familiar, wonderful vibration returned to the craft still without noise of engine. Myron's death grip on my leg began to hurt.

"Hang on, Doc, we're going to crash." The machine gunner leaned to my ear from his position behind me. "We're going to hit down."

I didn't respond. I knew we were going to crash. My only thought was that now we had a chance of surviving. All I wanted was a chance. That crazy, high school dropout, kid pilot had somehow checked our free fall.

There was no need to prepare for crash. Every muscle was involuntarily tense and spastic. The ground rushed up toward us at a less ominous pace, and we crashed.

The noise was made by metal, but it felt as if it were my back that was breaking. My head snapped forward. The electric tingle that shot to both feet confirmed that I was alive. I was immediately euphoric.

The machine gunners were out of the craft and kneeling in the grass, carrying their heavy machine guns with them. Pilot and copilot unstrapped and leaped to the ground with M16's in hand.

"Everybody out," they screamed.

We unstrapped and jumped out. Captain Street stretched and began to talk about his fear, his crash.

"Get down, Sir. We're in unfriendly country. Get away from the craft."

"Any of you Docs know how to use an M16?"

"I do," I lied.

"Here." An M16 was thrust across my chest. Crawling and looking far into the distance the machine gunners were twenty meters from each side of the craft. The pilot and I went to the front of the craft. The copilot took the other doctors far to the rear of the craft and had them huddle on the ground while he set up the rear of our new circular perimeter.

We could see men moving in the tree line two hundred meters to our left. The land was completely flat in all directions.

I was so glad to be alive, that I could care less if the tree line was full of VC. I began trying to figure out how to shoot the damn M16. It looked simple enough. I was ready for a fight. Visions of heroism danced in my head. I was alive. I was fucking alive. I could crouch and crawl and kneel and look and feel and fear and fight. I was alive!

The copilot threw a smoke grenade, and we watched the green smoke lift skyward. Now all the enemy and friendly within miles knew where we were. They knew we were alive.

For fifteen to twenty minutes we knelt in our circular perimeter far enough away from our crippled helicopter that, if it were mortared, we would be missed by most of the shrapnel. The pilot was constantly talking on his radio.

I could not help but study the pilot. He was a little older than his colleagues, probably in his early to mid-twenties. His build was slight, but he looked strong. His tan face was marked by old acne scars, but the basic features were good. He was busy in a determined, self-confident way.

He had saved my life. He had somehow averted that crash. I felt as though I knew him. I felt confident that he would get us out of this jam.

Who was in that tree line? Arvan? VC? Peasant farmers? Women? Marines?

Nothing happened.

I almost wished that something would happen. I had to demonstrate, to act, to use my new lease on life; to fight, to run, to die, to do anything. I did not want to just sit.

A single-engine spotter plane approached from our rear, circled once, and swooped down over us only thirty feet above the ground. The pilot threw a weighted piece of paper out of his window and disappeared to the south. The copilot crawled to the message. "Hold your position. Chopper en route to extract you. You are in unfriendly territory."

Minutes later a beautiful H-34 marine helicopter with ugly eyes painted on its front appeared at low level from the southeast and prepared to land just beyond the huddled doctors.

We ran toward the chopper. The other doctors climbed inside. I arrived at the side of the chopper before the pilot and one of the machine gunners.

I stopped, turned around in a half crouch, and pointing

my M16 toward the tree line, gave a head signal for the others to enter before me.

I was going to cover the rear. I was John Wayne. I was covering the retreat from the beaches of World War II. I was the star of War Comics. I was the salt-of-the-earth. I was playing the game like a champ. I was playing the role of some kind of goddamn hero. I was alive, goddamnit, and I was living.

The pilot and machine gunner ignored my heroism and leaped into the craft. I followed. When I was two steps from the open door the craft began to lift. To leave. To escape.

I leaped and my upper body and weapon flew into the helicopter as its rising floor caught me in the midsection and lifted me straight up from the earth, legs dangling ten, twenty, thirty, forty, fifty feet above the earth. Two marines caught my arms and pulled me in.

I lay on my belly in the helicopter. Its vibrating floor cut my lip and nose, but I felt no pain. The blood that ran down my chin was mine, and my heart was pumping the same kind of stuff all over my body. I was very happy.

We circled around the crippled craft. Round and round. Circle after circle. I didn't ask why. I didn't care. Finally two other helicopters arrived and landed on either side of our original helicopter and we left.

We returned to Phu Bai to get another army helicopter to take us to Da Nang. Myron, visibly a shaken man, elected not to continue and returned to the hooch. His plan of escape had failed him.

Our rescheduled flight to Da Nang was uneventful.

The 1 Corps Medical Society meeting was obviously just a preliminary to a social hour for all, and a drunk for some. War stories, beer, and cigarette smoke filled the large, modern Officers' Club. At night there was a live combo, more alcohol, prostitutes in all price ranges, steak dinners, and more war stories.

Jim Veesar was there. I hadn't seen him since R & R. He was very drunk, moderately loud, and successfully encountering an ugly Red Cross worker who was three inches taller than he.

I got separated from the rest of the Phu Bai doctors, and, consequently, lost out on the prearranged accommodations

and helicopter return flight. Jim and I spent the first night in
Da Nang in a small, one-bedroom apartment shared by three
American Red Cross girls. Two girls were asleep in the
bedroom when we arrived. I slept on the floor of the living
room listening to Jim and his tall, ugly chick screw on the
couch all night. It was a lovely, safe night with no incoming
rounds, no casualties, no fevers. A great night with the
sounds of the heated sexual intercourse of strangers complete
with whispers, panting, squeaking springs, real and feigned
orgasms, and occasional barefoot trips to the head.

The next morning Jim and I met the other two girls.
Breakfast, newspaper, cigarettes, chatting, and lots of coffee
filled the morning.

Jim accepted his hangover with stoic, quiet suffering. We
spent the afternoon walking the streets of Da Nang and
sitting in the sun on the banks of the Da Nang River in front
of the White Elephant, the large military administrative
building. Jim was so easy to talk to I was beginning to forget
how weird he looked.

We stripped to the waist and played outdoor basketball
against two army enlisted men who beat us easily.

That night we went to the Stone Elephant, an elegant
Officers' Club, for more music and alcohol. Jim disappeared
about nine o'clock (probably another chick), and I hitchhiked
to the navy hospital for a fantastic eight hours of uninterrupted sleep. When I awoke I walked to the airstrip across the
highway from the hospital to catch a ride to Phu Bai.

I had thrown away my overnight bag. The wide, externally
attached pockets of the jungle fatigues could easily hold a
razor, toothbrush, toothpaste, T-shirt, socks, pencil and paper, and still have room for a good time-killing paperback
book.

The wide cartridge belt with .45 on one side and canteen
on the other had become such a part of my dress that I felt
only partially dressed without them. The flak jacket and
helmet, however, always seemed like cumbersome extra gear.
I lay the flak gear in the sand next to me as I sat watching for
aircraft.

In Vietnam the heat can feel humid while the ground is
powder-dry sand that seems to evaporate into a dust that
sticks in your eyes and mouth and nose. It was already like
that by eight o'clock on the morning I left Da Nang. Hot as it

**Giant Flying Crane**

was, I wanted that cup of coffee I had missed in hurrying out to catch an early helicopter. I was alone at the end of the airstrip near a helicopter pad for over an hour without any success. Three marine choppers landed and took off again. One was full, one was not headed in my direction, and one had instructions not to carry passengers.

A giant flying crane landed. Two marines leaped out, and it was off again before I could could approach. The sand-blasting cyclone created by its flight temporarily hid the H-34 landing just beyond the bigger craft. One marine was loading some boxes as the blades kept turning.

Putting on my flak gear, I ran over to the marine. I was careful that the lieutenant bars on my collar showed over the edge of my flak jacket. The marine was a lance corporal with jet-black hair, surprisingly little tan and a thoroughly sweat-soaked shirt. He must have been new and unacclimatized.

"Hi! I'm Doctor Parrish."

I always used "doctor," not "lieutenant" in a situation like this. A marine lance corporal might just love to refuse a ride to a navy lieutenant, but would probably give a "doc" a break. I really wanted this ride. It was not unusual to spend whole days trying to get plane rides and my orders stated that I was due back in Phu Bai. Trying to look sincere, hurried, and important, I approached him all smiles.

"I need a ride to Phu Bai."

"We're going that way, if we don't get diverted." His accent was deep South. "We're taking supplies to A Med."

"That's my outfit. That's where I'm headed." I waited.

He turned without answering. After talking it over with the pilot, he motioned me to enter. I helped him load the remaining gear and climbed into the vibrating craft which lifted as we were still entering. The airstrip and hospital grew smaller and disappeared.

The pilot and copilot sat in the nose of the ship. The open-sided rear cabin housed the lance corporal, a machine gunner on each side, and me. Both of the gunners stared vacantly out the open doors, and, although they appeared to be bored and sleepy, they did not interrupt their focus from infinity even when they lit a cigarette. The lance corporal was busy securing the gear and talking on the headset. He offered me a headset which I refused, and he explained to me that we were going to make one stop before Phu Bai in order to leave most of the gear and to pick up a legal officer.

As we approached the landing site for the first leg of the mission, several puffs of smoke could be seen rising just beyond the tree line in the distance. Apparently the machine gunner on my side was not as unattentive as he appeared, because he was already pointing toward the smoke and talking on his headset. Suddenly we swerved away from the landing site, began to climb again, and headed toward the river on our right. Expecting me to know their meaning, the lance corporal pointed to the puffs of smoke.

As we approached the river, we lost altitude as our ground speed increased. We flew lower and faster until it seemed we were headed into the river. We turned to follow the course of the river and clipped along just above the sandpan and small crafts dotting the water. Both machine gunners were tense and ready, both hands on their weapons. They seemed to be looking for something in their boats. The lance corporal slipped a clip into his M16 and crouched down next to the open door opposite me. Then the chatter of small arms fire began in front of us, reached a crescendo, and then quickly passed beneath us, all in a matter of seconds.

The helicopter flew lower and lower until its wheels seemed only three or four feet from the water. I was really scared. If one wheel caught the water, we were dead. Was it necessary to fly so low, so fast? We rode each bend with the river; sometimes I was not sure we were going to stay in the valley created by the trees on each side. On one U-curve I noticed that another chopper was following close behind us.

I jammed a full clip into my .45. My reflexes kept me rearing back my head and shoulders as if my weight would influence us upward away from the water which raced below my feet. I was so damn scared that I considered jumping out. Was the pilot screening the vessels? Staying below tree line to avoid being fired upon? He couldn't be just playing. I felt weak and sweaty. The lance corporal handed me a set of headphones.

Then it came to me. I suddenly realized that I was the senior officer—the only officer—present. The senior officer present had no idea what the hell was going on. Was I going to be put in charge because of the silly bars on my collar?

I was inside a machine whose upkeep was maintained by kids who wanted to go to war. The pilot chose to fly in Vietnam instead of changing tires or going to college. How well did he know his skill? Was he quick thinking, bright? Did he have a hangover? Was he on pot? Whatever this was all about, I didn't want to be a part of it.

"Do you read me, Sir?" The copilot repeated, "Do you read me?"

"Do you read?" I thought to myself. "You can drop me off at the next stop. I want to pick up some cigarettes."

The copilot told me about the situation which had caused our change in course. It was good to have something to think about, and it did take a lot of concentration to obtain the story by headset. He was interrupted twice by messages coming from the ground. It was difficult to think beyond the fact that we were hurling through space between the water about to touch my feet and the whirling steel blades just above my head. If the two came any closer together, we would have no room between them.

A platoon of marines had left the main body of a company-sized sweep. The plan was to cross the river and move parallel to the main body up the opposite bank. However, the platoon made contact with the enemy, pursued him into the brush, and ran into a trap. Having fought their way back to the river at a point where it was too wide and deep for crossing, they were pinned down by an unknown number of enemy. They were under heavy fire. Several men were badly wounded.

At least two were killed in the initial contact. Two others died fighting back toward the river. Now the enemy was lobbing mortar shells at short range into the riverbank area. The marines could tell that the mortar positions were close, because they could hear the shells leaving the tubes. They called in artillery fire on the mortar positions, but it was questionable if the artillery could find the mortars before the mortars finished off the marines.

To make things worse, the first lieutenant in charge was wounded in the leg and drowned while trying to cross the river with full pack and flak gear. Helicopter extraction was being considered, but the fire seemed too heavy and the enemy too close. The gunny sergeant in charge would not attempt a crossing because of three severely wounded men who could not make it. The corpsmen were requesting medical evacuation at once. We were the closest helicopter at the time and just happened to have a doctor on board.

"They say that one area of the riverbank has a beach big enough for us to land." Copilot was painting a very clear picture.

A voice broke in from the ground again. One of the three had already died but now another man had been hit—head injury—serious. Eight walking wounded. They could wait; they could still fight.

I wasn't sure what all this had to do with our low flying, but what we had been asked to do was very clear. We were being requested—begged—to fly into that fire fight and to extract three men who might die without our help. If we were downed, we might all die with them. I still wasn't sure if these kids in the helicopter were asking me or telling me what we were up to. It was obvious that they were ready to go as if no other choice was really possible. And it seemed that we were rapidly headed there now.

We gained some altitude; the water seemed a safer distance away.

"Yes" was all I said.

I don't know if they interpreted this as my saying "yes, go ahead," or "yes, I understand," or "yes, thank-you-very-much, pull up and stop skimming the water." I wasn't sure which I meant and, finally, was a little surprised I had been able to say anything. I heard small arms fire again and incoming rounds. This time it did not pass beneath us. It increased in loudness. We slowed, turned toward the bank, and approached for landing. With all of its guns going full blast the helicopter previously behind us veered off to our left and swept around us. Marines were scattered all about the beach behind the trees. They shot into the woods as if their lives depended on the number of rounds they fired. Their activity was frantic but determined. There was a lot of rapid chatter and static on the headset, most of which I couldn't understand. Bullets, explosions, gunfire were everywhere. It was the middle of hell. I saw one boy get shot right in the middle of his chest. He flew backward and landed on his back. His trunk seemed to have been jerked directly to the ground and his arms and head flopped along behind.

Before we touched, four marines carrying the corners of a blanket ran toward us in a crouch with weapons in one hand and a corner of the blanket in the other. Two more men carried another wounded by the arms and legs. They fell to the ground as a mortar exploded in the river next to them and then they crawled along dragging the wounded man the rest of the way.

As I helped the blanket into the craft a bullet or a piece of shrapnel went through the helicopter just above my head. A marine carried the body of one of his buddies in a fireman's carry and dumped him into the opposite side of our helicopter. The pilot was screaming all kinds of profanities into the headset, all connected to the word "hurry." Surrounded only by a plexiglass shield and a flak jacket, he and his co-pilot were strapped into their seats in the cockpit. Waiting. Waiting for the wounded to be loaded. Every second on the ground was too long for them.

Another explosion in the river shook the helicopter and sprayed water over us. As the marines ran for cover, a corpsman turned to motion toward his right lateral chest, probably trying to show me where the entrance wound was on one of the wounded. He saluted. I waved in a manner to tell him to get the hell down on the ground.

We were up and out of there so fast that it was all I could do to keep the wounded and myself in the helicopter.

I'm sure we were on the ground for only twenty or thirty seconds, but that twenty seconds was incredibly draining and frightening. I wondered how those poor kids could have been there all afternoon, maybe all night tonight. Why hadn't they

clamored for escape on our chopper? Why did the corpsman
stand up and salute?

The lance corporal opened the first-aid kit as I examined
the wounded. Somehow another body had been thrown
aboard unnoticed, because there were two men obviously
dead, one with a large gaping neck wound, the other with
blood soaked pants (I didn't look for the wound). A third man
had an entrance wound in his right temple with brains
protruding. No exit wound was visible. He had dilated pupils, irregular breathing with long periods of apnea, but a
good pounding pulse. All four limbs were flaccid although I
had seen some decerebrate posturing as he was dragged into
the chopper. I didn't spend any time with him. He was
obviously going to die, and if he didn't, it would be too
bad, for he would never think again.

The man in the blanket was awake, quite short of breath,
and anxious. His pulse was rapid but easily palpable. He had
a sucking chest wound in his right lower chest and an exit
wound in his right lower back. He had a chance if his liver
was not torn up. I found a vaseline gauze and sealed the
wound. I could do no more until we returned to the hospital.
A good corpsman can usually do as much in the battlefield as
a doctor.

The machine gunners resumed their vacant stares and
smoked. The lance corporal took each of the dead men's belts
off and wrapped them around their ankles. He stuck their
hands and arms inside their cartridge belts. Thus the bodies
were easier to load, unload, and carry. He worked so
mechanically that it was evident he had done it many times
before. This was all in a morning's work for these kids. They
didn't consider themselves heroes. They were just doing a
job. They had probably saved the life of one marine but
would never even know for sure, because they would just
leave him at the hospital. I got the feeling that they would
never try to find out if he lived. It was as if they did not care.
But the next time a wounded marine needed them, they
would break their ass and again endanger their lives to help.
It was their job. Maybe they had learned that personal
involvement brings pain and that a job well done brings a
relative pleasure. I looked at the two gunners poised in the
doorways. Maybe they weren't thinking about it at all, but
about R & R or home or chow. Maybe they were reliving

those twenty seconds. Whatever their thoughts, they had the same bored, sleepy look which they had when I joined them. Amazing kids.

We returned to the Da Nang hospital where stretcher bearers took our wounded. I accompanied the chest wound until the hospital doctors were with him. He was probably going to live. The two bodies were carried directly to Graves. The head wound went to triage where he would wait several hours before joining his two colleagues. At Graves the three of them would be washed down, identified, pronounced dead, put in green bags, and left in the cold room until next flight home.

The form letters and official notifications would be initiated later today. By tomorrow friends and family would be crushed. The family would remember them with images of childhood, a picture on the piano, an empty chair at the dinner table, and the cold sheets of a double bed. Their marine friends would relive the moment of impact again and again. But otherwise they would become a number, a pink slip, a typewritten line, a fact. War's maximum efficiency is the reduction of twenty years and one hundred sixty pounds into a telegram and a statistic.

I returned to the helicopter pad where the copilot and the lance corporal were examining some large holes torn in the tail section. They decided not to fly on but to hop over to the maintenance area for repairs.

I again returned to the hospital area. I still needed a cup of coffee and a ride to Phu Bai. I forgot to ask why we were flying so low.

# NINE

"Well, guys, it's happened." I threw my hat on my bunk as I entered the hooch. "I got my orders. I'm going out into the field."

"No shit."

"Oh, no."

"Really?"

"Uh oh."

"Yep." I stood in the center of the room and waved the orders. "It says right here. Forward unit. Battalion aid station (BAS). It's an infantry outfit. That means out in the bush."

I sat on my bunk and looked at the floor.

After an awkward silence Myron broke the ice. "Maybe you'll be in a secure area."

"Cam Lo, the wash out, and headed west," I answered. "Not exactly Quiet City."

"When do you go?"

"In two days."

"Why you?"

"It's my turn, I guess."

"How long?"

"Don't know."

"We'll save your bunk."

"Thanks."

"Take tomorrow off to pack and rest up," Myron said.

"Don't need to pack. I'm not taking anything with me. And how the hell do you take a day off in Phu Bai?"

Bill walked to the fridge, removed two beers, opened one, and handed it to me. "How about some hearts tonight?"

"Sure. Why not." I forced a smile. "Why the hell not."

We didn't talk about the field anymore that night but

spoke often of how great it would be "when John gets back."

"When John gets back we'll all start getting up and going to breakfast together."

"When you get back, John," said Myron, "I'll even start taking a run with you now and then."

"We'll even get Prince to do some exercise," I added. "When I get back."

"If you stay too long, you'll miss me," taunted Roland. "I've only got ninety-one days left."

Although my hoochmates were concerned about my being out on the front lines with the infantry and would probably even miss me, an important aspect of my trip for them was that they would be "shorter" when I returned. Time would pass measured by days of my adventures, days of my absence. Time sometimes seemed more important than morals, religion, or even one's own self. The subconscious defense mechanisms of denial, fantasy, escape, and withdrawal were given something real to work with—the 365-day tour.

The 365-day tour became one of the most fixed and permanent things about one's whole existence. The war was unpredictable. The enemy could be doing your wash, selling you a stolen coke, or sneaking toward you in the jungle. Your health might deteriorate from diarrhea, fever, malaria, or pneumonia. Your friends may be transferred or killed. Your hooch may be blown away. You yourself might die, or go crazy. But the 365-day year, the one year tour, the rotation date, became fixed in our minds as an undisputed fact of nature. If someone wanted to or could change that fact we didn't want to think about it.

And our tour was 366 days. It was leap year.

After another frightening C-130 ride, I joined the rear elements of the infantry battalion in Dong Ha. From there I was taken by jeep over miles of flat country to Cam Lo and then west to the "wash out" just beyond the Cam Lo River.

I rode shotgun as we rode without much conversation. When we got beyond the outer perimeter of the Dong Ha military base I noticed that the driver and the marine in the back seat put a clip into their M16's. The other passenger in the back seat, a corpsman who had just arrived in country, slipped a clip into his rifle too. His hands were shaking so that I thought he was going to shoot us all. Trying to act like I knew what I was doing and trying to hide my own fear, I slid a full clip into my .45.

As we bumped along on what seemed an endless journey, I studied every bush and tree on the side of the road. I turned my collar devices into my shirt so as not to let my rank flash in the sun to aid a sniper's selection of candidates. What the hell was I going to do if the enemy started firing? What good would a .45 be against snipers or a surprise attack?

My thighs ached from the tension produced by fear and from trying to keep my balance. I expected to be shot at any minute or to hit a land mine and be blown away. For some strange reason I felt obligated not to express my anxiety. I wanted to ask the driver about our chances of getting lost or being fired at, but his answers would not have helped me or even frightened me any more than I was no matter what he might have said.

Instead, I made conversation with the new corpsman who was also headed for the same battalion aid station (BAS), which would be his first assignment in Vietnam. His name was Robby Wills. He was a nineteen-year-old, fair-skinned, small, black-haired boy from Albany, Georgia. Robby looked sixteen, frightened, and insecure.

Robby Wills looked upon me as a seasoned veteran, a doctor, an officer, and an adult. I played all those roles for him even though I felt like we were both helpless orphans.

The wash out was a flat, dry basin housing a few tents and many partially underground bunkers. From its center a small dirt road led directly west to the hills surrounding Con Thien. The hills seemed all too close.

My new home was a tent with a dirt floor, surrounded by a double sandbag wall about three feet high. The front half of the tent was used for sick call and the back half had three canvass cots—one for me, one for the chief and one for the first class corpsman. Robby Wills slept next door in a tent shared by four or five corpsmen.

The infantry battalion was scattered all around us; marines slept in bunkers, tents, and on the ground. The mess hall tent and kitchen tent were in the lowest part of the basin about fifty meters from my own. My first official act was to have the mess hall tent moved to a slightly higher location because it sat squarely in the middle of the only mud puddle

106 mm recoilless on mule.

in the area and the grease, water, heat, and men had attracted an army of flies. Within a few days that move made no difference because the monsoons had changed the whole basin into one large mud sea.

I met the colonel and his staff. The colonel was a small, thin man in his late forties, with piercing eyes, a sardonic smile, a big cigar butt, and a practiced nasty disposition. He was unable to speak to anyone, even the chaplain, without using unnecessarily abusive and profane adjectives and his lack of tact was so obvious that it insulted no one. The officers tolerated him and did everything he said without resentment and usually without much question. The enlisted men did not hate him but dislike, distrust, fear, and rank made them avoid eye contact with him. He called me "Doc," as did everyone else in the unit, and never had much to say to me outside of our professional encounters.

The first class hospitalman my new tentmate, a twenty-two-year-old college dropout from Connecticut took me on a tour of my new home. At one edge of the perimeter a recoiless rifle team was preparing to fire across the barbed wire into a group of trees about a hundred meters away. Not

knowing any better, I walked up behind them to watch. As I
heard a marine yell "All clear to the rear—fire," the first class
suddenly knocked me to the ground and fell next to me. Just
as he did so the backblast of flame, dirt, and debris from the
recoiless rifle flew over our prone bodies.

"Oh, and another thing, Sir, don't ever stand behind a
recoiless rifle. The backblast will kill a man up to twenty feet
away."

"Thanks."

"And you, you stupid ass grunt," the first class was
standing again and yelling at the marine sitting on the
four-wheel mule carrying the rifle. "Don't yell 'all clear to the
rear—fire' unless it's all clear to the rear."

"Shove it up your navy ass," someone yelled. We kept
walking.

The western perimeter of the camp bordered on a
"free-fire zone." Anyone or anything that moves in that area
is free game and can be shot, mortared, or bombed. All of
the military maps had it marked as such and supposedly all
civilians in the area had been informed.

The camp dump was in this "free-fire zone." Each morning at the same time a truck drove out to the dump and all of
the tin cans, cardboard containers, wrappers, and garbage
from the camp was dumped about fifty meters inside the
zone. Within minutes, the dump was filled with Vietnamese
from nearby villes gathering cans and garbage. The marines
in the watchtower would fire close to them to frighten them
away. A few days earlier, an eight-year-old Vietnamese boy
had been wounded by these warning shots and was brought
to the aid station where he was kept until his wounds were
healed. One day he stole an orange soda from a marine who
shot and killed him as he tried to run away.

The first class was a smooth operator. He was small in
stature but strong, persuasive, and an excellent manipulator.
He had marines twice his size jumping at his command.
Although his face was very plain, he somehow had the
appearance of that one person in the room everyone should
try to impress. He was bright and worked hard. He spoke
Vietnamese and knew all the right people, especially girls, in
the nearby ville. He knew all the angles, rules, ropes, and
right people, and could obtain or get away with anything.

The only thing that worried me about him was that he

seemed to enjoy what he was doing. A touch of inappropriate euphoria, stubborn dedication, and feigned sincerity seemed out of place in the environment of a forward BAS.

The chief, like many chiefs in the navy, did as little as possible. He spent most of his time telling dirty jokes, cooking meals to compete with the mess sergeant, and yelling at people.

"Your ass is on report," he would say to anybody whose actions he did not approve. He said it so often that no one paid any attention. I never saw him actually put anyone on report.

"Wills, if I find one goddamn band aid out of place, your ass is on report."

He even threatened to put my ass on report when I did things like eat chow hall food instead of one of his awful C ration home-cooked concoctions, or refused to skip the colonel's daily briefings just to play blackjack. Pretty soon, we were all putting each other's asses on report for everything.

It was the chief who picked the corpsmen to go out on patrols. Usually it was pretty automatic because each marine squad had certain corpsmen assigned to it but the week before I arrived, four corpsmen had been killed in one operation and some juggling around was necessary. He assigned Robby Wills to me to help with sick call until he got used to his new job and his new environment.

Each morning at dawn a large group of expressionless marines with full pack, extra ammunition, heavy gear, radios, and mortars walked, half awake, single file, past our tent and out into the trees in the distance. Each night they returned. Tired, dirty, with the salt of dried sweat on their fatigues, and with far-away blank stares. Often fewer returned than left and it was always the marine carrying two M16's that had a hurt, confused, and bitter look. His buddy had fallen. The sick, wounded, and dead were taken by helicopters directly from the place they fell and simply did not return with the rest of the marines at dusk.

The patrols left everyday. Their exits and returns were without conversation, without drama, without heroism, without question. Those who died, died. Those who lived didn't die. They filed back past us, ate, cleaned their weapons, and went to sleep waiting for dawn and the gunny sergeant to return them to the rice paddies, the woods, the jungle, the

**M 110 8″ Self propelled**

hills. Waiting to walk and sweat through another day to end up again back at camp, if they were lucky.

Patrols, sweeps, missions, search and destroy. It continued everyday as if part of sunlight itself. I went to the colonel's briefings everyday. He explained how effectively we were keeping the enemy off balance, not allowing them to move in, set up mortar sites, and gather for attack. He didn't seem to hate them. They were to him like pests or insects that had to be kept away. It seemed that one important purpose of patrols was just for them to take place, to happen, to exist; there had to be patrols. It gave the men something to do. Find the enemy, make contact, kill, be killed, and return. Trap, block, hold. Air support, artillery support. Movement, forward observers, reports, intelligence. A game played from the colonel's tent by telephone and by second-hand stories. In the first five days, I lost six corpsmen—two killed, four wounded.

We never saw the wounded or dead. The helicopters returned them directly from the field to the rear. My friends in Phu Bai were probably taking care of them. Usually my corpsmen came back from patrols. Sometimes they didn't.

My days at the BAS were very boring. The first class corpsman ran the sick call for two hours each morning and afternoon, and he only called on me for problems he could not handle. Most of my business was minor illness, injuries, and malingerers. The high point of the day was one of the chief's special C-rat combination lunches, or a patrol coming back early with nobody missing.

I tried to read or nap during the day. The conversations around me were repetitive and uninteresting and I was always behind on sleep. There was a battery of six of the big eight-inch guns dug into the hillside just behind my tent. The closest one was about twenty meters from my rack and it fired outgoing shells intermittently all through the night. I could feel the sound with my whole body. A sharp crack that seemed to lift me out of bed and stop my heart and fire every synapse in my brain at once, a quick metal convulsion followed by a postictal, psychic weakness. A hundred sound-shock therapies every night.

The men with whom I lived had high school educations at best. They talked of sex, fist fights, descriptions of wounds and fire fights, and told detailed short stories of how other corpsmen had gotten killed. The same comments and stories were told at least daily. My new tentmates seemed to understand when I didn't join in every conversation. We generally got along very well and when we weren't putting each other's asses on report were mutually helping each other pass the time.

The first class corpsman was excellent at making time pass for himself and he always dreamed up something that it was "important" for me to do. Inspect the latrines, make out a report on the chow tent, check the evacuation routes through the barbed wire, talk with the colonel about this or that, or spend some time in the watchtower getting to know the men. I would accept almost any invitation to do almost anything to pass time.

One day the colonel sent for me to meet him on the bank of the Cam Lo River just south of the bridge. He wanted to show me four Vietnamese bodies which had washed up on shore during the night. When I arrived the colonel was standing over the bodies and started asking me questions as I approached.

"Okay, Doc, how long have these NVA been dead? How old are they? Were they dead before they hit the water or did they drown?"

I didn't answer. I had some questions of my own. "How do you know they're NVA?" I asked.

"Too fucking fat and healthy looking to be VC. Short-ass haircuts. One of them had on fucking fatigue pants. Villagers said they never saw the cock suckers before. Four young men found all at once, and nobody's missing from the ville. Shit. Peasants probably caught the bastards stealing rice and killed their ass and threw 'em in the goddamn river. Or maybe..." he paused. "Hell, I'm the one sposed to be asking the goddamn questions. Just examine the fuckers, Doc. Come to my tent when you finish." He walked back to his jeep and was gone.

Four nude, markedly swollen, water-logged bodies lay side by side on their backs. Each had a massively swollen face. Eyes seemed to try to bulge out of sockets whose contents were as big as apples. Their lips were three times normal size and each mouth was open and round like that of a fish, with a massive splitting tongue protruding skyward. A thin, bloody fluid trickled from their nostrils.

Massive edema and rigor mortis held their arms up and out in front of them with fat fingers reaching toward the clouds. Their scrota were the size of softballs, and their swollen penises stood as if erect. Their knees were bent in identical frog-leg positions. The smell was overwhelming and hundreds of flies circled around those which were already busy inspecting the mouths and nostrils. There was not a mark on the front of their bodies.

I tried to turn one of them over but he must have weighed several hundred pounds. My driver helped me and the body flipped over face down in the sand without really changing its fixed position.

No signs of trauma.

I didn't bother to flip the others. I had to stand back because the smell was making me sick. I walked down and rinsed my hands in the river and walked back to the road and leaned against the jeep.

Several small children approached and began to throw rocks at the bodies and strike the bodies with sticks. The older ones yelled profanities in broken English for our benefit.

"Fuckin' NVA."

"VC, number ten."

"Fuckin' bastards."

"Number ten."

The younger kids began to sing and chant as they

skipped and danced in circles around the bodies. What a great game. They laughed and screamed and struck out at the bodies.

We watched in silence for several minutes. The villagers across the river ignored us and the bodies. The bored marines on the nearby bridge paced back and forth as they stood watch. Several jeeps and troop transport trucks vibrated across the wooden bridge. A Vietnamese family passed by in a small boat allowing the clear current to carry them toward the bridge. The kids continued their happy dance.

My driver studied my face. "What do you think, Doc?"

"I don't know what to think anymore."

"I mean were they dead when they hit the water?"

"I don't know. Does it matter? I mean, who gives a shit?"

"The colonel does."

"Oh, I'll make up a story that the colonel will love. It'll make his whole day."

The first class hospitalman managed to go into the ville for two or three hours everyday to "run errands." His visits usually included a few small shops, a whorehouse, and a certain Vietnamese family—an old lady and two young boys—which he had adopted and supported with food and money. One day he convinced me to go into the ville with him to make his usual rounds. We skipped the whorehouse that day.

Many of the villagers knew him and seemed genuinely glad to see him. He joked and played with the children and chatted in good Vietnamese with the elders. As we drove slowly down one crowded little side street, a four-year-old boy walked out and threw a crude wooden box with metal casing, wires, and a flashlight battery taped to its side. It landed in the back seat of our jeep right next to where I was sitting. I didn't realize at first what it was.

The driver stopped the jeep. "Jump! It's a fucking bomb." He curled up in a ball with his face between his legs.

By the time the jeep stopped moving I was headed over the side rail.

"Don't move, Doc!" yelled the corpsman from the shotgun seat. "Don't touch it!"

I froze for a second. The first class corpsman carefully picked up the crude device and flung it into a field next to us. We all curled and covered and waited. It didn't go off.

The driver picked up his M16, turned in his seat, and carefully aimed at the boy who was running back down the street.

"No, don't!" The corpsman grabbed the barrel of the gun and shoved it toward the floor of the jeep.

Without answering the driver struggled to free the gun from the corpsman's grip. They both looked at me at the same time to settle their dispute. I shook my head side to side, the driver lay down his gun, and we proceeded in silence.

The next day that same driver was mysteriously blown away in the same part of the ville.

On occasion I climbed up the wooden watchtower to pass the time watching the world around me through the powerful field glasses. One afternoon I caught sight of a straggly line of marines slowly snaking through a rice paddy far to the southwest. Two Vietnamese women were bending over working in the mud and seemed not to notice the marines passing by at wide intervals. One appeared to be an older woman, the other a girl.

The older woman was approached by one of the marines who reached inside his shirt and gave her something. The woman bent over at the waist again as if resuming her work. The marine pulled up her long skirt, opened his fly, and entered her from the rear. He proceeded to have intercourse with her as she continued to work in the rice water with both hands. The marine pressed behind her kept both hands on his M16 and looked straight ahead as they rocked back and forth to the rhythm of his thrusts. A second marine further back in the straggly column did the same thing when he approached the woman. The girl continued her work.

A few minutes later a second small group of marines filed through the same paddy. The woman waved to one of them and lifted her skirt. The marine closest to her picked up a rock and hit her with it.

"Hey, Doc," the marine lieutenant put his hand on my shoulder. "See any VC?"

"Nope, just marines."

"Wanna shoot somebody?"

"Nope."

"Seriously, I mean it."

I looked at the marine without answering.

"Colonel says we gotta wound one of them garbage rats," he smiled and shrugged his shoulders. "The Vietnamese are getting to where they ignore our warning shots. So we gotta show them we mean business. Either they get away from the dump or we shoot 'em."

"Let them have the fucking garbage, will you," I said. "Maybe they're hungry."

"It's a free-fire zone, Doc. You go letting people walk around in there and next thing you know we're getting mortared from close range. And the garbage truck hits a land mine."

"Yeah, I guess you're right."

"Damn right I am. It's our own asses I'm concerned about."

"Why don't you just throw some smoke or tear gas or something?"

"They'll just come back when it's cleared. You gotta wound or kill one of them. Show 'em we mean business."

"Not me."

"I'm just looking out for my men, Doc."

I looked down at the platform floor.

"Doc, you gotta take care of the one we hit, so you might as well pick a site and shoot him yourself."

"No thanks," I almost smiled. "I've been trying to quit."


At first it started just like any other rainstorm. Late one afternoon it rained hard for over an hour then tapered off to a steady drizzle which lasted all night. It didn't stop raining again for seven weeks. The baseline was a steady, cold, misty, shifting rain. Superimposed on that were sheets of solid water that lasted for hours. Once everyone accepted the constantly wet state and the mud up above the ankle level, then life went on as usual. The cold chill at night could not be kept out of one's bones even by long underwear, fatigues, boots, and two blankets.

Patrols kept going.

"If we can't keep the fuckers away from us, then we'll have to pull the fuck out," said the colonel.

Patrols didn't, however, go as far or as often and made

less contact. The outgoing artillery guns kept up their relent-
less work. The chief kept cooking. Robby Wills kept helping
around the BAS.

"Wills, I want to talk to you." The chief seemed upset.

"It's time isn't it, Chief?" Robby had been expecting it.
"I knew it had to come sooner or later."

"Well, kid," the chief looked right at him and then at the
floor, "it's time."

"When?"

"Tomorrow morning. Company B is sending a platoon on
an all day patrol. They lost their corpsman last time out
and——"

"And I just joined Company B. Right, Chief?"

"Right, Wills." The chief tried to smile. "Now get over
and find the sergeant and get your ass briefed before I put
your ass on report."

"Yes, Sir." He left at a fast walk.

The chief looked over to me shaking his head. "Doc, do
you know how many of those goddamn kids I've sent out who
never came back?" It's the first time I'd ever heard his voice
tremble.

"I don't want to know," I said.

"Hot dogs or hamburger patties?"

"Hamburger patties, please, Chief."

"Coming right up, Doc. And wait till you taste this
sauce."

Next morning I watched another patrol leave into the
curtain of rain. The fourth man in line was Robby Wills. Full
gear, brave smile, and M16. But he really looked like a little
boy.

The marines spent most of the day in an undefended
ville on the Cam Lo River. No contact. Nothing special. On
the way back to base they were ambushed. The point was
killed, the others pinned down.

"Greenleaf two, Greenleaf two. We are under fire. Small
arms and mortars. No X. It is an L, but the river is to our
right flank and open paddies behind. I repeat. L to our west
flank and our north. Heavy fire. Number not known."

Helicopters could not function in the heavy rain and
wind. The colonel decided to take a company-sized force and
try to relieve the trapped marines. At the same time he

hoped to pin the enemy between him and the trapped marines. The colonel wanted me to go. If he got hit he wanted a doctor to be on hand. I elected to stay at the BAS and wait. It was after three in the afternoon by the time the company got organized and left.

I waited.

About dark the company returned. The NVA had disappeared as soon as the reinforcements had made contact, but not before they had wiped out half the original marine patrol. Wills was unhurt but visibly shaken. I was surprised that he didn't have much to say that night. No war stories.

About 2 A.M. somebody woke me. It was Wills. He whispered that he had to talk to me. We went up to the front of my BAS tent. No one could hear us above the steady pounding of the rain.

Wills started to talk and then quickly, completely broke down, sobbing and shaking. It took him some time to tell me his story between bursts of uncontrollable crying. In the ville that day he had watched a black marine rape a Vietnamese teen-age girl and later, when the fire fight broke out he saw the same marine hiding behind a tree. In his state of panic he was suddenly overcome by rage, prejudice, and hate, and had shot at the marine himself. Wills thought that it was he and not the enemy who had killed the black marine.

He had to tell me his story. He wanted me to tell him what to do. He wanted me to do an autopsy to see whose bullet it was that downed the marine. He wanted to confess.

I quieted him down. We decided to do nothing until morning after we had talked again, and Wills disappeared under the tent flap into the rain. I sat on the ground right where I was and lit a cigarette. The big eight-inch guns opened up several long volleys.

I wasn't sure what to do with this piece of information. Was Wills a scared, confused kid, a victim? A racist murderer? A self-appointed judge and executioner? Insane? If we decided that the yellow man's bullet had killed the black boy then it would be a sad but routine casualty of war. If it was the white boy from Albany, Georgia, whose bullet struck the marine, then it was a murder. Bullets everywhere. Why should I be the judge? How could I judge? Who will judge the NVA? Who will accuse the colonel? Who will try the congressman? Who will execute the voter?

Bombs are murdering thousands of civilians. Four-year-old boys try to kill me. Children dance around the bodies of their uncles and cousins. If I had one chance to stop the chain of murders, didn't I have the right to do so?

Wills walked about in the rain the rest of the night. At dawn he again came into my tent, shaking with cold, fear, and guilt.

"Doc, Doc," he whispered, "let's go to the chow hall. They'll be open in a minute. I gotta talk to you some more."

"Coming." I threw a rain slicker over my shoulders and we sloshed through the mud toward the chow tent just as first light was breaking into the rain. The cooks were moving around by kerosene lamps.

We sat on the edge of the elevated deck and drank coffee.

"What are you going to do to me, Doc?"

"I don't know. What are you going to do, Robby?"

"I don't know."

It began to rain harder.

The shadowy forms of a few sleepy marines began to move through the chow line.

Robby Wills bolted to his feet. "Doc, it's him. It's him! Big as life!"

"What?"

"In line. The big black mother. Big as life. He's not dead. Big and black and ugly as ever. I love him."

Wills ran over and threw a running bear hug on a big lance corporal. His tray went flying into the air and they both went to the floor covered with coffee and powdered eggs. The surprised lance corporal got to his feet first and let swing with a wild right hook that caught Wills in the side of the head just as he was getting up. He went sprawling toward me.

"You crazy fucker, what the hell are you doing?" The marine brushed the eggs off his wet T-shirt.

Wills crawled over to where I stood. He was laughing and crying at the same time. Everybody started to laugh. They didn't know why they were laughing. The lance corporal was laughing too.

I hit Wills in the shoulder and knocked him down again and I started laughing too.

"I love him," Wills said as he rolled in the mud. "I fucking love him."

**B-52**

Wills and I never mentioned the incident again.

Wills went on several more patrols. He got to be a good corpsman. A great corpsman. And a good soldier. What continually amazed me, and pissed me off a little, was that these kids were good soldiers. So good it made tears come to your eyes. Wills started to feel like he was part of Company B. He began to bug the guys to take their malaria pills. He began to volunteer for missions and carry less ammo and more medical supplies. It was the coldest night of the rainy season when Wills found a permanent place in the history of Company B and joined a long line of young heroes. Some living, some dead.

It was cold as hell and the rain had increased from its stormlike baseline to full-fledged monsoon. The mud in the shallowest places was ankle deep and in the basins one could sink up to his waist and not be able to walk. A two-company sweep started early in the morning. The marines were to join up with a company of Arvans and walk to the highway to provide protection for the bridge and ville and highway. The battalion which had been providing this security was pulling back toward the rear. The rains had made it impossible to hold all that had been held two weeks earlier. It was a routine operation. No contact was expected.

The Arvans didn't show up. The marines waited three hours in the rain before continuing without them. Because of the delay and the mud it became clear that they would not reach the objective by dark. When it grew too dark to see adequately it was decided to kneel in place and wait until first light.

It was too muddy to dig in. Anyone who lay down or fell asleep without positioning his head correctly on his helmet would drown. A loose perimeter was established hoping that the mud would prevent any enemy attack. It was hoped, above all, that the NVA mortar bearers did not know the exact position of the marines because they were in open, unprotected country.

A no light, no fire, red alert was established and man-to-man communication in the darkness was by occasional touch or whisper. Whenever a form sloshed by no one could be sure if it was friend or foe.

Suddenly automatic weapon fire began cracking repeatedly about two hundred meters from the main body of marines. No one was sure if it was marine or NVA. Soldiers began yelling at one another. One marine opened up in the direction of the automatic weapons. Then all hell broke loose.

Weapons were firing everywhere. Creatures sloshed back and forth in the mud in all directions. No one was sure who was moving and where they were going.

The marine captain started screaming orders. Just then enemy mortar rounds began to sock into the mud making dull, deep, sickening belches. Screams of fear and pain added to the mass confusion. Everyone was firing now.

A B-52 bombing raid began in the mountains several miles to the north, and the rumble occasionally lighted the whole northern sky. Under the cover of the confusion and the mortars NVA began to wade in from nowhere right into the midst of the marines while the shelling continued.

The marines started firing flares into the air. As they intermittently floated to earth, bright light and good visibility alternated with complete darkness. Just as one flare exploded Wills saw two NVA who had already passed by him. He stood, turned, and fired his M16 from the hip and cut them down at close range.

Now everybody was firing at anything that moved. Each marine did not move but just squeezed deeper into the mud and kept firing.

"Corpsman up." A cry about twenty meters from Wills. He began crawling toward the cry. Automatic weapon fire whizzed by him. Probably marines and NVA were shooting at him. A mortar shell socked into the mud just behind him and pushed him face forward deep into the mud, wounding him in the buttocks and propelling him closer to the wounded man.

"Corpsman up!" A black lance corporal had a chest wound, a missing left hand, and a smashed M16. Wills pulled up beside him.

"Hey, Doc, I got it in the chest, man. I can't breathe."

Wills found a vaseline gauze in his pack and dressed the chest wound as he lay on his side next to the lance corporal.

"I'm freezing. I'm cold as hell, Doc." The lance corporal was shaking. Most of what Wills did was by feel and not by sight.

"This should plug the hole."

"Hurry, Doc. Can't breathe."

Wills put a tourniquet on the left wrist and gave the marine a shot of morphine.

"Doc, I gotta stay out here all night, don't I?"

"Right."

"Doc, stay here with me. I don't wanna die."

"You'll make it, man."

"I'm cold as hell, Doc."

Wills didn't answer. He crawled back to the two NVA bodies. Bullets flew everywhere. The NVA were walking the mortar shells systematically back and forth in rows across the mud plain. Wills froze as they came closer to him on one pass. He put his whole body face down as low as he could in the mud. A mortar shell landed fifteen to twenty meters to his left in the mud, the next one twenty meters to his right and then he began to crawl again. He dragged one of the NVA bodies back to the wounded marine and curled it around his upper body for protection. The marine let his legs and hips slide down deeper into the mud and hid his upper body in the crook of the NVA's body.

"Corpsman up! Corpsman up!" from behind Wills. "Corpsman up, goddamnit, hurry!" Wills was off again.

Wills was at it all night. When first light arrived the enemy fled. Wills was found nude except for his boots. Six wounded marines were huddled in a pile in a mud hole protected on three sides by bodies (two NVA and one marine). They all had well placed battle dressings and were covered up with the clothes and the flak gear of Wills and the three bodies.

Wills lay face up next to his human-body-and-mud-

bunker with his head resting on the dead marine's leg. The
rain beating on his face had washed it clean. The rest of his
nude body was partially submerged in the sea of mud.

The marines began to pick up the wounded and carry
them to the highway and ground transportation to Dong Ha.
Wills came to while they were being loaded on litters. He
refused to be helped or dressed until all the marines were
loaded. Then he bandaged his own ass, wrapped himself in a
blanket, and got in the truck to attend the wounded en route
to the clearing station.

Three of six men in Will's homemade fortress were dead
when they arrived in Dong Ha. Two had died during the long
night and one more died en route to the clearing station.

When the truck pulled up at Dong Ha Wills looked over
at the lance corporal with no left hand. "You got it made now,
man. Doctors. Gear. Operating rooms. You've made it."

"Thanks, man," the lance corporal said holding out his
one hand palm up.

"Three for six," Wills slapped his palm. "Fifty percent."
He hopped off the truck to help with the litters. "I'll do
better next time."


"John! You made it back in time for Christmas. How was
it?" Myron rubbed his eyes; he'd been napping as usual.

"Not too bad. Kinda wet and cold."

"Busy?"

"No. All the casualties came here. And all the real
sickies came to you."

"Yeah. I saw your name on some medevac tags."

Myron and I talked for a few minutes and then made
rounds on the medical wards. We ended up back at the desk
in the corner with a cup of coffee.

"Some things I'll never forget, Myron. One is the look
on those kids' faces when they leave and come back from
those damn patrols everyday. And I'll never forget how it is to
be cold all the time—day and night. I occasionally got dry but
I wasn't warm once all that time.

"And there is a sound that will haunt me forever."

"What's that, John?"

"It's the nauseating sound a mortar shell makes when it
lands in the mud. It makes me sick, Myron, it really makes
me sick."

*In those days a decree went out from Caesar Augustus,
that all the world should be taxed.*

*(And this taxing was first made when Cyrenius
was governor of Syria.)*

*And all went to be taxed, every one into his
own city.*

(Luke 2:1–3)

The chaplain was reading by candlelight. He had a King
James southern accent.

*And Joseph also went up from Galilee, out of the
city of Nazareth, into Judaea, unto the city of
David, which is called Bethlehem; (because he was
of the house and lineage of David:)*

*To be taxed with Mary his espoused wife, being
great with child.*

*And so it was, that, while they were there, the
days were accomplished that she should be delivered.*

(Luke 2:4–6)

The crowd was small. Four to five doctors, eight or ten
corpsman, a couple of marines all sitting on the benches with
hats in hands.

*And she brought forth her firstborn son, and
wrapped him in swaddling clothes, and laid him in a
manger; because there was no room for them in the
inn.*

(Luke 2:7)

I wondered if everything was quiet up in triage. I was
getting nervous.

*And there were in the same country shepherds
abiding in the field, keeping watch over their flock
by night.*

(Luke 2:8)

I thought of all those marines who were out in the field right
now. Kids in the mud.

> *And, lo, the angel of the Lord came upon them,
> and the glory of the Lord shone round about them:
> and they were sore afraid.*
>
> (Luke 2:9)

Those kids were scared shitless out in that black night
and cold as hell. I knew how cold they were.

> *And the angel said unto them, Fear not: for,
> behold, I bring you good tidings of great joy, which
> shall be to all people.*
>
> (Luke 2:10)

My mind began to replay the mortars socking into the
mud. I thought I heard screams.

> *For unto you is born this day in the city of
> David a Saviour, which is Christ the Lord.*
>
> (Luke 2:11)

Merry Christmas, you poor bastards out there. God
knows I wish you weren't out there.

> *And this shall be a sign unto you; Ye shall find
> the babe wrapped in swaddling clothes, lying in a
> manger.*
>
> (Luke 2:12)

I wrinkled and twisted my hat. I looked down at my
hands. Mud and blood and shit.

> *And suddenly there was with the angel a multi-
> tude of the heavenly host praising God, and saying,*
>
> (Luke 2:13)

Mortars socking into the mud. Machine gun fire, flares,
screams. Kids getting hit and drowning in the mud. I could
see them plainly in my mind.

> *Glory to God in the highest, and on earth
> peace, good will toward men.*
>
> (Luke 2:14)

I couldn't stand it any longer. I left the chapel.

*And it came to pass, as the angels were gone away from them into heaven, the shepherds said one to another, Let us now go even unto Bethlehem, and see this thing which is come to pass, which the Lord hath made known unto us.*

(Luke 2:15)

One good thing about the rain is that nobody can tell when you're crying.

# TEN

Monday, January 29, 192 days left. The housemice were chattering louder and working faster than usual as they tried to finish their day's work by noon. They were going to miss the next two days work to enjoy the Tet holidays at home with family and friends. Some planned to see cousins from the north supposedly taking an intermission from war games. Even the most reserved of the Vietnamese on our base were caught up in a contagious euphoria. The war seemed far away. Hooch 75 had given our housemouse, Cô Ngai, a thousand piasters, and I had bought four cases of beer and two cartons of Salems with which Sun could impress her friends—a small donation to the drive for prostitution of the Vietnamese, lest they forget the Americans on this traditional holiday. Roland took Sun, her roommate, the beer, the Salems, and Dai úy Bác Sĩ Parrish to Hue for Monday morning rounds at the TB hospital.

The traffic was heavier than usual. It was hot by mid-morning, and I was tired to start the day. I had gone to visit Sun on Saturday night and had smoked, talked, made love, and intermittently napped until time for my early morning trip to Graves. It had been my turn to spend all day Sunday in triage, and although it had been a slow day, there were always plenty of war wounds, accidents, and illnesses to keep one man busy all day. We made it a point of honor not to ask the other doctors to help on Sunday unless we were markedly overwhelmed with work. Sunday night I had assisted the hospital company's slowest surgeon on a midnight hunt for shrapnel holes in the small bowel of a twenty-year-old Jewish marine from New Jersey—eight holes discovered, three closed, two small sections of small bowel removed. Blood loss: four

208

units. Time: three hours and fifteen minutes. Sleep loss, heat, and a big morning load at Graves, made my "Tet" seem less than happy.

The huts crowded along the side of the highway increased in number as we approached the city. Kids up to the age of six or seven ran naked or wore ragged shirts with no pants. Their barefooted mothers wore their one pair of all-season, twenty-four-hour, black silk pants, their braless breasts made low set impressions in their loose-fitting cotton shirts. A few old men sat about in baggy short pants or in old, faded and worn green fatigues. Fatigues all look alike after several hundred washes and years of wear. They could have come from anybody's army. They may have been sadly retrieved from the body of a fallen comrade or a son. They may have been stolen by a grandson or traded for a piece of ass by a granddaughter.

As we entered Hue, the huts crowded even closer together. Floors changed from dirt to straw or wood, and roofs from thatch to tin, sheet metal, or flattened coke and beer cans. Walls appeared and joined together as the huts merged into continuous seas of one-story, haphazard, simple constructions.

There seemed to be an increased number of men on the streets. They walked among the women and children, but they did not seem to be accompanying any of them. They moved with an air of purpose and expectation that seemed more serious than that of a holiday spirit.

A Vietnamese man in civilian clothes stared hatefully from the rear standing rail of an old Vietnamese bus bumping along in front of our jeep. His look was one of contempt. His body acted as a shock absorber to hold his stare knifing directly toward me, the friendly Dai úy Bác Si en route to fight disease in a backward country. I wondered if this man was not a "cousin" from the north returning for Tet. I considered putting a clip in my .45, but instead I snapped up my flak jacket. I thought that I had made the wrong decision when I saw the Vietnamese man reach inside his loose-fitting green shirt. Roland had been watching the man, too. His foot went for the brake as his right hand reached for his M16 on the floor beside him.

Without interrupting his stare, the man pulled out a package of Salems. Continuing the nonverbal communication

with his eyes, he lit and inhaled the mentholated media of
modern exchange. It soon became evident that this man was
only a more obvious member of a large, unfriendly audience.
The usual accepting, pseudo-friendly or disinterested crowds
lining the highway were spotted with unfamiliar, poorly-
hidden glances of curiosity, hate, and study.

"Maybe the Sisters and patients have gone home for Tet.
Why don't you skip your rounds today," said Roland while he
was waiting to be waved over a bridge.

"Sun and her roommate have to get all this beer home,
and I told the Sisters I'd be there. I won't stay long. Are you
going to wait, or drop me and come back? A quick piece of
ass today?"

"I'll wait. I think we'd better get the hell back to the
base."

We dropped Sun and her roommate at their houses and
drove on toward the hospital. Downtown Hue had pink,
white, and brown stucco or mud-concrete homes and buildings, some with a second story. Young Vietnamese men in
uniform were everywhere with polished boots, clean uniforms, and colorful ascots. The young women wore colorful ao
dais and thick, wooden-heeled sandals. Their non-bouncing,
perfect pyramid breasts were set higher than those of their
rural fellow-women. The children wore pants. Motor scooters, bikes, and jeeps were everywhere.

The Sisters were childishly excited. They hurried the
Bác Sĩ through his rounds. Despite the Sisters' protest, several patients had gone for the holidays. They left their medicine, but took their infective sputum to the close family
reunions. The one VC patient had gone.

The Sisters had planned a Tet luncheon for their doctor
and his driver. We were invited to their quarters where they
served traditional foods, rice wine, sugared palm, and homemade breads. My Vietnamese was not adequate to follow all
of the nonmedical and nonbastardized conversation. If the
Sisters wished me to understand, they would speak slowly
and simply, and add what English they could. I was beginning to like the bright young nurses. I admired their dedication and unselfish attitude. They did the best with what they
had.

An older Sister arrived out of breath at the door. She
spoke too quickly for me to understand. Excusing themselves

**Armored Troop Carrier M-113**

appropriately, the Sisters all began to leave the room. Maria reached into a drawer and returned our weapons. She explained that holiday celebrations were beginning and that families were arriving to visit the patients. She thought it would be best if we returned to our base at once. Her urgency was frightening. She backed out of the room saying "pray for us" in English.

"Let's get the fuck out of here," said Roland as he hastily slapped his holster, weapon, and hat onto the appropriate places.

"I guess if trouble starts we'd best be back at the base. We should let the Vietnamese celebrate their own holidays without American clods screwing it up. Happy Tet, you marine bastard."

"Happy Tet yourself, you navy son-of-a-bitch. Let's get out of this awful city and back to sweet old Phu Bai-in-the-Sky."

\*　　　\*　　　\*

Automatic weapon fire could be heard just to the north of the hospital. Roland drove very fast and civilians hurried to get out of his way. The automatic weapon fire stuttered again, this time somewhat closer. A convoy of ten to twelve marine-filled troop transport trucks sped by us in the opposite direction. Small arms fire broke out east of Highway One. Too much rice wine, fatigue, anxiety, and heat limited my body movements to those of keeping my balance in the jeep.

Civilians and Vietnamese soldiers hurried in all directions. No one seemed to know exactly where they were going or why they were hurrying. It was obvious that something was changing the excited holiday spirit to a confused, ominous fear. Another convoy of marines passed us followed by two armored troop carriers and a tank traveling at top speed. The dust and noise set children into wild panic as the metal tracks gouged into the thin asphalt.

The lead truck of the convoy motioned us off the road to make way. The second truck motioned us to turn around and follow. The turret gunner of the tank motioned us to get the hell out and pointed back toward Phu Bai. When we reached the bridge, the marine sentries ignored us. One of them was talking on the radio headset. The others were running down the riverbank with about a dozen Arvan soldiers. They were shooting into the water. A steady stream of helicopters flew at low altitude toward the heart of the city. The small arms fire faded behind us as we fled from the city on Highway One.

We arrived at Phu Bai in record time, and to our surprise, Phu Bai was quiet. Sick bay was open, and all of the real and unreal minor problems of the marines were being solved: "drip," low-back pain, congressional inquiries. Triage was moderately busy taking care of some off-duty marines who had gone into Hue to take some pictures and had come across a VC mortar team just north of the city limits. Before we could finish telling our colleagues about the excitement in Hue, an army truck came speeding down the road. Three Arvan soldiers and five civilians had been wounded in a brief skirmish with a group of armed North Vietnamese visitors inside the city of Hue.

As usual, large numbers of family members accompanied the wounded. While segregating and calming the nonwounded civilians, I was interrupted by the arrival of a marine from Dong Ha with a through and through wound of his upper arm. He was stripped to the waist. A bloody tourniquet encompassed his shoulder and upper arm. Wide-eyed and scared, he watched every move I made. I drew blood for type and crossmatch and started an IV in the good arm before I even looked at the wound. I pinched his hand.

"Do you feel that, buddy?"

"Yes, Sir."

"Can you move your fingers?"

"Yes, Sir." He grimaced in effort, but I didn't see any movement.

"Shrapnel or a round?"

"I think it was a round, Sir. A sniper."

I unwrapped the battle dressing tourniquet. He had a false joint at the upper third of his humerus. When I moved his arm, he stiffened with pain. As the bandage loosened, blood seeped through and then belched out in a rhythmical geyser of warm red. I put two fingers of my right hand over the torn vessel and pressed tightly. In order to apply firmer pressure to the pulsating artery, I reached over his chest and grasped the opposite side of the litter for stability.

"I need two stretcher bearers and an operating room. Right now." I spoke slowly and loudly. "Tell the lab tech to bring the blood directly to the O.R. Get a surgeon." Each command initiated activity.

The stretcher bearers started us toward the operating area as I kept my position with my fingers inside the wound.

"We're going to operate on your arm now, buddy."

"Am I going to lose my arm, Sir?"

"Not if we can help it."

"Thank you, Sir."

The anesthesiologist put the marine to sleep while the corpsman prepped his arm with my hand still in the wound. A high-pressure tourniquet was carefully placed just distal to the shoulder, and I removed my hand. The skin of my fingers was red and wrinkled.

Bill stuck his head in the door.

"What you got, Big John?"

"A through and through of the upper arm, severed and retracted brachial artery, and a shattered segment of upper humerus. I don't know about the vein or nerves. Some sensation may be preserved."

"Good, we'll take a look. I'm in the mood for a little

vascular surgery. You gonna help me, Big John? I'll teach you
something." He knew that surgery was not one of my favorite
pastimes.

"Sure, I guess I'm sort of involved now."

"I'll scrub and take a look around. A six pack says I can
repair the vessel. That should make it interesting. Prep his
whole arm and hand. Did you listen to his lungs yet? Got any
X rays?"

"He's breathing on both sides. Didn't take time for
pictures. He was exsanguinating and the wound was too high
for a good tourniquet." I yelled from inside the operating
room to Bill who was already in the hall scrubbing his hands.

"We'll worry about the bones later. Call an orthopod and
get a portable chest and an arm shot. We've got to be through
by happy hour. I'll teach you how to tie onehanded knots.
Better yet, maybe I'd better teach this kid. Ha! You goddamn
corpsmen had better have some size eight gloves around. I'm
not squeezing into seven and a halfs again. Hey, Big John,
you gonna scrub or not?"

An uninterrupted flight of sentences. I didn't answer.
This was going to be a long operation.

As the hours passed, I grew so tired that I somehow
forgot about what might be happening in Hue. My back felt
as if it were breaking. Bill kept operating and talking. I knew
that an amputation would have taken twenty to thirty minutes, and we would have been through long ago. I wondered
if it were concern for a young boy's arm, Bill's pride as a
surgeon, or just automatic learned responses that kept us
glued to the operating table. After seeing hundreds of amputations result from such nebulous causes as "saving face,"
"police action," and "man power support," could we not
sacrifice just one more limb for a concrete reason like getting
some sleep when we were tired?

How many times had I seen these kids wake up and look
for their missing extremities? How many of these kids had we
put to sleep in this room who never woke up? How many
times had I been awakened in the middle of the night to see a
severely wounded casualty and had actually been relieved to
see that he was already dead and required no extensive care?
I had played no role in his death, and I would have broken
my ass to save him had there been a chance, but I was glad

that circumstances had taken the responsibility of hours of work and emotional strain away from me before I could start. I could go back to sleep—uninvolved. The value of life and limb decreases when you see them wasted day after day, and night after night. The dead were not our business, and nonviable, unsalvageable arms and legs could not occupy our time. If this were one of those arms, we could stop, and I could lie down. I was making myself sick with my own thoughts.

Another hour passed.

"Hey, Big John, maybe another save, huh? Nice job, if I do say so myself. Let's go for a late night snack. I was really dreaming when I said we'd be through by happy hour. I hope the goddamn mess sergeant saved us some chow, I'm starving." Bill was talking as he worked. He didn't notice my far-away look and my failure to answer.

"Hey, you're not a bad surgeon. Why don't you give up that internal medicine shit and go where the action is? You didn't think I'd pull this one out did you?"

"You're the greatest," I said, as I stretched and yawned.

We both knew that neither of us would ever know if this operation were successful or not. The kid would be evacuated to the rear first thing the next morning, and we would never hear of him again.

Bill and the O.R. crew went for a snack. I went back to my hooch and fell onto my sandy rack. Rumors were circulating that NVA were in and around Hue. I drank a warm beer as I struggled to take off my boots. My socks were stiff with dried blood, and I smelled like a real marine. I stripped naked and walked out to the water buffalo where I enjoyed a sponge bath with several helmetfuls of water. I smoked a cigarette, had another warm beer, climbed into my sand-covered bed, and closed my eyes. My hoochmates were playing cards, but I was soon oblivious to their presence.

As I lay in bed, my mind cruelly continued to analyze the long day. Maybe Sun and Maria and the Sisters were in trouble. I sat up.

"Roland, can we go to Hue?"

"We can't go anywhere outside the perimeter at night, you dumb shit. Besides Intelligence says the VC are everywhere tonight. We're on red alert."

"I thought it was truce time," I argued.

"You were in Hue yourself today. You know trouble is brewing. Now go to sleep, you dumb tit."

I did.

"Am I going to lose my arm, Sir?"

"Not if we can help it, buddy."

"Thank you, Sir."

"Not if we can help it, buddy." I rolled over and put my sandy pillow over my head. But the voice was my own, and it grew louder. "Not if we can help it, buddy. Not if we can help it, buddy." I was in Graves crawling among the twisted, mangled bodies, over miles of bowels, mountains of brains, and giant tongues.

"We couldn't help it, buddy," I whispered to each one. "We couldn't help it, buddy." Somehow I felt I was lying.

I was awakened about dawn the next morning with the sound of the corpsmen running from hooch to hooch with the all too familiar cry of "mass casualties." With jerky, clumsy movements, I rapidly put on my fatigues and laced up my jungle boots. In a fog of sleepy depression, I joined the group of running, unshaven, partially dressed doctors as they converged on triage still buttoning flys and shirts.

For the next three hours, helicopters landed and took off continuously in a noisy, swirling storm of dust. Before the day was over, three hundred wounded and dead were delivered within that small landing square. Hue had been taken during the night, and the marines were trying to regain it. Civilians were being shot in the streets in brutal cross fire. Vietnamese who worked for, or were sympathetic toward Americans were being systematically slaughtered in a door-to-door roll call. Hue had been infiltrated by all those staring eyes we had noticed the day before, and, on the holiday night, Hue had been captured. Even the sacred walled city had been taken by NVA.

If Sun did not get out of Hue, she would not have a chance. Her whole neighborhood knew that she worked for the Americans, and many of them had seen me coming and going several times. But the casualties were pouring in. There was more work than we could do. I could not leave. Roland approached as I automatically put in another chest tube.

"I know what you're thinking, John, and it's impossible.

A whole company of marines can't fight its way into Hue now, and I sure as hell couldn't get a jeep in there."

I shook my head and Roland left to help carry litters.

D.J. approached as I knelt over another casualty. I looked up.

"Not in a million years, Doc. Don't you realize the city has fallen. It's in enemy hands. A helicopter would be an easy target."

Goddamnit, D.J. I didn't say a word.

The chest tube popped through the pleura, and the blood rushed out onto my thigh. I continued to stabilize casualties as fast and efficiently as possible. D.J. watched my every move.

"I know about your Vietnamese friends, Doc." He was out of breath. "I'm awfully sorry but I can't go in there. It would be impossible."

I didn't stop working. I didn't even look up.

"I don't know where they live. There would be no place to land. They're probably not home. They're probably hiding somewhere. And even if I did find them, the chance of getting them onto a helicopter is . . . is . . . it's crazy."

I hopped over to the next casualty. D.J. followed. He spoke apologetically.

"Gee, I'm sorry, Doc. Don't you know if there was anything I could do, I would? Don't you know that, Doc?"

I shook my head. "Just trying to get you a medal, old man." I tried to smile at my own sick joke. Nobody else did.

"Medal! Shit! I'd get court-martialed, I'd never get clearance to go in there. Look, Doc, if there was a way I could help——"

"Here, hold his leg up while I wrap it."

I never missed a stroke. It took one corpsman full time just to keep me with the appropriate gear. D.J. held the wounded leg.

"D.J., old man, do you know where the TB hospital is?"

"Yes."

"There are nine Catholic Sisters who run the hospital. I've been helping them lately, which is reason enough for them to be killed by the NVA."

"Well, that's a long way from the walled city where most of the fighting is. But I'd never get clearance. The Sisters will have fled by now."

"They won't leave the hospital. They'll be working when the NVA shoot them," I said. "You go there and tell them Bác Sĩ Parrish said for them to come with you."

D.J. thought for a long time as he watched me work. "If my C.O. told me to do this, with clearance, I'd tell him to shove it. But if you really want me to try it, Doc, I will."

"Just fly in close enough to see if it's possible. If you get in, tell the one named Maria that I said to come with you. The others will follow. If you can't get in, forget it."

"If anybody ever told me I might die for a bunch of Vietnamese women..."

I turned to another casualty. When I looked up, D.J. was gone..

Fixed-wing aircraft took large numbers of the stable wounded to the rear, and choppers moved some to the hospital ships, but the flow constantly increased. By 11 A.M., the hospital compound was totally jammed. All O.R.'s were full, and all hallways were lined with wounded awaiting X ray and surgery. Triage had a wall-to-wall carpet of wounded bodies with doctors and corpsmen skipping over, between, and around them; kneeling, sitting, and standing, but never stopping. The sea of litters spilled out onto the parking lot and the helicopter pad. Many of the wounded lay on the ground. The dead lay with the wounded, and some wounded joined the dead.

The triage officer system broke down completely. Each doctor picked and stepped among the prone bodies choosing who to work on, who could be saved, who could wait, and who would be a waste of precious time. Rapid, scientific and professional appraisal of the torn bodies seldom gave way to the emotional tug of an outstretched, begging hand or a trembling cry. All of the doctors knew that under the circumstances compassion was best shown by cold, hard efficiency.

All of the cries were treated with a squeeze of the hand or a sympathetic glance, but they had to be ignored. The corpsmen fell behind the endless flow of rapid-fire commands, and several marines who had come to help fell all over themselves with too much good intention and not enough medical training.

"I want that chest tube now, goddamnit."

"Type and cross for eight units and bring me the first two after a rapid spin."

"Get those two back to Graves."

"Put that one with brains all over his chest in the corner."

"Put your finger in this hole and don't move it until I get this chest tube in."

"Turn his head, he's puking!"

"Will you please station a corpsman at the chopper to keep those goddamned bodies out of here and send them directly to Graves."

"Leave those goddamn civilians alone; there are dying marines all around you. I'll court-martial the next one who touches a wounded civilian!"

"Cut down set!"

"Trach set."

"One hundred milligrams Phenobarbital."

"Seventy-five milligrams Demerol."

My boots were soaked with blood; my toes sloshed around inside. Blood, vomit, and sweat covered my clothing. My hands got so sticky with dried blood that it became difficult to work. The only part that really bothered me was the brains under my fingernails.

A marine with a partially blown-away hand got up from his blanket and, with his good hand, fumbled with his canteen. Without saying a word, he held the canteen up to my mouth as both my hands sorted through the ragged stump of a blown-off leg attached to a screaming kid. As I turned my head sideways to gulp the fluid, I looked out of the corner of my eye at my work. The marine poured the remainder of the canteen on my back and neck and returned to his blanket.

By mid-afternoon it was obvious that there was no end in sight. At the time there was enough work to be done in the operating room and debridement room for another twenty-four hours, and casualties still arrived in groups of three to thirty. Wounded, wailing, and whining, over one hundred civilians waited outside. Piled outside its door, the Graves customers waited quietly, grotesquely.

A well-muscled, large, black marine limped in at a running pace from a recently landed chopper.

"Bandage my leg, like fast! I'm going back and get me one of them yellow bastards. This will be the last Tet for some poor mother fucker when I get back to Hue. Those yellow pricks have pissed off the wrong nigger this time."

Sensing that this theatrical entrance was poorly accepted, the marine paused and looked about him. The smell of bodies, the sound of pain, the sights of freshly ripped and mangled tissues, and the total wastefulness of the whole scene converted one angry militant into a thinking man.

If I allowed myself to think beyond my immediate task, the sense of waste was overwhelming—nineteen-year-old bodies with firm muscles and years of learning. My eyes scanned the surrounding bodies as I finished up a hastily applied pressure dressing. It was time to choose my next patient. Next to me lay a young man with a right angle bend in the mid-shaft of his shin and with an absent left foot. The foot, still inside his boot, sat between his outstretched legs. Small shrapnel wounds peppered his trunk and thighs, and his left eyelid closed over a bulging, purple swelling. The intricate, fascinating and unreplaceable unit, which used to be his left hand, was an oozing, meaty mass of twisted bones. The fingers were charred a dry, dark black. His carotid pulse was faint, but present, and his remaining eye had a reacting pupil. My numbed senses registered: possible salvageability, twenty percent chance; needs both legs amputated below the knee, left hand amputated, will lose his left eye; lung probably not penetrated; rigid abdomen, requires a laparotomy; needs first aid now, tie his bleeders; O.R. time with amputation and exploration at least three hours. At best he will be a one-armed, one-eyed, wheelchair job. As I started an IV on him, I was interrupted by the man next to me who began to spurt blood from his neck and to gasp and gurgle as he vomited blood. I put my finger in his neck and yelled for an operating room. All were full. One of the surgeons came over and worked around in his neck with a Kelly clamp. The marine screamed and struggled. I reached over to help, but I was knocked down by a clumsy, stumbling group of panic-stricken marines carrying a wounded man on a stretcher and applying cardiac massage and mouth-to-mouth resuscitation. The man giving the artificial respiration spit the vomitus and blood out of his mouth to scream something about the man's being hit seconds ago on the other side of the air strip. "Too late," I said. "Keep going on back to Graves in the back."

"But, Doc, he was just talking to me, Doc."

"Well, he is dead now."

"Please, Doc, please."

I was already kneeling next to another. A thin boy grimaced as he held a moistened pad over his belly under which I could see eviscerated small bowel. Putting a chest tube in another man without anesthesia, I ignored his screams and did not even try to get out of the way of the gush of blood which flowed through the tube as the clamp ripped through his pleura.

The priest could not give last rites fast enough. He blessed some who lived and missed some who died. More blessed living than unblessed dead. Better blessed and living than unblessed and dead. I only wished that the father could start an IV.

In the early afternoon D.J. came limping in. Grinning like a child, he held up six fingers. He seemed not to notice that he was picking his way through a sea of bodies.

"Hey, Doc, I got them. Six of them, they're outside treating the civilian wounded."

"Is Maria among them?"

"How the hell do I know their names?"

"She speaks English."

"I couldn't hear anything above the chopper, and Hue is like a big battlefield."

"D.J., that was a wonderful thing to do. Thanks."

"It was a stupid thing to do, but you're welcome."

He was gone again. I knew we would discuss it over beers someday, probably more than once. I wanted to go see the Sisters, but every second in triage was too precious. The pace kept up until dark when the helicopters could no longer get into the city. One chopper did manage to bring one dead and six wounded in at 2 A.M. Surgery and debridement continued uninterrupted despite the decreased load in triage. As soon as all were stabilized in triage, I went to the debridement room to begin work. Already the delay in those who came in early in the day would increase the rate of infection in the minor wounds. About 3 A.M., a corpsman brought me a sandwich and black coffee, which I consumed while the corpsman prepared the next case, a marine lieutenant with several shrapnel wounds in his left hand.

Incoming rounds were heard just beyond the airstrip. Rumors were circulating that Hue had fallen and Phu Bai was next. It appeared that the enemy would probably attempt to seize the airstrip after "prepping" it with mortar fire. I gave the lieutenant some gauze to hold in his good hand. If we received incoming rounds while debriding his injured hand, he was to cover the wound with the gauze and roll off the litter onto the floor.

No sooner had I finished my instructions, than a deafening, nauseating crunch shook the building. We all lay on the floor without moving as several rounds landed on the airstrip next to the hospital. When quiet returned, several people headed for the bunkers, but most of us continued working. The sequence repeated itself four times. With each group of shells my heart beat faster. My hands shook so, that it was difficult to continue my work, but there was so much work yet to be done. We had no place to carry the wounded to safety.

A fifth series of incoming rounds began. They did not let up as the earlier bursts had done. They seemed to be getting closer. Shrapnel and dirt sprayed the hospital building. Many of the wounded began dragging themselves toward the bunkers. I held my helmet on with one hand and crawled on my belly toward the retaining wall. The mortar shells began to go beyond us toward headquarters battalion. I could hear them whistling above me. The high-pitched ones went beyond us. Others sounded like a roaring freight train and landed nearby. The jarring explosion was followed by the sound of dirt and metal spraying against the building and the blast wall.

The long, crunching sound of the incoming explosions was interrupted by the sharp crack of our own guns as we returned the fire. As the shells whistled over my head, I became confused between the whistling in and the whistling out. I lay frozen on the ground about halfway to the retaining wall. I didn't seem able to move any farther. I was totally paralyzed with my face in the dirt. I could taste the dirt in my mouth and could feel the sweat and tears rolling along the side of my nose. For some crazy reason I thought of the Code of Military Justice. Is this what happens to people when they are declared cowards? Unable to advance in the face of the enemy? Unable to retreat? Unable to move? I lay transfixed on the ground for a long time. I may have even slept, for the next thing I knew the sun was coming up, and the noisy parade of choppers had resumed.

During the next two days, the nightmare of the day before was repeated and even magnified. On the second day alone we received five hundred casualties including many civilians. My responses were more automatic than reasoned. I functioned in a zombie state. I don't remember much of the third day. Late in the afternoon I was found unconsciously slumped over a dead marine with a chest tube and a Kelly clamp gripped tightly in my hands.

Our commanding officer set up a compulsory sleep schedule. All doctors and corpsmen were to return to their quarters for a six-hour period out of each twenty-four hours. Work continued at a frantic pace for another eight days, and, despite my total physical fatigue, I had insomnia during my compulsory sleep period. I lay in my hooch staring blankly at the ceiling and listening to the helicopters come and go. I often clenched my fists and cursed aloud when no one was around to listen. At times I cried. But most of the time, I just lay on my bed or on the ground in the bunker and thought.

For ten days the endless line of wounded marines continued. We could not keep up. On those rare occasions when triage was empty except for brain injuries awaiting death, there were always hours of work waiting in the operating rooms and the debridement rooms. Many of the wounded did not reach us until their wounds had become infected. Thus their treatment was complicated. Our work was hindered further by occasional incoming shells, one group of which included irritating nausea gas. The heat, flak gear, and gas masks made the volume of work even more overwhelming. General medical problems were squeezed in when possible. Frightened, hysterical, confused, and stunned civilian casualties were brought by the truckload. We could provide them with only basic first aid before sending them to the provincial hospitals.

Several miles away, the city of Hue was in ruins. Initially, Vietnamese college students provided information and pictures to the NVA. They acted as guides in a house-to-house search for the families of Arvan soldiers, and family and friends of those who worked with the Americans. Those people were killed in their homes or marched into the streets for mass slaughter. One day, over a hundred civilians were lined up against the outer wall of the Catholic church and mowed down with machine guns. The NVA entered the TB hospital where I had worked and moved from ward to ward killing any patients who had not fled.

The urban civilians were learning lessons about this war that the peasants had known for years. The most certain method of self-survival was to avoid involvement. Punishment for ties with the Americans was quick and final. Many of our interpreters and housemice were killed. Our Vietnamese barber was brought in with both hands cut off. There was no word from Sun, except for several rumors of her ceremonial rape and murder.

At the high cost of their own lives, North Vietnamese soldiers had captured the ancient Vietnamese capital from their fellow South Vietnamese. The marines had helped to return the city to the stalemate of the week before. The cost of the assistance was the hundreds of casualties flowing through triage everyday. American boys were scattered among the decomposing bodies lining the streets of downtown Hue. In the brutal house-to-house battle to reclaim the city, women and children were caught in the fierce cross fire. American tanks, mortars, and rockets destroyed whole buildings and their occupants as they "liberated" the city.

All of this useless loss of arms, legs, and life was to reestablish some absurd equilibrium shown by the events of the last few days to be a very fragile one at best.

# ELEVEN

"Parrish!"

I wheeled around. "Yes, Sir."

"I want to talk to you." The new Division Surgeon had been standing behind me in triage. "Come to the 'O' Club when you get caught up, I'll buy you a beer."

"Yes, Sir."

I had not seen the new Division Surgeon since the good-bye drunk that Captain Street gave in honor of his own departure for home. Not only was he new in country, but he was also unsure enough to be all business. He was sitting at a corner table when I arrived at the 'O' Club. He started talking before I greeted him or even sat down.

"We're sending you up to Dong Ha."

"Oh." That was all I could manage to say at first. Everybody knew that Dong Ha was within range of the big guns in the DMZ.

"Things are beginning to slow down here a bit, Parrish, and everybody has to do his bit up front you know."

"Well, Captain Street had sort of suggested that I might——"

"Captain Street is gone. I am the Division Surgeon now."

"Yes, I know, but I've got so many extra jobs here. Vietnamese sick call, MEDCAP, medicine ward, the TB hospital in Hue, the——"

"I'm sure the hospital in Hue has been destroyed. We don't have time for MEDCAP's or Vietnamese sick call anymore. Tet has changed all that."

"Well, I hope Myron can handle all the malaria and fevers by himself."

"He'll have help soon enough. They're sending another

fully-trained internist this week in addition to the one that will replace Myron next month. We rate two internists now for some reason."

"Well, we need two internists. I guess you don't need me as much now." He obviously didn't need me at all if he was sending me away.

"Well, to be completely honest, we'd like to keep you here. But a couple of the GMO's at Dong Ha are beginning to wear down under the pressure of too many casualties and too much incoming artillery. They've been very busy, too, you know."

"Yeah." I was too emotionally tired and empty to react further or to resist. Besides, there was nothing I could do.

"You will act chiefly as a GMO, but you will also be the only internist there."

"When do I leave?"

"Tomorrow. First flight tomorrow morning."

"Yes, Sir." I excuse myself and left the club. I had to tell my hoochies about my leaving. Again, I had to go. No choice. Dong Ha. The rear. A person could get killed by being in the wrong place at the wrong time.

"Well, gee, John, we'll miss you." Myron had been napping when I awoke him. "But I'm sure you'll be okay. It won't be as bad as you think." We both knew that despite what Myron was saying he would worry his ass off about me.

Bill had worked at Dong Ha before. He gave me all kinds of advice about where to sleep, where to hide, and who to know. Roland decided that he would have time to squeeze in a couple of visits to Dong Ha before he went home thirty-one days later. Prince gave me a big hug that smelled like scotch and Mennen aftershave.

Again my seabag was packed. The hooch had been quiet for an hour and it was well past midnight when I tried unsuccessfully to get to sleep. I thought about my first days at Phu Bai. Was it only six months ago?

I had invested six months in building a world that would allow me to survive my tour. A world built around Hue and Phu Bai. Now, suddenly, it was all gone—my Vietnamese clinic, my TB hospital, my position as Myron's partner, my affair with Sun.

I was frightened and lonely. Phu Bai was slipping away from me. It wasn't much but it was all I had. I grew more and more homesick. I didn't know what was ahead of me, but whatever it was it could be for six more months.

I knew now how long six months could be. I had trouble remembering little details of life before Vietnam. I had been here through thousands of slow, frightening hours. The line of casualties I had seen stretched to infinity. I had endured millions of minutes of helplessness during which I had no control over the source of pain and destruction.

I looked at each of my hoochies sleeping in his gritty, lumpy, cramped rack. Alarm clocks or corpsmen or helicopters would wake them soon for another day's work. I realized that I might never see any of them again. I wanted to leave them a present or a note or somehow let them know that I appreciated them and really cared if they survived their tours. I wanted them to know that they had supported my mental health for six months. I wanted them to know that they were doing good work, amazing work under really shitty conditions and that they were some kind of fucking heroes... sleeping there in their racks... waiting for another awful day... together... in Phu Bai.

I wanted them to know that I would really miss them and that I—those fucking tears again—I actually .. I would buy them a beer someday, and I'd tell them about Sun, and we'd laugh, and we'd tease good old Myron, and I'd beat the shit out of Roland—pin him in sixty seconds—and we'd play monopoly and hearts and run and lift weights and drink and...

Bill Bond started to wake so I quickly tiptoed out of the hooch. I stood out behind the hooch as the sun climbed

C-130

behind the shitters. My helmet and flak jacket and seabag felt
heavy already. Phu Bai was still quiet. Sun would not come
by at toothbrush time. I did not go to Graves. I stood and
looked at Hooch 75 for several minutes, turned, and walked
out to the airstrip. I ate my last can of Prince's Vienna
sausages as I waited for the first flight to Dong Ha.

The big C-130 delivered my sweaty armored body to the
airstrip at Dong Ha. I walked over to the hospital compound
expecting to be blown away any moment. I stepped up the
pace as I left the vicinity of one bunker and slowed as I
neared the next ready to dive at any moment. Everybody
seemed to be carrying on his life as in Phu Bai. But I couldn't
relax knowing that somewhere in those hills in plain sight just
to the north were some giant guns pointing toward me. Some
Vietnamese men, women, and children were carrying shells
down to the guns. Even now they could be loading the shell
that would blow me to bits.

It was mid-morning when I arrived at the hospital compound. I met the hospital commander and the GMO's. The
casualties and the marines in sick call looked the same as the
ones in Phu Bai. Even GMO's were beginning to look alike.
Sweaty, busy, older than the other soldiers. Concerned, confident, dedicated. Intelligent, educated, articulate. Smooth,
sensitive and . . .

"Well, fuck me. I'll be a son-of-a-bitching-bastard ant. If
it isn't John-fucking-Parrish."

That voice. That grin. It was Jim Veesar. He continued.

"You old fart. What the fuck are you doing here, John,
you old whoremonger? You some kind of crazy mother——"

"Hi, Jim."

"What the fuck are you doing here?"

"How are you, Jim? I've been assigned to Dong Ha."

"So have I! Can you imagine that? From the field to
Dong Ha."

Jim Veesar had arrived at Dong Ha three days earlier.
He showed me around the place, ushered me through a day
in sick call, and offered me a rack in his quarters. One small
hooch was divided in half by a plywood wall. The front was
the "O" Club consisting of a bench, a bar, a fan, and a small
refrigerator. Our quarters were in the back and had two
collapsible metal frame beds and two plywood hot boxes. I

poured the contents of my seabag into a hot box and was drinking a beer and unlacing my jungle boots before I realized that Jim was talking.

"I get to scrub a lot. I'm doing all kinds of procedures. The surgeons let me do everything. It's fantastic."

"That's great, Jim." As always, he did not notice my lack of enthusiasm. "Is there much incoming?"

"Everyday. Every fucking day." Jim opened another beer. "Two noises you'll learn to hate here. One is the fucking incoming artillery. The whistle is higher pitched than the rockets and the crunch is much louder and longer than mortar shells. The other sound you'll hate is that of a landing helicopter."

"Why?"

"It means business." Jim leaned forward, stopped grinning, and said, "Everytime a chopper lands on that pad everybody in our compound goes to triage. There aren't many of us, so we're all on call all the time. Every chopper is met by every doctor."

"Even in the middle of the night?"

"Even in the middle of the night, John. And they come in at all hours. You get sick of it. And the landing pad is right behind our hooch. Sand and wind and noise throw you out of your rack anyway; you might as well go up to triage."

"Sounds awful."

"You get to where you just automatically start walking toward triage in your sleep whenever noise and sand blasting your face awakens you. You get to where——"

"Jim, you talk like some kind of goddamn veteran, and you've only been here three days."

"Three days longer than you, you simple cunt."

"You're right."

"And three days can be as long as hell. Wait and see."

"We'd better get some sleep. Sounds like this is the kind of place where you'd better get sleep whenever you can."

"If you can."

"It's after midnight, Big Jim. Let's hit it."

"You mean the rack?"

"Both."

The sound of an approaching helicopter made Jim put down the beer he was about to open. "Goddamnit. Son-of-a-bitch. Here comes one of the fuckers now."

The chopper landed on the pad behind our hooch. The dust and sand and noise were all over us as he had warned. We moved toward triage where we were met by the other doctors. Some only wore T-shirts, undershorts, and sandals.

The litter bearers brought in a Vietnamese woman with both legs missing at about mid-thigh. She was naked below the waist, and the stringy jelly stumps were no longer bleeding.

"No need to stop here. She's dead."

"Good enough. A legless woman in this society couldn't survive."

A Vietnamese woman with a missing right hand and several flank and thigh wounds was carried past me. With her good arm she held a baby to her breast. Both were covered with dirt and blood. The mother lost consciousness, and the baby slid away from her breast and began to cry.

Then it began. More choppers landed, and for the next two hours we received a steady stream of women and children blown apart, badly burned, and dead. Women wailed, children cried. The smell of burnt flesh was so piercing that some of the doctors had to wear masks. I could tell when the sounds and smells went into my brain that they were there to stay and would come back when I least wanted them.

Dead baby, charred black. A six-year-old girl with a missing leg refused to let go of her unharmed two-year-old brother. The body of a teen-age girl nine months pregnant with a missing head and right breast, and with amniotic fluid dripping from her vagina. Old ladies with chest wounds. Mothers mourning dead children, and frightened children clinging to dead mothers.

"Today is Saint Valentine's Day," said Jim. "We can call this our Saint Valentine's Day Massacre."

I couldn't answer. Horror, disgust, anger. I barely had time to experience any of my emotions much less express them. Efficiency permitted a sincere professional concern at most. I could react later. Maybe for years.

I was making an incision in a little boy's thigh to find a vein for administration of fluids. Each time he strained to cry, another inch of small bowel snaked out of the two inch hole in his anterior abdominal wall. He tried to reach his belly, but had no left hand. A big pair of hands across from me was preparing a saline dressing and packing the abdominal wound.

"This is really a shitty introduction for you, but anyway—welcome to Dong Ha."

I looked up to see a great big doctor with a mustache whose rank suggested that he must have been the hospital commander.

"Thanks," I said without stopping my work. "I've got a vein here, if you'll connect me to that IV tube we'll be all set."

"Sure. There." He began to examine the arm stump. "This scene was caused by our accidentally bombing a friendly ville. We napalmed these folks."

"Oh, no." I was sick.

"It doesn't matter," he said coldly, "whether it was their own people from the north unifying the country or their good friends from across the sea saving them from communism. It doesn't matter to them. They don't know who did it and don't know why anybody does anything."

I hung up some blood for the boy. "I guess the casualties would look the same if the correct ville had been bombed. And it would be just as tragic."

The C.O. moved on to another casualty. He turned back toward me as he walked away, peered over his glasses, and asked, "I wonder if we can add them to our body count?"

Third-degree burns of the face, chest, and arm of a six-year-old. Shooky needed IV fluids. Hopefully he was the last. The sun had risen and the choppers were probably out in the field right now gathering up the wounded. Jim beat me back to the rack.

"Catch a couple of hours sleep before sick call," said Jim. "If the casualties don't start in too early."

"I'm dead," I fell fully dressed onto my new sandy rack. "I don't think I'm going to like Dong Ha. If you ask me this place——"

CRUNCH!

Jim rolled onto the floor.

An explosion shook my whole body. A high-pitched, piercing scream was followed by a second ear-shattering explosion.

I rolled onto the floor and covered my head. Jim started

to reach for the nail where his flak gear hung, but just as he touched it another explosion brought him and all his gear crashing back to the wooden floor.

"Jesus Christ! Those bastards are at it again." He began sliding on his stomach toward the back door of the hooch. "That's your fuckin' incoming shells, Big John, hear it for yourself."

I didn't try to get my flak gear. I just slid out the back door and fell the one foot to the ground where I lay face down making my body as flat and as small as possible.

A group of five or six more shells crashed in. I couldn't believe a single explosion could last so long. Crrrrrunch. It was a loud, dull, nauseating sound.

"Those bastards up in the hills knew we were up all night. They know everything about us." Jim seemed more angry than scared.

A few seconds of quiet. Jim broke into a crouched run for the closest bunker which was the large triage bunker just next to the helicopter landing pad. He just made it inside when more shells began slamming into the ground. I was too frightened to follow him.

A full minute of silence. I finally crawled rapidly toward the bunker. By the time I reached the bunker entrance, Jim and several other doctors casually walked out.

Jim stretched, yawned and looked down at me as I crawled past them. "Well, good morning, Crawling Turtle." He grinned. "The attack is over and Chief Giant Dork invites you to be his guest at breakfast. The boom-boom gods of the hills have told us that the sun rises and another day is here."

I stood up very cautiously. "You mean that's it! It's over and we just go on about our work and pretend we didn't just get shot at. Those shells could have killed us!"

"Happens everyday sometimes all day, Big John, but we have work to do. Come on. It's over for now. That may be all for today or they may be loading those mothers right now."

"Someone just tried to kill us!" I protested.

"Almost like it was a war or something," laughed Jim.

"I don't think I like Dong Ha."

"It's not the bush, Big John. Just remember, it's not the bush."

The chow hall hooch was like all the hooches except that it was filled with long wooden tables and wooden benches.

Like the other hooches, it had a sandbag bunker at its front and back doors. The enlisted men ate in the front half, the officers in the back. Most people straddled the bench with one leg in the aisle in preparation for a quick exit to the bunkers.

Jim had two feet squarely under the table, both hands full of toast, and his chin covered with jelly. "Three hot meals a day, here, Big John. It may be shit, but it's hot."

"Why isn't this whole compound underground?" I was still shaking from the fact that someone had just tried to kill me.

"Don't know, too much trouble, I guess, to sink a whole compound."

"Our hooch isn't even sandbagged," I challenged.

"Well, I just moved in there three days ago. Everybody has to sandbag his own hooch, you know."

"Well, let's do it then. If I'm going to live here, I'm going to sandbag my hooch or sleep in the bunker. You've got jelly on your chin."

"The Vietnamese women in the ville will fill sandbags for one piaster each, we could stack them after work." Jim pulled at his dirty handkerchief and wiped his chin.

"And there's no blast wall between our hooch and the helicopter pad." I spoke with disbelief. "I'd think that the helo pad would be a prime target and——"

"Those NVA gunners don't want to bust up our hospital. They get treated here if they get captured. They want the airstrip, the oil bladders, the Air Force Compound, the headquarters, the——"

"I don't care what they want, they might get me by mistake. If the C.O. won't get his marines to make a blast wall, we'll make our own. It might keep the damn helicopter sandstorm off our beds anyway."

Jim was amused by my enthusiasm and concern. "If you're crazy enough to build your own fucking blast wall, I'll be crazy enough to help you."

As he was talking the flapping chatter of approaching choppers drew closer and finally put down amidst a sandy whirlwind.

"Let's go to work," yelled Jim. "That's business."

"I haven't eaten my breakfast," I complained as I stood.

"You'll soon learn that most of what you eat here is what

you can carry in your hand and eat as you walk to triage or run to a bunker." Jim spoke as a veteran of four days now. I didn't bother to tell him he had grape jelly on his chin again.

I didn't think I was going to like Dong Ha.

About 10 A.M. we received more incoming shells. At the time we had about six casualties set up on litters in triage. It was amazing how everyone reacted automatically, quickly, efficiently, and without speaking, to carry the litters first to the floor, and then quickly into the triage bunkers, to continue work. When alone or in the hooches, no one would consider an extra fraction of a second of upright posture to get flak gear, step over a bench or even to break into a run for a bunker. But in triage—and I saw it with my own eyes time and time again—people actually carried litters into a triage bunker while someone else ran alongside with IV bottles or blood, an act that took ten to fifteen seconds, time enough to die a thousand times. The wounded were our extra responsibility. Whenever we thought of survival, we had to consider that extra burden.

And the extra emotional burden of being constantly aware of the sick and wounded was more intense at Dong Ha. There was no time off, no holiday, no hour of being not on call. No trips to Hue. No meal, shower, movie, reading time, thinking time, time on the shitter, sleep time, or anytime that we were not available for that chopper coming from anywhere. Triage was right there. The O.R.'s were right there. The wards always had somebody in them waiting for surgery, waiting for medevac south, waiting for that fever to break, waiting to die. Waiting. Sweating. Hurting.

Marines usually hurt quietly. If you couldn't see them, you could try to forget. You could try to forget that any second you might join the hurting when that shell comes in. You could try to forget that any second you might die. The thought you just had may have been your last. The thing you are doing now may be your final act. Now is where it's at. And now is full of hurting. But when it's all you've got you cling to it. Hang on and hope you don't get blown up or blow your mind.

"I can't forget, even for one lousy second, that choppers full of dying kids are about to land, and that an artillery shell is headed this way." I passed Jim a beer and took one of his Salems.

"Well, you get used to it," Jim said. "You get used to anything."

"You mean it becomes part of the background noise of your psyche, and you don't hear it anymore?" I wasn't convinced.

"You can learn to live with anything." Jim really believed what he was saying. "Humans are good that way. Those who can't accept things the way they go crazy."

"They lose, I guess." I was confused.

"They lose big, Big John," Jim grinned. "Besides we are sitting here right now having a beer. Right?"

"Right, Jim."

"And a fucking good cigarette."

"Right."

"And we're not dead. Not even wounded."

"Okay, okay, Jim, that's enough."

"And we actually help a lot of those kids, Big John. I mean we actually save some fucking lives. Do you know how few people actually get to save a life?"

"You can stop, Jim. I really don't need all that shit."

"Actually save a life! When you're a kid you have fantasies of rescuing babies from the paths of runaway trucks, carrying cripples from fires, diving into the water to rescue a beautiful girl——"

I joined the psychotherapy. "Who just happens to be the only daughter of the world's richest man. The girl falls in love with you and you are rich."

"But mainly you have saved a life. I mean, that's a real turn on. Someone could be dead, but you intervened and now he lives."

"Jim, you're too much. You——"

"Everyday, you save lives. You save five people before breakfast and don't even think about it. While you're trying to decide between apple or grape jelly on your toast, those five guys are in this world living. They may be hurting, but they are breathing, living, experiencing, thinking."

"I know, Jim, but think about——"

"Think, schmink. Think of all the kids who will go home to see their families, thanks to you. They may limp, or hop, or not play the piano, but they will be going home. And feel, and touch, and screw, and turn on."

"Next you'll be saying we're some kind of fucking heroes." I actually did feel much better now. "Any schmuck who is stupid enough to spend half of his life studying and training could do what we're doing here."

"But that's just it, Big John, it's not just any schmuck. It's you and me. And we're here doing it. Sure, it's because we have to. But we're still here doing it. And hacking it. We can hack anything if we have to."

"Question is," I reached for another Salem, "do we have to?"

"Of course we do," snapped Jim.

"Bigger question. Do those kids have to get shot in the first place? Do those guys in the hills have to shoot at us?"

"Hell, I don't know. Pass me another beer."

Nearly thirty tiny shrapnel wounds all over the trunk and extremities. He was wide awake and very uncomfortable. By the time I finished debriding all the wounds, the marine and I were both exhausted. I went back to the hooch. Jim was just coming back from the O.R.

Although I missed Hooch 75, Jim became my new family. He was always in a good mood, worked too hard, and occasionally got too drunk. But he always suffered through his hangovers without a single complaint. However, he gave himself away by doubling his cigarette and coffee consumption. He played basketball with me for half an hour every afternoon and scrubbed in the O.R. any chance he got day or night. At night he studied Russian or read airplane magazines.

"When I get out of this shithole, I'm going to buy a fucking airplane—a little Cessna—and fly over and see you, Big John. I've got a pilot's license you know. Where will you be?"

"I've requested California for my next duty station, but who the hell knows. Do you really fly?"

"No, but I can pilot an airplane. I've got a fucking license, you know."

"You can't afford an airplane."

Jim stretched out on his rack. "Well, Big John, I'm single. Right? I'm getting ten thousand dollars plus combat pay for this year. It's physically impossible for me to spend a goddamn cent over here, and I'm sure as hell not sending my money to anybody."

"I guess you're right."

"It's the same as the government's saying, 'I'll give you a ten thousand dollar check for your year.'"

"I wouldn't do it for ten million. I wouldn't do it for ten governments."

"You're doing it for one," Jim laughed.

Tiny entrance wound at the right temple. Large exit wound at right occiput with brain sliding out and matting with the blood in his black hair. Start a slow drip IV, put in an endotracheal airway, and put him in the corner.

Dong Ha had about twelve doctors, half of whom were GMO's, the rest some kind of surgeons. We shared the compound with several dentists and an oral surgeon. After dark the front half of our hooch was filled with dentists drinking beer. They never had any business at night, but they occasionally helped us when we had a big load of casualties. Their abilities ranged from that of a poorly trained corpsman to that of a pretty good surgeon.

Another one of the "O" Club regulars was a chaplain. Two chaplains lived in the hospital compound with us. It took two of them to keep up with the demand—blessing the dead and the dying; comforting the scared and the sorry; supporting the mental and spiritual health of commander doctors and Pfc. riflemen; reading letters from home to those without eyes, and writing them for those without arms; explaining to a bitter nineteen-year-old boy that even though he had no legs at least he could be grateful that he was alive, and then watching him die. They even made time for Sunday services.

One of the chaplains was a Catholic priest who was low-key, friendly, human, manly, supportive, and generally "with it." Everyone enjoyed talking with him over a beer. Even the marines liked him. He would laugh at their jokes and understand their rage and their tears. He had the magic ability to make a wounded marine relax and talk—even smile. Half of the time the casualties didn't even realize he was a chaplain. He didn't push religion but somehow made it known that support and comfort and talk and God and all that stuff were available if he needed them.

The other chaplain, Father Daugherty, was older, a little

less worldly (or a little more pious), quieter, and slightly distant, partly because of insecurity. Yet, it was obvious that he was concerned and ready to help. He was so eager to help that he sometimes frightened or embarrassed the wounded kids. They sometimes couldn't easily relate to him.

When it was unusually busy in triage the chaplain would help remove clothing from casualties, carry litters, supply bandages, hold patients down, and help in very tangible ways. One such day when the room was filled with casualties, corpsmen were removing the flak gear from a wounded marine when a grenade rolled out of his webbing and onto the floor.

"Grenade!" yelled a corpsman.

Several people hit the deck.

Without hesitating, Father Daugherty scooped up the grenade, clamped it tightly against his belly, and ran out of triage.

Silence. We waited.

Slowly, Father Daugherty walked back in with an embarrassed grin. The pin was still in the grenade. Father Daugherty had assumed it was a live grenade when he heard the corpsman's yell. A marine with a missing left leg laughed. Father Daugherty shrugged his shoulders and smiled. Everyone else continued to work.

A marine stationed practically in the DMZ could drop by to get his teeth worked on, and with his near-perfect smile and five hundred piasters, get laid in the nearby ville, drop by to confess his sins to the father, and return in two to three days to get his VD treated by a real physician. All the comforts of home.

The military base at Dong Ha had no housemice, no bargirls, no laundry girls. No women. I had no one with whom to speak Vietnamese. I never had time to venture into the ville outside the compound. For some reason I didn't really want to.

The NVA gunners hidden in the hills did not let us forget that they were there. Anytime could be incoming time. Lunch, dawn, midnight, midday. Reactions were automatic. Sometimes the shells were close, sometimes farther away, but always overwhelmingly frightening. Jim and I spent every spare minute sandbagging our hooch and building a sandbag blast wall between us and the helicopter pad. The casualties, the basketball games, and the sandbagging engendered enough real physical fatigue so that it took only a beer or two to get to sleep at night.

Nevertheless, the nights were still tough to handle. The sun helped to keep away that awful depression and homesickness. At night I tried movies, books, Jim Veesar, dentists, doctors, work—anything to keep from the frightening, quiet, self-withdrawal. I even read a textbook of dermatology.

I was really homesick and lonely. I often sat alone on top of the blast wall so carefully designed and constructed by Parrish and Veesar and looked across the helicopter pad to Graves. The naked lightbulbs would catch my eye as I watched the Graves marines work into the night. Tagging, typing, hosing down bodies, playing cards, waiting. Keeping watch over the dead.

Not all were killed by the enemy. Some were killed by other marines both by accident and on purpose. On one occasion one of our own helicopters wiped out a Marine reconnaissance squad spotted just north of the DMZ and thought to be enemy. Some were killed by Vietnamese civilians. Some were killed by a well-meaning, frightened, overzealous and anxious corpsman who accidentally gave too much morphine to his wounded buddies. Some were killed by vehicles, snakes, plane crashes, overdose of hard drugs, mud, water, bacteria, falls, bunker cave-ins, or even tigers. But they were everyone killed by whoever and whatever had us in this country. Greed or politics or foreign policy or mistakes or sacrifice or democracy or freedom or dictatorship or love or hate or something was really doing a job on these boys. They were dead as hell. You can't get much deader than being headless, having your whole body swollen from lying in the mud for three days, getting hosed down, tagged, zipped in a green bag and flipped into a freezer. You're never more dead than when you're completely blown away. You can't get more dead than when you cradle your head in the hands of some poor navy doctor, barf blood in his lap and then, as your fingers start to relax from their grip on his shirt, just stop breathing.

Swollen, boggy, tender nose with steady stream of blood coming from the left nostril. Several abrasions on the forehead. Point tenderness of second metacarpal of a big, black, right hand.

"I don't care what he called you, buddy," I put a pack in his nose, "we don't have time for you guys beating up on each other."

"Nobody calls me a nigger without getting stomped."

"It's not worth it, buddy. Look, you've got a bloody nose and probably a broken hand. Move your fingers, open and close." I palpated the bones of his hand. "Does that hurt?"

"Ow, yes! Jesus Christ, yes!"

"And your friend there probably has a broken jaw." I pointed to his opponent on the next litter. "He's got a missing tooth and the jaw is still swelling. So what have you gained?"

"He won't call me nigger again."

"That's cause his jaw's too swollen. If you guys would just . . ." The noise of the approaching chopper made it impossible to carry on. I examined the two fist fighters in silence.

Three litters were rushed in from the chopper. Just as one was carried by me, the patient's femoral artery broke open and blood spurted to the ceiling and all over the litter. I ran to the wounded marine's side and stuck my fingers in the hole in his thigh.

"Get me two IV's. Hurry! Get me some blood and a fast spin."

The corpsmen undressed the marine with the high wound while I kept one hand in the wound. He had a hole in his belly and a sucking chest wound. He had no measurable blood pressure but I could still feel a thready pulse against my fingers in his thigh.

We bought some time with pressure dressings and two liters of fluids.

"Let's go to the O.R.," I yelled to get people moving. "Now!"

"No more O-negative blood, sir," said the corpsman from the lab. "He's O-negative."

"How can you be out of blood? Find some! We need ten units. Find some now."

"We could chopper some in from the hospital ship if they have it. We could look for donors. Half an hour at the least, if we're lucky."

"I don't care where it comes from. Just get it!"

"Yes, Sir."

The patient went to X ray on his way to the operating room. Jim Veesar went with him. I turned back to finish up with my fist fighters.

They were gone. Probably back behind triage fighting again, I thought to myself. I helped with the other two casualties from the most recent chopper until they were stable and ready for transport south.

The black marine with the broken hand walked up to me. His nose was still bleeding. "Come here, quick, Sir," he said.

I walked to the triage door where I was surprised to see thirty or more marines in a single line outside the triage door. More were still coming and joining the line.

"Will this be enough, Sir?" said the big marine wiping the blood off his upper lip with his sleeve. "These guys all want to give blood. We can get more if you want."

I looked at the first guy in line. "What's your blood type?" I asked.

He couldn't answer. By now his jaw was too swollen.

I started to pump on the dead marine's chest as I quickly surveyed the situation. Right pelvis and right leg not present— no trace—probably still lying out in the field somewhere; multiple penetrating wounds of the left chest and left flank; right mastoid area missing, multiple wounds of the scalp, probably penetrating the skull. Not salvageable. I shook my head to the corpsmen who already knew. We moved on to the next casualty.

Through and through of the left upper arm with unstable fracture of the humerus and no pulse at the radial artery. Sensation intact, some finger motion present. Stabilize arm, IV, blood, X ray, and then to O.R. Probably need to reoperate again later in the rear.

As I worked I could hear the muffled grunts, heavy breathing, and staccato cursing of pain behind me. I didn't turn to see the face. My curiosity factor for seeing the face of such victims was approaching zero. I was busy.

I finished up with the arm injury by writing on a tag at the foot of his litter. "Humerus, AP and lat. Right shoulder PA, chest PA, lat."

"Take him from X ray to the O.R."

"Yes, Sir. Will do."

"Your ass is on report, Sir." The voice behind me sounded too familiar. It was the pain voice I had just heard.

"Your ass is on report, Doctor Parrish, Sir," he repeated.

I turned in disbelief. Behind me lay Robby Wills, my corpsman in the field. I was surprised to see an old friend. By now I had learned that most relationships in Nam, no matter how intense, are over forever when they are over.

"Robby Wills, what the hell are you doing here?"

"Collecting my third purple heart. I got a couple of little dings in my leg."

By now the corpsmen had undressed him and washed the dirt and blood off of his leg. Two small shrapnel wounds—right inner thigh, right calf. Pulses good, sensation and muscle strength good. Could be debrided under local if frags not too far in.

"Well, we'll get some X rays of your leg and fix you right up. How are you? Is this really your third heart?"

"Yeah, about a week after you left us, I took a round through my scalp. Knocked my helmet off, creased my skull bone and kept on going. Same shell hit Green in the shoulder. Remember him?"

"No." I put on a temporary dressing, ordered X rays and signaled for two stretcher bearers. "Good to see you again, Wills. How's the old outfit?"

"Lots of new faces. We really got wiped out last month at LZ Dottie. Lots of new faces."

"I'll be in later to get those dings out. We'll get a couple of X rays first. You'll be fine."

"Oh, I know I'll be okay. Now that I see you're here."

"One more cornball comment like that, and your ass if on report, Wills."

"Yes, Sir," he laughed.

"And Wills," I put my hand on his shoulder and smiled, "thanks for dropping by."

Left foot still in his boot, but connected to his knee only by a few strands of skin. The corpsman clipped it free with a giant pair of scissors while I applied a pressure tourniquet, drew blood for type and crossmatch and started an intravenous in his massive muscular neck. He was already shocky, and we had to hurry. It was one of those days when Jim

Veesar spent the whole day in the operating room. From dawn to dark, he came out only long enough to get involved with another case and scrub again. Finally, at about 10 P.M., leaning against our new blast wall we had time for a beer together.

"Jim, you must be sick and tired of operating. You've been in there all day."

"Oh, it's not bad. It's fun. They let me do a lot. Good experience."

"Who needs it?" I protested.

"But it's interfering with my study. You'll have to help me since you're in triage most of the time."

"Study?" I lit up a Winston, I was carrying cigarettes that day.

"Yeah, I'm doing a survey. Trying to find out what percentage of marines eat out chicks."

"You're kidding."

"No, these are middle-American eighteen- and nineteen-year-old kids. I'd like to know what the incidence of oral-genital sex is."

"Who cares?"

"I'll never get a chance to interview such a large cross section. Thousands of kids."

"In triage?"

"Sure, I ask every marine that comes through here if he eats out chicks."

CH-46

"You're crazy."

"So you've got to help me with my survey," Jim was serious despite his grin.

"Well, okay. If I think of it. I usually make some small talk with the kids anyway."

"Good, I'll get you another beer." Jim was up and headed to the hooch.

"You're crazy. No shit, Jim, you're crazy."

I knew Jim would never be back with that beer, because I had seen the light in the sky approaching for some time. Now I could hear the flap-flap hum of the chopper engine. I knew somehow it was headed for our pad. The noise grew louder, and a big "46" four-wheeled helicopter landed amidst the usual blasting sandstorm. I crouched behind the blast wall until the mechanical storm was over and then headed for triage.

About a dozen wounded. Four bad litter cases, the rest not serious. We went back to work. The first doctors to arrive in triage automatically began to care for the litter cases. I sat down next to a fever patient on the long bench against the wall. After asking him some questions, I had him lie down on the concrete floor in order to examine him. As I knelt over him to feel his belly, I looked up to see Jim bending over to speak to a legless black boy as he put a needle in his arm to administer fluids. The boy at first raised his head in disbelief. Then he smiled. Then he started talking and actually laughed. Jim passed by where I was as he helped carry the litter to X ray.

"Black boys just don't eat pussy," he said as he passed by. "They think it's dirty."

Sucking chest wound. Vaseline gauze dressing, chest tube. Type and cross. Blood and fluids. Medevac tag.

"Greetings from Phu Bai." A familiar voice entered triage.

"Roland Ames! What are you doing here?"

"Came up to see you." Roland shook my hand and then hooked his thumbs into his holster belt. "Made up a story about checking on Dong Ha Motor T and just came-the-hell up."

"Well, good." I sidestepped as the Kelly clamp ripped through the pleura with a popping noise and the blood shot to the floor. "It's good to see you. How's Hooch 75?"

"Fine. Same as ever. I'm going home next month."

"Excellent." I was sewing the chest tube in place. "I'll be glad to see you go, 'cause I'll be one month shorter then."

"All the hoochies send their best. We're keeping your rack empty in case you come back." Roland had unthinkingly put his hand on the wounded marine's leg.

"Go put your gear in the rear of the "O" Club. That's where I'm staying now." I took off the bloody gloves and threw them at Roland. "I'll meet you in the chow hall in fifteen minutes."

Roland ignored the gloves and turned to the wounded marine. "You're in good hands, buddy. You'll be all right."

The marine coughed, winced, and raised his head and grunted, "If he puts another one of those goddamn tubes in my chest, I'm taking my business elsewhere."

I pushed his head back down on the litter. "Lie down and shut up. At least you can breathe now." I smiled so he would know I was kidding him.

He grabbed the sides of the litter and drove the back of his head into the canvass. "Next time, I'm going to one of those painless docs. All I needed was a goddamn nuther hole in my chest."

"Next time, don't get hit in the chest," said Roland.

"Better yet," I added, "stay home next time."

Roland and I had lunch over Hooch 75 stories, war stories, incoming stories, and R & R stories. A chopper came in as we were having coffee, and I got up to leave. The hospital commander walked by me and motioned me to sit back down.

"Stay here and finish your coffee. You've got company. We'll send for you if we need you."

"Thanks." I sat. Another chopper came in.

Roland was just lighting up his second after-lunch cigarette when a corpsman came running up to our table.

"We need you in triage, Doctor Parrish. The room's full of casualties and more are coming in."

I shrugged apologetically toward Roland and got up to leave.

"That big lunch and this heat make me want to take a nap anyway," yawned Roland. "Don't feel much like inspecting Motor Transport. Too depressing."

"Try walking into a room full of abused, hurting, human

lumber, to the sounds of pain and vomiting and the hot smell
of sweat, shit, and blood knowing you may be there for the
next ten or twelve hours." I left. I had a chill on my way to
triage and stuck a thermometer in my mouth as I worked.
The oral temperature was 102°.

Sometimes the only way I could handle the casualty
scene was to ignore the big picture around me and just keep
busy mechanically moving from one task to another. Patching
holes, putting intravenous drips in arms, necks, groins. Putting in chest tubes. Talking to scared marines when the lump
in my throat was not too big. Ripping off clothes. Splinting
limbs. Examining. Working. Touching.

They kept coming. After about three hours, I stopped for
some water and a couple of salt tablets. My fatigues were
soaked with my sweat and and marines' blood. I smoked a
cigarette that was soon stiff with the matted blood, crap, and
vomit from my fingers. I coughed repeatedly. I had been
coughing for several days. The right side of my chest had
been hurting all day and it felt like it was going to tear open
with each cough. Between helicopters I listened to my own
chest with a stethoscope and was startled to hear a friction
rub. I had pleurisy or pneumonia or both. I could feel the
friction rub with my hand placed on my right chest.

I spotted an Intelligence man I had known in Hue. He
was talking to one of the corpsmen in the corner. I hustled
over to ask him about the fate of my civilian friends.

"Well, Doc Parrish, it was a real bad scene. I mean like
the VC went through the hospitals room by room and shot all
the patients who had not fled. That bargirl friend of yours was
stood up alongside the Catholic church and executed by an
NVA firing squad. Her and about forty or fifty others. I barely
got my ass out of there alive. I was trapped in Hue for three
days in house-to-house hiding and fighting. Twice I had to
shoot my way out of a house as they came in. Why one time
I . . ."

I walked away. I didn't want to hear his war stories—true
or not. I returned to work and mechanically moved from task
to task. Sun was dead. I was in a daze. I could hear nothing
but the steady beat of the helicopter and the horror around
me no longer seemed real. I began to have chills again and
my head was pounding. The red blood and green fatigues and
brown mud and crystal-clear intravenous fluids all seemed to

fade into dull grays of an old black-and-white movie. I suddenly felt very tired and wanted to lie down and quit.

A through and through of the thigh with a busted femur. Massive hematoma. Sensation intact. Peripheral pulse present. I did all the right things quickly. I had all the moves.

"Doc. Doc. You can save my leg, can't you?"

"We'll give it a hell of a try, buddy"

"It hurts like hell. Can I have a shot? Don't touch it!"

"Relax. I have to touch it. Once I get it stabilized it won't hurt so much." A corpsman helped me raise his hips to apply a long splint. The marine screamed and grabbed a handful of my shirt. We kept working.

"Them yellow bastards. I hate 'em. I'm going to kill every fucking Vietnamese I see. Them worthless yellow bastards." He was still pulling at my shirt.

I thought of sitting in the grass with Sun and talking in broken English and worse Vietnamese. We actually used to laugh.

"Them yellow turds. You could blow up this whole fucking country and not miss it." No one seemed to be listening to the marine. We had heard it all before.

I thought of driving Sun to Hue and seeing her float around the "O" Club like everybody's sweetheart. I thought of our secret meetings. Sometimes as friends. Sometimes as lovers. Sometimes as two lonely children.

"Yellow cock suckers. I'm going to empty a whole clip in the next one I see." He was in severe pain. I took his hand firmly from my shirt.

"Your pain will be less now, buddy. Try to quiet down."

"My fucking leg is ruined. I hate them yellow assholes. My leg . . ."

I moved on to another casualty.

"Doctor Parrish. Position one! We've got a doctor in coma. A navy doctor. I think he's been poisoned. Hurry!"

One of my classmates from Camp Pendleton was in coma. I examined him quickly and tried to arouse him. Some withdrawal to deep pain was the only response I could elicit.

The medevac tag was written in ballpoint pen. "Barbiturates overdose, ?time." The tag was from one of the infantry outfits which had been taking heavy casualties for several weeks.

Suicide gesture to get the hell out of the fire? Suicide

attempt because he was through with life? Temporary psychosis? Acute depression? I didn't know. Probably he didn't
know. All the possibilities were equally sane in this insane
world, and the difference between them was very thin. Pump
his stomach. Diurese him. Send him back to Prince Edwards.
Maybe back home to his family.

A hundred more little tasks followed. A thousand more
partly subdued cries of pain. A lot more blood. A few more
fevers. A little more shit, and two more blobs of brains.

Roland walked in as I pushed in another chest tube. He
watched for a minute. "This is where I came in, I think."

I didn't answer.

"Pretty busy, John?"

"Get me a cup of coffee."

"I'm going to the chow hall. I guess you're too busy to
eat. I'll fix you a sandwich and put it in your hooch."

"Yeah."

"You tired or pissed off or something, John?"

"Just bring me a fucking cup of coffee, will you, and
three aspirin."

"Okay, okay."

"And a cigarette"

"Okay."

"Lighted!"

"Yes. Yes."

Entrance wound in the right femoral triangle. No exit
wound. Helicopter pilot still in lead vest, helmet, and full
gear. Too late. Fixed dilated pupils. No heartbeat. Dead.
Take him away to Graves.

Hopefully that was the last one. The sun was already up.
I walked slowly back to my hooch. My back hurt and my eyes
were filled with sand and sleep loss.

There was a note on my bed.

Dear John,
    Sorry we didn't get to visit. Had to take the
first morning flight back to Phu Bai. Looked for you
late last night. You were in the operating room.
Come see me in Phu Bai before I go home.
    Next time I come to see you, don't work all
night.
                                          Roland

I sprawled out fully dressed. I was freezing and sweating at the same time. My bed was so full of sand that my boots didn't matter. I was so tired I didn't care anyway.

E-E-E-E-E-E- K-Krrrump.

Incoming! I rolled onto the floor. More shells came in. Where the hell was Jim? Probably still in the O.R. I slid on my belly to the back door and out against my new blast wall.

Silence. Several people ran past me into the bunker. I did not want to move. Some people began to leave the bunkers. I just wanted to lie right where I was. I was too tired to move.

At first it was a distant buzz, then a close chatter-chatter, then a loud sandblast. A chopper landed next to my wall. Time to go back to work.

By noon we had received another thirty or forty casualties and had been interrupted by incoming artillery three times. One of the shells hit an oil bladder killing two marines and badly burning another five.

By early afternoon things slowed down enough to allow us to clean out the sick call line and have some chow. Green Kool-Aid, beans and baloney sandwiches were interrupted by more incoming artillery, a fist fight between two of the cooks and, finally, by more helicopters. By now, I knew I didn't like Dong Ha.

We were greeted in triage by a smiling Arvan soldier with his arm around the waist of a limping, staggering companion. They were standing in the middle of the room waiting for the corpsmen to set up a litter for the wounded Arvan. For some reason the corpsmen were refusing to set up a litter.

The hospital C.O. approaching with sandwich in hand was first to speak. "What the hell's going on here. Set up a litter for this wounded man."

"But, Sir. He's just got a ding in his wrist. He can sit on the bench."

"But he looks hurt. He was medevaced by chopper."

"I know. But he's got one small shrapnel wound in his wrist."

"Better strip him down and examine him. Don't want to miss anything. Parrish. You question him. See what's wrong."

"Okay, Sir," the corpsman complained. "But I'm telling you, he's got one goddamn ding in his wrist and that's all."

Mumbling so the C.O. couldn't hear, a second corpsman helped set up the litter with equal absence of enthusiasm. "Goddamn queer fairy. Risks a whole chopper crew for a goddamn ding in the wrist, so small he coulda treated it himself in the field."

I questioned the Arvan soldier and examined him completely. He was very dramatic and appeared in great distress. His colleague stood by looking brave and sincere. He pointed to the wounded Arvan and talked to the corpsmen in Vietnamese. At first they ignored him. Finally, one of them answered, "I don't know what you're saying, shitbird, but if you medevaced out of the field to carry that fairy in here leaving some marine flank unprotected, I oughta kick your ass and make your trip to the hospital worthwhile. I oughta——"

"Quiet." The C.O. walked up to the litter. "Well, what's the trouble, John? What's the story?"

"It seems that our friend here has a superficial shrapnel wound of the wrist."

Eviscerated black kid holding his belly as little slips of small intestine worked their way between his fingers. IV, type and cross, saline pad, and off to the O.R.

A helicopter pilot in full gear ran into the triage removing his helmet as he approached me, all grins with hand extended.

"D.J.! You old shit. How are you?" I was pleasantly surprised.

"Great. Just wanted to say hello. My crew is waiting. Can't stay."

"Come back when you can. We need to talk."

"I will." He turned and ran. "Sun sends her best. She's working in Da Nang."

"What? Wait! D.J.!"

He was gone.

# TWELVE

For awhile I was used as a kind of trouble shooter. I filled in for the GMO's of several outfits while they went on R & R, went out into the field, or had emotional breakdowns. This allowed me to spend time in the rear with the Headquarters Battalion, the Third Shore Party, the engineers, and the rear resting station for the reconnaissance unit.

My life was essentially the same in each outfit. Sick call for two to three hours each morning and afternoon. No casualties. Lunch with lieutenants and captains. Dinner with colonels, majors, and generals. Movies at night. The new people were moderately interesting for a night or two but I usually kept pretty much to myself and ran, read, and thought alone.

The marines in the rear also had more time to get VD, use and abuse drugs, to have racial brawls, and to shoot each other. When a nineteen-year-old bundle of frustration trained to react quickly, kill efficiently, and to lead a purely physical life gets angry after too many beers and happens to be carrying his weapon, he shoots somebody.

By being in the wrong place at the right time, I somehow managed to get involved as an expert witness in a murder trial. I was involved in a case in which a sergeant had shot one of his own unarmed men in the chest at short range and claimed self-defense because of the threatening words and gestures used by the boy. After many accounts from witnesses, diagrams, angle of fire studies, descriptions of wounds, a logical prosecution, and a theatrical defense, the sergeant was found not guilty.

The obvious major advantage to being in the rear was the relative safety. It was so great to be away from the

incoming artillery of Dong Ha. Occasionally enemy mortar
teams managed to slip in close enough to shell us, but that
was unusual.

It was good to get away from the seriously sick and
wounded but for some reason I felt more lonely, frustrated,
and helpless with each of these assignments.

Killing time was a problem in the marine rear in I Corps
because large military bases had been created in the middle
of nowhere next to small villes. No big city life. It simply was
not a full-time job trying to stay alive. There seemed to be
more use of marijuana by the enlisted men in the rear. A
marine caught smoking grass on watch out in the field was
likely to get the shit kicked out of him by his own colleagues.
No such internal control was present in the rear.

My own job with these rear elements was boring. Sick
call was not just an ever present line of snotty noses, drip,
fevers, and skin infections to be fitted in between casualties.
It was now my only job. Regular hours. Patients were logged
in and seen only at certain times, some even by appointment.
The complaints included more headaches, chest pain, back
pain, and nonspecific complaints; and the average sick call
population was older. Twenty-eight-year-old captains, thirty-
five-year-old majors, forty-two-year-old colonels, and fifty-
five-year-old generals.

Another major difference in these sick call patients was
that I actually saw the same patient more than once. The
patients were not medevaced, shipped out or transferred to
the rear. I actually knew if they got better or worse. I even
accumulated my share of problem patients who don't, or don't
want to get a better. Like the old general practitioner back
home, I had a few recurrent, bitchy, pain-in-the-ass patients.

The emotional problems were not the acute situational
anxiety attacks of the front lines. They were the deep seated,
chronic, ulcer-and-headache-producing career, success, bitterness, and competition kind of problems. I nursed one colonel
through some severe stomach pains which were relieved only
by large doses of narcotics, sedation, and bed rest. After
repeated normal physical exams, I discovered that because
the colonel had recently lost most of an entire company, he
had been pulled back to a post in the rear. He was literally
eating his guts out and was one of the most miserable people
I saw in Vietnam. Between attacks of severe depression,

guilt, and stomach pains, he carried on his job with a blank stare and cold efficiency.

Travel was more easily available to those in the rear. I managed to make several trips to Da Nang. The I Corps Medical Society. The big navy hospital. One weekend I managed to find Sun. She was working at an NCO club just outside Da Nang.

Sun had managed to survive the Tet disaster in Hue. During the first few days of house-to-house searching and murder she had managed to hide. During the days of "liberation" she set up shop and sold cokes and beer—my beer—to marines. When things got hot again, she fled to Da Nang.

I spent one night in her new apartment. Being off limits at night in Da Nang proved to be a frightening experience. I ducked from alleyway to doorway expecting any minute to be shot by a VC, PF, or American MP. Once I was in Sun's house a group of angry Vietnamese men came to the door. I hid in one room while Sun had a long, angry, and heated interchange with the midnight visitors. After they finally left Sun would not tell me the nature of their visit.

The next night we decided it would be safer for me if we stayed in a downtown hotel. As luck would have it, Da Nang was shelled that night for the first time in months and shrapnel, small arms fire in the streets, and people running up and down the halls of the hotel kept us hiding under the bed most of the night.

Although I had more than four months left in Vietnam, I told Sun that I had to say goodbye to her. My ability to get to Da Nang was unpredictable. My visits were inconvenient and even dangerous, and it would only be a matter of time until I left country.

The farewell was not a particularly painful one. Sun was hurt that I chose to say goodbye before it was absolutely necessary but respected my judgment. Still, she made the whole scene easy for me. She knew that the reasons for the end of our relationship was a trip that would make me very happy and would only remind her of the helpless dependency which her personal allegiances, her country's politics, and the war had thrust upon her. She had no escape.

Sun was brave. She was getting pretty good at saying goodbye. I tried to give her some money but she refused it. She did allow me to give money for the children to the old lady who kept them. I never saw or heard from Sun again.

On my return from one of my Da Nang weekends I flew into Dong Ha to get some gear from my hot box and take ground transportation back to Quang Tri and the headquarters area. We were about to land on the airstrip near D Med when the whole world seemed to explode around us. We pulled into an all-effort climb with jet assists going full blast and returned to the sky. An enemy artillery shell had landed directly in the ammo dump.

We climbed to a safe height and circled repeatedly while watching the awesome fireworks show below. The dump continued to explode midst clouds of black smoke, belching fire, and flying debris. It continued so long that we had to return to Da Nang and refuel.

When I did make it to D Med later that day, I discovered my desk overturned and my books and papers all over the room. There was a large shrapnel hole in the wall immediately above the desk. When I sat in my chair to examine it more closely, I couldn't help but notice that it was exactly head high. I hurried off to Quang Tri.

The easiest assignment I had in the rear was the sick call for the reconnaissance unit, the Special Forces of the Marine Corps. The toughest of the tough were highly trained in all the skills of survival and the art of killing. Very few of these men come to sick call. Those who did were usually treated or mistreated by an enlisted man who made it a point of honor not to need my help. The men spent all of their time in the rear impressing one another with their ruggedness by using friendly abusive banter and stories of their most dangerous missions, or by broadcasting a practiced stern quiet stoicism.

The rear was merely a place where the reconnaissance teams rested and waited between missions. Real life was out in the jungle, and rice paddies, the rivers, the choppers. The important things were behind enemy lines and in forbidden places. Out there they were against the whole world. They had to conquer the elements, the enemy, their own fears and come back alive. They had to do it over and over again. Constantly retesting of oneself was not just important, it was somehow necessary.

The enemy was only part of the picture. Charlie was to be spied upon, avoided, fooled, killed if necessary but he was not as important as the whole experience in itself. It was important to go and come back. It was important to be ready to go. The more severe the test, the better. Barely making it back was a good kind of victory. Barely making it back and being ready to go again was the best kind of victory. I saw two men have a fist fight over who was going to get to volunteer for the last man on a behind-the-line helicopter drop. As punishment, neither was allowed to go. They left for the chow line arm in arm.

Many of the kids were in their second or third tour in Vietnam. Some would stay until the war was over, until they had been killed or wounded, or until they arrived at a point where they no longer needed to test and be tested. Often, those who signed up for another tour were awarded an extra R & R and leave time that amounted to thirty days paid vacation in the port of choice. The stories of the beautiful women in Hong Kong and Bangkok, the cheap ass in Taipei, the nude group sex parties with round-eyes in Australia and screwing American school teachers in Hawaii were enough to make these boys sign anything. A number of young men later died paying back the government for their free trip and their wild sex. Some came back to Vietnam because they thought they were in love with a Vietnamese girl and had to see her again. Often they couldn't find her or when they did she was with another soldier. One marine admitted that he finally found his woman after four months of searching. She was living with a Vietnamese man in a small ville. The marine backed up, set up his bazooka, and blew them and their hut out of existence.

A large number of marines did not sign up for repeated tours until after they had been in the States for some time. They often compared the frustrations and boredom while in the rear with that of the States. They had very ambivalent feelings toward returning to the front lines. The jungle and the bush offered maximum excitement, independence and comradery, physical exercise, chance at heroism, and documentation of manliness. At the same time, it was a place where one might die.

"I don't really know why I came back, Doc," the lance corporal had his right boot off so that I could check his infected foot. "I just did."

"You married?" I felt his foot to see if it was warm.

"Nope," he said, "almost was once."

"Drop your pants so I can check your groin for nodes."

He hopped off the litter and dropped his fatigue trousers. Most marines don't wear underpants to prevent jock itch.

"How long has your foot been like that?"

He held up three fingers. The corpsman had stuck a thermometer in his mouth.

"Three days?"

He shook his head. I examined his foot again. Mild emersion foot with some fissuring had led to a moderate cellulitis.

"You're going to have to take some antibiotic pills and stay off your feet for awhile. Just wait here 'til I write something in your record and write a note to your sarge."

"Yes, Sir," he mumbled.

He got dressed and sat on the bench with his hat in his hand. "I tried to go back to school but nothing seemed relevant or interesting. Those damn kids in class were so fucking sincere and got all worked up over such unimportant things."

I kept writing in silence.

"Nobody cared that I had been getting my ass shot at. Only people who wanted to hear my war stories were a bunch of hoods who hung around the drive-in pizza joints."

I stopped writing and looked at him. He continued.

"My girl married some insurance creep while I was gone." He looked down at the floor. "I pumped gas for a couple of months. Didn't have any real friends."

"Old gang was gone?" I asked.

"They were still around. But they were different, Doc."

"Maybe you were different."

"Yeah, guess so. Can I smoke in here?"

"If you give me one," I answered.

We both lit up and I put my feet up on my desk.

"You know, Doc, nothing seemed important. I mean like nothing. My job, my paycheck, school, my friends. Nothing. They were all a drag."

"So?"

"So, here, everything is important. I mean it's important as hell if you wear your helmet or not. An untied boot lace may cost you your life. It's important where you sleep, when you sleep, and who's next to you and who's awake while you sleep.

"It's important how and where I walk, when and how much I eat. My job here is important as hell. And my buddies really need me to do a good job. They don't think I'm a piece of shit putting gas in their car."

"If I met you in my office in the States I wouldn't think you were a piece of shit."

"Yeah, but somehow it's just different, Doc. Back home nothing I did was important and here every fucking little thing I do is important as hell."

"So you came back."

"And the people at home just don't understand us, Doc."

"Do the people over here understand you?"

"Yes, I really think they do."

"I'm not sure I do."

"With you it's different, Doc. You probably got a wife and kids. You go back to a ready-made family, a respected job and position. You don't understand what it is to be a piece of shit in a society that doesn't understand you and somehow tries to pretend you don't exist. That the whole fucking war doesn't exist."

"But what can you prove by coming back? How does that help?"

"We're supposed to be fighting this shitty war for them bastards you know." He ignored my questions. "A fucking lot they appreciate it."

"So why come back to this shitty war?"

"I don't fit in in the States, Doc. Here I do. I fit in just fine. I might get my ass killed but I fit in just fine."

I stood and handed him his record without comment.

"Do you think I'm wrong to try to be where I fit in, Doc?"

"No, kid. I think it's wrong that you don't fit in at home. Now stay off that foot and see me tomorrow."

"Yes, Sir," he limped out.

A major advantage and disadvantage to being in the rear was that there was a lot of time to think. Empty daytime hours and totally vacant nights. Too much time for bad thoughts. Too long until the good thoughts could come true.

I thought about Hooch 75. All but Roland had gone home and he was a short-timer. I'm sure he could have told me how many more hours. I thought about my Camp Pendleton class. The dentist with whom I had thumbed a ride that first night was dead. I had personally seen four of my classmates medevaced out for psychiatric reasons.

I thought of all my Vietnamese friends. Sun. Maria and the Sisters. Our housemouse. I felt as though I were deserting them. My country could afford to remove me from this mess as easily as it inserted me into it and at the same time play some part in maximizing and prolonging the involvement of certain Vietnamese.

I thought of the armless, legless, and psychotic people that I had seen come through triage. Thousands of them. Their war would never be over no matter what happened to this land. And I thought of all the dead I had seen in Graves. Hundreds of them. I could picture almost every one of them. Their war was over.

I thought. I dreamed. I philosophized. I planned. I schemed. I read my notebook over and over. Notes on malaria, EKG interpretations, history of Vietnam, voluminous lists of English and Vietnamese words and their dictionary meanings, various calendar schemes to mark off days, a map of Vietnam, a sketchy diary, a list of intestinal parasites and their treatment, a few proverbs, notes on VD, a few newspaper clippings and some nude pictures cut from Playboy.

It was in the rear that I began to get the notion that I was really going to go home someday. Counting days became a really serious and exciting business. When I had less than a hundred days to go I began to think like a shorttimer.

I reread letters from home and wrote long letters saying nothing. I designed the house I would someday build for my family. A pool, a big study, a weight room and pool table in the basement, a big playroom for the kids, a giant dressing room for my wife, and an extra bedroom for the son I might have someday.

R & R's were easier to get in the rear. However, despite much effort, I was never able to land a Hawaii billet to meet my wife. I took an R & R to Hong Kong. This time I did rest and relax. I shopped and toured and played it straight. Myron and Joan would have been proud of me. I began to really believe that I would see Joan again someday and decided that if I did I would work at making her very happy.

Husband. Father. Me? I could reclaim all that. My life before and after Vietnam was not just fantasy, not just another escape. It was a happy thought.

When the world around me became less frantic and frightening and I was not overwhelmed with the horror of dead and wounded, I became less frantic. I did not have to live hard, work hard, play hard, drink, run, and escape. It was just me for awhile. I grew up a lot in the rear.

Four thirty P.M., or 1630, was the relatively sacred goal of most people's day. Preparations for 1630 began about four o'clock and it was tough to get anything done by anybody for any reason after the magic hour. The clubs filled with untired bodies by 1631 and the next two hours were donated to social intercourse, drinking, and eating. I usually went for a run at four thirty for exercise and to avoid the social hour. By the time I showered and dressed most people were eating supper.

"Being in the rear is not exactly a piece of cake. But it's not getting your ass shot at either." The young marine lieutenant had sat down at my table uninvited. He was tearing apart his second steak.

"In this war, it's hard to say where the rear is." I spoke without looking up from the steak I was vigorously sawing. "Any civilian might kill you and any road might be mined. Mortars and rockets can come from open fields and friendly villes."

"Yeah, but look," talking with his mouth full, "here we sit with steak and beer," he shrugged his shoulders in amazement, "and a fucking tossed salad, in a fucking salad bowl, no less."

He left the table again and this time came back with two peach cobblers and three beers. He gave me one of the beers and continued talking.

"Can you imagine, Doc, yesterday at this time I was squatting in the tall grass trying to figure out how to get my men out of a fucking fire fight without losing half of them. Tomorrow we may be dropped into the DMZ," he switched to his second cobbler, "But today—steak and beer and a fucking tossed salad in a salad bowl."

**M 42 "Duster"**

"And a tablecloth and a bar and music," I added.

"You work here, Doc?"

"Temporarily."

"I'm out in the bush. The old man flies me back to the rear every few weeks for a hot steak, a shower, too many beers, and twelve hours sleep." The lieutenant had had his shower and steak and was working hard on the too many beers. "The old man says I should get away from my men every now and then."

"Maybe he's right."

"Yeah, Doc, I guess he is. I get kinda batty after awhile and take too many chances. Been out in the bush for over six months now."

I shook my head. "Why so long?"

"Oh, I don't know. I could of rotated back but I knew all those kids and nobody else can take care of 'em like I can." He lit up and opened another beer. "Why just yesterday half of 'em woulda been wiped out if I hadn't crawled around in tall grass yelling orders and getting our mortars set and all. We had twin forties and really kicked some ass. Cleaned out the tree line in twenty minutes."

"You have to leave them sometime."

"I know, Doc, but I love them kids. They're really great little soldiers. They fight their asses off when I tell them to. I really love the ignorant little bastards."

"Your luck is going to run out if you keep pushing it."

"It's not luck, Doc. I know what the fuck I'm doing. I stay outa trouble. Been wounded three times but they're not going to kill this marine."

"Three hearts? Why don't you go home?"

"Don't want to. My job is to kick some ass and keep my men alive and I'm damn good at it."

We drank for a few minutes without speaking.

"You think I'm crazy don't you, Doc?"

"I don't know what crazy means anymore."

"Well, I do crazy things because that's my job." He leaned forward and rapped his index finger on the table. "I kill, Doc. I kill. I mean that's crazy in itself. Right?"

"Right."

"My job is to keep my men alive and kick some ass. I do what has to be done to get those two jobs done. The brass back here wants me to do that. And I do it."

I agreed with a head shake.

"And they know how we do it. They're not blind and they're not dumb. They know just how stinky this whole shit is. They know the score."

"What do you mean?"

"I mean they know that pacification and body counts and trusts and friendly villes is all a bag of shit. A bunch of pure bullshit to feed the League of Women Voters and the senators and the peace freaks." The lieutenant obviously had a load on his mind and needed the beer, my ears, and some rest.

"I do things, Doc, which are totally insane. But I have to do them."

"It's a crazy war." I tried to help him.

"It's not so simple as that. It's so fucking complicated."

"I know. It's—"

"Doc, my sergeant was killed last week."

"I'm sorry. I——"

"Do you know how he died?"

"I——"

"He got his goddamn throat slit."

"Well——"

"Got his goddamn throat slit in his sleep."

I stopped trying to interrupt.

"We 'liberated' this friendly ville from the VC. The first night we stayed there four of my men were mysteriously blown up. The second night my fucking sergeant got his throat slit." His eyes were getting watery and he was talking faster. "The third night we decided we'd all better sleep a hundred meters outside the ville in the woods and nobody else would mysteriously die and we were mortared all night long from somewhere."

"The villagers were trying to tell you something."

"I know that if we go back to that ville tomorrow, there'll be a hundred new booby traps to get my men."

"Don't go back," I suggested.

"If we don't go back the VC live there, take their rice for supplies, store ammo and shell us from the friendly ville and we can't shoot back. A few weeks and a few villes later they'll be shelling you right here in the rear, Doc.

"Next time I take a fucking ville, I'm going to kill every fucker in it if I have to, to keep my men from dying after the fight is over. Enough of them die during the fight. It's the only safe way to take a ville."

"You can't just shoot all of the people. What kind of a victory is that?"

"There aren't any victories, Doc. You just try not to lose. 'Cause when you lose, you lose big."

"I guess we ought to go home."

"Fine with me. But as long as I'm here, I'm going to do my fucking job."

"Drink your beer and go get some sleep."

He left and returned with three more beers.

"Doc, I shoulda listened to the old man and killed the whole ville."

I couldn't answer.

"Half the time the old man is watching from his helicopter."

Again I didn't respond.

"If I hada done what the boss said, Doc, I wouldn't be

here drinking beer with you." He had watery eyes again. "You know where I'd be, Doc?"

"No."

"I'd be leaning against the enlisted men's hut getting smashed with the sarge. Like I did last month. The sarge would be alive and we'd be smashed and laughing our asses off. That big black mother was the best sergeant in the whole fucking corps.

"If I had wiped the ville, he'd still be here. I shoulda listened."

"But you can't kill women and kids."

"Doc, you don't understand. The people at their TV's don't understand. The brass and the grunts understand.

"You walk through the fucking bush for three days and nights without sleep. Watch your men, your buddies, your goddamn kids get booby trapped. Blown apart. Get thrown six feet in the air by a trap laid by an old lady and come down with no legs. And the only thing he says to you is 'I'm sorry lieutenant.' And then dies. Watch them die as you get more and more tired, and more and more scared, and more and more freaked out by no sleep. Watch the Bouncing Betty rip up three good men and watch your fucking corpsman bleed to death while he's trying to drag himself up to the other two.

"You finally take the fucking ville. The villagers welcome you and cheer you and then your men continue to die each night.

"All you want to do is sleep. And stay alive. And keep your men alive. All you want to do is sleep and not die. If you gotta kill every yellow thing that moves to do that you will. And you won't stop till you're out of ammo or your gun barrel burns your hands and every possible yellow shit is dead or gone. And then you think of your sarge and your corpsman and your buddy and you start in on the water buffalo and the huts and the dogs and chickens."

He crushed a beer can and wiped a tear from his cheek.

"You gotta sleep, Doc. You gotta sleep and you gotta stay alive."

I stared at the table for a minute, "I know, buddy, I——"

"You don't know, Doc. You don't know unless you've been there. Go to the village whorehouse and find three of your men nude and dead with their heads cut off and put between their legs with their dick and their balls stuffed in their mouth, and the next time you to into a village whorehouse you go in with your M16 blazing and chewing up teen-age girls.

"Take pity on a sick old man in a straw hut and have the walls of the hut come alive with machine gun bullets ripping up two of your men and your own goddamn calf and the next old man you see in this hut is as good as dead. Blow the fucker up."

"Maybe anybody would do the same." I tried to comfort the big marine.

"I didn't one time, Doc. Because I couldn't. And now my sergeant is one dead mother fucker."

"You can't blame yourself because your sergeant is dead. You can't shoot all the civilian population to make sure you kill all the VC."

The big marine paused. He rubbed his forehead and sat back. He lit a cigarette and stared at his marine corps lighter.

"I know, Doc. The poor peasant here doesn't want to kill anybody either. He wants to screw his wife, raise his rice and his kids and stay alive. He's just Joe Shit the Rag Picker."

"He's just like Joe Shit the Rag Picker back home." I added, "War is somebody else's business."

"But here, Doc, the war is forced down his goddamn throat. On Monday night the VC come through, take a third of his rice and his oldest boy. He thanks them, says he hates the American invaders and they leave. On Thursday afternoon the marines come through, screw his daughter, shoot his water buffalo, and push him around a little. He thanks them, says he hates the VC and they leave."

"You can't kill him for that," I said, "and you can't expect the peasant to trust us any more than we trust him."

The marine thought about the peasant for a minute, leaned forward again, pointed his finger at me and said slowly and carefully, "Doc, when the old man tells me to take his ville and I'm worried about my own goddamn men, I'll kill the fucker every time."

# THIRTEEN

The terrible noise was the alarm clock. On the second try I shut it off. My eyes finally focused on my wristwatch. 6:05, Thu 4. It was not just a nightmare, I really was in Dong Ha. It was the Fourth of July! Only thirty days until I was due to leave Vietnam. I threw a boot at Jim.

"Wake up, you twink. It's the Fourth of July!" Suddenly wide awake, I stood in the middle of the floor in my torn green undershorts.

> *"Thirty days has September,*
> *April, May, and Parrish.*
> *All the rest have more,*
> *Except Jim Veesar*
> *who also has thirty."*

Jim raised his head, "We're short-timers!"

"I'm so short I don't have time to talk about it—might miss my airplane." I put on gym shorts and laced up my boots.

"I'm so short I have to blouse my underwear." Jim rolled over. "In fact, I'm much too short to run today—might miss my plane." He went back to sleep.

No one else got up to run. What a wonderful feeling! For almost a year I had watched people become "short-timers" and leave Vietnam. Now I was a short-timer. Too late in my tour of duty for reassignment. Too late for another tour in the field. In thirty days a big CONUS bird would take me home, and my war would be over. Dong Ha could be tolerated for thirty more days. Anything could be tolerated for only thirty days.

I ran through the corner of the air force compound beneath the big tower and through the ankle-high grass to the dirt road. The road headed directly south, away from the DMZ. On the left were the oil bladders, giant rubber bags about ten-feet wide, fifteen-feet long and three-feet high filled with gasoline, oil, or other fuels. They lay side by side in holes dug deep enough that the top of the bladder was about one foot below ground level. Thus, laterally moving shrapnel could not reach them. Only a direct hit would tear or explode them. Pumps and large hoses ran in all directions. The air force bunkers were to my right separated from the road by a mesh of barbed wire.

I liked this part of my run the least. The oil bladders smelled. And, furthermore, if incoming shells were to interrupt my run at this point, it would be impossible to get to the air force bunkers through the barbed wire, and if those big oil tits were hit, it would be curtains for anyone close by. I usually sprinted this one hundred meter stretch.

I turned right on to a smaller road which wound through the rear elements of several of the infantry battalions. I was soaking wet, tired, and out of breath, but I continued. Tents, hooches, and bunkers lined both sides of the road. Troops were already lined up at the piss tubes. They walked about and stretched their limbs. The road led to the POW camp on the western border of the compound. A double wire fence about eight-feet high topped with another two or three feet of barbed wire surrounded the square compound. Vietnamese prisoners clothed in shorts, loin cloths, or fatigue pants lived on the ground under low thatched roofs. They squatted in small groups eating breakfast. They were used to seeing me come by, and we usually exchanged waves and smiles on my first lap around. The major part of my run was always round and round the prison compound, because there was very little traffic, and because that would be the least likely area for the enemy to aim his artillery pieces. On the Fourth of July my run was only two laps around, because it seemed hotter than usual and there was a burning, prickly sensation on my chest and back. My mouth felt like it was stuffed with cotton.

From the prison compound another dirt road headed east toward the airstrip. From there I headed north alongside the strip until it ended about one hundred yards east of D

Med. The last stretch cut behind Graves, across the helicopter pad, and back to my hooch. The course had become almost ritualistic. I had run it almost every day for several months.

I sat on the back steps of the hooch slowly unlacing my boots and recovering from my run. Suddenly, a piercing, freight-train noise whizzed overhead followed by a thundering crunch. Incoming rounds! I dove to the ground and froze. The explosion was followed immediately by some very familiar sounds inside my hooch. It was clear to me what each component of the commotion was, because I witnessed the noises being made many times from the floor of my hooch. Jim had rolled off his bed onto the floor, stood up to get his flak jacket, dropped his helmet, taken two steps toward the door, and finally decided to dive to the floor again.

Three more shells crashed in. I remained on the ground and belly-crawled toward the big triage bunker. Several seconds of silence followed. I broke into a crouched run toward the bunker. Jim came flying out of the hooch and ran panting and cursing right behind me. Before I had taken two steps, another shell whistled overhead, and I fell to the ground again just outside the bunker entrance. Having gathered considerable ground speed, Jim decided not to stop until inside the bunker. When I fell to the ground at his feet, he tripped over me and crashed into the wall of the bunker.

"Nice block, you fuckin' gringo." Without stopping he crawled toward the bunker entrance as two more shells exploded.

"Stay down, you dumb shit," I yelled, but he was already in the bunker. I crawled in behind him.

"Nice block." He cocked his fist. We leaned against the inside bunker wall and laughed. Shells continued to explode all around and the bunker filled with barefooted doctors in T-shirts and flak gear.

"Good morning."

"Happy Fourth."

"Firecrackers, yes; cherry bombs, okay; but this is ridiculous!"

"Somebody's declaring his independence."

"Where are they hitting? Sounds like they're on the airstrip."

"What the hell are you two farts laughing about?"

"We're short-timers," said Jim. "This time next month we'll be reading 'bout this shit in the papers."

"And we won't believe a word of it," I added.

"And we won't fucking believe it," laughed Jim. "We won't fucking believe it."

A shell landed close enough to spray the bunker with dirt and shrapnel. The conversation stopped. Another shell shook the ground.

"Jesus Christ!"

Everybody flattened on the ground inside the bunker except Jim and I. We maintained our sitting positions against the inside bunker wall.

"Do you believe this shit?" I asked Jim as two more shells hit at very close range.

"Do you believe that in one month this will all be a bad dream?" Jim looked around him. "I'm going to eat every girl in San Francisco. Then I'm going to eat my way to the Midwest. By that time I'll have such an erection, I can pole vault to New York City."

"You're not horny are you, Big Jim?"

"Well let's put it this way. I hope my mother doesn't meet my airplane. That might be embarrassing. I . . ."

A steady rhythmical banging of outgoing shells began. Our return fire lasted about three minutes without interruption. The spotters must have seen where the incoming rounds originated, because when our big guns finally stopped, there was a long silence—no more incoming shells. Cheers went up within two bunkers.

"Sorry about that, Charlie."

"What a hell of a Fourth of July celebration."

"The Green machine bangs out a few rounds."

"Happy Fourth."

"I hope they blew the shit out of those DMZ guns. Those bastards."

"That's the last Fourth I'm going to spend in this country."

We heard several trucks approaching at high speed and honking. We knew what that meant. There are no celebrations for doctors in a war. The trucks pulled up beside the triage bunker. Sixteen soldiers had been hit by the incoming shells. Our day's work had begun.

After the wounded were stabilized, I showered, ate breakfast, and made hasty rounds on the ambulatory fever patients. (Ambulatory status meant that they could run to the bunker if necessary. All leg injuries had to be sent farther to the rear.) The men who still had high fever were "medevaced" south by fixed-wing aircraft, while those who were improved were returned to their rear elements. It seemed wise to keep as many men between D Med and the DMZ as possible.

After a second cup of coffee, I headed for triage to begin sick call. A long line of marines prepared stories of woe and sickness: headaches, back pain, exaggerated limps, sore throats, rashes, and colds. Those with diarrhea or gonorrhea dropped out of line periodically to visit the head. The first patient I saw was a marine first lieutenant with gonorrhea. He had just returned from R & R in Hawaii with his wife. She was the only woman he had touched since he left California four months earlier.

As usual, sick call was interrupted by several helicopter loads of wounded marines and fevers. At about 9:30 A.M. we received two unconscious marines with normal temperature, slight hypotension, and pale, dry skin. They reacted to painful stimuli and their cranial nerves were intact. They looked like victims of heat exhaustion, but it was early in the day for heat exhaustion, and the unconsciousness was bothersome. We started IV saline and kept them at D Med even though a morning medevac was leaving shortly. Within twenty minutes another chopper arrived with four marines who were too weak to ambulate, but were not unconscious. One was confused. One was dry-heaving. All had a normal temperature and blood pressure, but were sweaty and pale. Questioning revealed a history comparable with heat exhaustion. I remembered how quickly I had "overheated" when running earlier that morning.

At six fifteen two companies of marines had begun chase of a battalion of NVA spotted by helicopters. They had proceeded at a fast pace with full pack up and down shadeless hills without rest the whole morning. Their canteens were dry by midmorning, and salt pills without water are nauseating. Several men had fallen exhausted and overheated. The corpsmen allowed them to rest for several minutes, but those who could not continue were medevaced to us because the outfit had to keep moving.

Pale and exhausted marines started arriving by fives and sixes. Some were sweating profusely, but the more seriously

ill boys felt dry. Central nervous system status ranged from
fully awake, to combative and delirious, to frank unconsciousness. Seeing people medevaced to water, rest, and safety, and
knowing the rewards of pushing on would be total collapse or
encounter with the NVA, some had chosen the easier, and
perhaps wiser, way out, and had simply lain down in exhaustion. Others had truly become seriously dehydrated. At this
point a chopper from the beach area at the mouth of the
Quang Tri River arrived with two exhausted marines from the
tank battalion. We were already being overrun by heat casualties, and the hottest part of the day was still two hours away.
We shut down sick call and began to organize.

The "coolest" place in the compound was the sandbag
lined hallway between the operating rooms. We lined up the
casualties side by side in the area. The conscious and oriented
were given three or four salt pills and led to the water pipe to
drink ad lib. The others were given intravenous fluids. The
corpsmen were instructed: "Two liters IV over the first two
hours, then one liter over two hours. Then check with the
doctor. If the patient wakes up, he may have water or
Kool-Aid." IV fluids were continued for those who remained
disoriented or unconscious. Some required more than four
liters of fluid before they urinated and felt well. A few
remained unconscious for several hours. Some spiked fevers
after fluid replacement was well underway. The latter turned
out to have malaria in addition to heat exhaustion.

The volume increased. By late afternoon, we had received over seventy-five heat casualties in addition to the
usual forty wounded and ten malaria victims. At six o'clock,
an additional twelve marines arrived with minor heat exhaustion. Two of them had severe muscle cramps. One had such
painful abdominal cramping that our surgeon contemplated
exploring his abdomen, but his symptoms disappeared with
intravenous fluids and sedation. The next hot appendix that
came in would be watched as a heat casualty for several hours.

Although three medevac fixed-wing planes flew south
that day, we elected to keep all the heat casualties in Dong
Ha. Most of them went back to their outfits later that same
day. We feared that if the medevac scene was too much of a
holiday, word would spread, and heat "casualties" would
increase. Those who stayed overnight were not even allowed

to watch the movie. This was real denial to the marines; it was a World War II movie with John Wayne.

The malaria victims, a self-inflicted foot wound, and a combative drunk kept me busy the rest of the evening. After a beer with Jim, I went to bed. Jim stayed up to drink with a friend of his who was visiting from the hospital ship.

Early the next morning I faithfully but reluctantly responded to my 6:05 alarm clock and Jim and I put on our boots to go for a run. We were stopped by a newspaper man who wanted to interview us for a story to send the folks at home. The interview was a farce because Jim kept cutting up and giving false, corny, patriotic, pseudosincere, heroic answers. The newspaper man loved it and didn't realize that Jim was pulling his leg. He even took pictures of us in our boots and shorts to send to the States.

I was a little upset by the delay until two artillery shells pounded into the road by the runway strip right where we may have been if our run had not been delayed. Just when we finally did get underway, before we had passed the oil bladders, we saw a chopper coming toward D Med and turned back to receive the casualties.

The only passenger was a Vietnamese woman carrying her dead baby. The doctors who had automatically stumbled out of their hooches when they heard the chopper returned to bed. I approached the woman and tried to explain to her that we could not help. The baby with a small hole in his abdomen was dead.

She somehow expected me to restore life to the child. Surely, the Americans with their jets and oil bladders and operating rooms and fantastic scientific weapons of destruction could fix one small baby.

She was crushed when I sent her away. She in fact did not know where she was and had no way of getting back to her own ville. In her own country she stood stranded in the middle of America without food, money, transportation, friends, or sympathy.

Had brave American soldiers risked their lives to save the woman and her village from the hands of the enemy? Or had tired, frightened, confused, hate-filled American boys burned her village, raped her daughters, and killed her child? In this war the baby may have been wounded while the ville was being liberated by the VC, or while the Allied Forces were shelling an unfriendly ville? This woman could not hope to understand these things.

It was time to shower and dress before sick call. The morning was unusually hot again, and we received several heat casualties by ten o'clock. A few were repeaters from the morning before.

A "54" landed with twelve wounded and four dead. Two of the wounded were NVA officers, a valuable treasure. One of them talked to me as I bandaged a shrapnel wound in his leg. He was a doctor who had walked from Hanoi to the DMZ to help in an underground hospital. Moving from one hospital area to another that morning, he was wounded and captured. He was not afraid, and his wound was not serious. I left him to work on another wounded man, but, when things quieted, I returned again to talk. He was dead. How could that be? His wound was superficial, and his blood loss had been minimal. The marine on the next litter had seen him take a pill. He must have committed suicide.

His colleague spoke out in slow, simple Vietnamese. "The doctor of North Vietnam walks a hundred miles to serve. The soldier of South Vietnam will not defend his own village."

Intelligence officers arrived full of excitement, self-importance, and drama. Two NVA officers, one of them a doctor—the best find in weeks. Disappointed to find the doctor dead, they quickly gathered around his colleague.

The major in charge looked toward me. "How bad is this one?"

"Through and through of the ankle. He'll lose his foot. Should have it amputated in the next few hours." I stated the facts.

"Don't do anything for him until we've questioned him."

"I've already stopped the bleeding."

"Don't you know you can't show him that you're going to help unless he talks?" The major's tone was that of scolding.

I started unwrapping the wound. "Here, you make it bleed again if you want. Any wounded man brought to my triage I fix. You can't play Dick Tracy with a dead man anyway."

He stopped me. "Just leave him alone. We'll call you when we're finished."

I stood back and watched. The major talked to the interpreter. The interpreter talked to the NVA. The Intelligence men talked to one another. The major talked. The interpreter talked. The NVA was silent.

The major grew angry. "Tell him he's going to die. Tell him we won't help him unless he talks. Tell him his only chance is to talk, and then we'll fix his foot."

The interpreter rambled on. The NVA was silent. The major struck the wounded ankle with his clip board, and the prisoner grimaced in silent pain. I went back to the sick call area.

Ninety minutes later the major stormed into sick call. "What happens if you don't operate today?"

"He probably won't die, but he may lose more of his leg."

"Don't do anything. We'll put a guard on him and be back to talk to him this afternoon." He turned and stomped out. "It's lunch time anyway."

Lunch consisted of a sandwich and purple Kool-Aid, the same damn purple Kool-Aid we'd had every day that month. Purple Kool-Aid with breakfast, lunch, dinner, and midnight snack. Purple Kool-Aid and coffee.

The NVA artillery men in the DMZ had favorite times to throw in a few rounds. For psychological reasons, lunchtime was one of them. Six o'clock on Sunday morning and suppertime were other popular choices.

That noontime, a deafening overhead whistle followed by a sickening crunch cleared the chow hall in seconds. I had learned to carry food with me so I could finish lunch in the bunker. Several more shells came in; one of them close enough to make me spill my Kool-Aid.

Still in the chow hall bunker, we heard a helicopter approach the landing pad. Running for triage, we met the stretcher bearers with an air force major still clad in lead vest, helmet, and sunglasses. The handsome, crew-cut, middle-aged man was wide awake, but was experiencing considerable pain. There was a penetrating wound in the right upper quadrant of his abdomen.

"Hi, fellows. I'm really glad to see some doctors. I'm really hurting, and I must admit, a little scared, too."

I started an IV while one of the surgeons examined his wound. "Looks like the liver. We'd better get him out to the ship. We can't start a long surgical procedure with all this 'incoming.'"

"But he's likely to shock any minute. Maybe we'd better keep him."

"No, we'll start blood and send a corpsman with him. Call the ship and get a helicopter."

I explained to the major what the conversation was all about.

"Whatever you think best, Doc. I'm in no position to argue. I don't even feel like debating."

I went back to my hooch and stretched out for a minute before afternoon sick call. I heard a helicopter land. Purely out of habit, I got up and started for triage before I realized that it was the chopper to take the major to the ship. I returned to the rack, but minutes later I heard the familiar rattle of another helicopter. Out on the pad the corpsmen were rushing the major back to triage.

"He went into shock as soon as we got up, Sir. I gave him the whole unit of blood and started another. I told the pilot to bring him back. We would never have made the ship, Sir."

The surgeon took over. "Get me an O.R. crew." He turned to me. "John, scrub in and help me." The corpsmen began prepping him as he rolled through the operating room doors. The litter had barely come to a halt when the anesthesiologist inserted an endotracheal tube and began to force-breathe oxygen and air. By the time we got him on the O.R. table, the surgeon was scrubbed, gloved, and ready. He had already made an incision when I joined him. His movements were fast and accurate. He reached inside the incision and paused. All of the hurry was over. The surgeon shook his head and stepped back. "Put your hand in that incision, John. Palpate the liver."

My whole hand passed through the fist-sized hole in the surface of the liver and into a bowl of jelly. His entire liver was destroyed, blown apart, torn from its supports. "Nothing we can do about that," I said sadly.

The surgeon signaled the anesthesiologist to stop pumping. He turned to the corpsmen. "Leave him here till his heart stops, and then take him to Graves. I'm sorry, boys."

The operating room doors banged open. A corpsman came running in. "O.R. Two, Sir. A carotid artery! Doctor Veesar's got his finger in it now, but it's still bleeding."

We ran to the adjacent operating room. Holding an endotracheal tube in place, Jim had one hand in a struggling marine's mouth. The other was in a neck wound where blood welled between his fingers. Both men were covered with blood and vomitus. This time it was Jim giving the orders.

"Somebody pump up the goddamn thing on the endotracheal tube—the balloon or cuff or whatever the fuck you call it. John, start an IV and do a femoral stick to get some blood."

The surgeon put on fresh gloves and gown while a corpsman prepped the wound with Jim's hands still in place. The anesthesiologist took care of the endotracheal tube and began to administer gases. I put a needle into the marine's femoral artery, drew blood for type and crossmatch, and started an IV in each arm. He stopped struggling and became motionless as the anesthesia took effect. The surgeon got a clamp on the vessel, and things calmed down a bit.

"He's hypotensive. We'd better pump the first couple of units in."

Without answering, I hung up a unit of blood for each arm and pumped them manually. Jim and the surgeon began the repair of the vessels.

At that moment two incoming artillery rounds ripped into the compound. The corpsmen hit the floor. We heard patients and doctors running for the bunkers. The surgeon didn't even look up. He continued to operate. Jim stood across from him. The anesthesiologist lay on his back and operated the breathing bag from the floor. Kneeling on the floor, I continued to pump the blood with my hands.

Two more shells landed close by.

"We can't stop now. The clamps are on too many things." The surgeon looked at Jim. "I've got to keep going."

Jim answered, "As long as you stand on that side operating, I'll stand on this side assisting."

There was a long silent period. The surgeon moved rapidly and efficiently. The sweat dripped from his forehead. Jim's hands were shaking.

A shell ripped into the ground just outside the operating room wall and shook the floor. Shrapnel ripped through the

wall and ceiling at several places, and the lights went out.
Sunlight streaked through the newly-made holes in the roof.
Another shell hit the retaining wall and sprayed dirt over the
roof. Then the emergency generator kicked in. As the lights
came on, Jim and the surgeon were still standing. Pale and
motionless, both were still looking into the wound. The
surgeon's hands began to move again.

"Jesus, Christ, I'm scared." Jim's voice cracked. I crawled
across the floor to get another unit of blood. Another shell
whistled in, and I froze face down. The ground shook so that
I skinned my nose on the floor. Another shower of dirt
followed.

"We're gonna have to put this fellow on the floor," I said,
"or he'll be killed by the shrapnel." We pulled the unconscious marine onto the floor. The surgeon lay on his belly. Jim
faced him from the other side as they continued to operate.
Pumping gas and blood, the anesthesiologist and I joined
them on the floor.

Three more shells landed in the distance. Then it was
over. We returned the marine to the operating table,
rescrubbed, and finished the procedure.

"That's what I call earning your combat pay," I said.

"That's what I call being scared shitless," added Jim.
His face didn't seem so ugly now. It was partially covered by a
mask.

The surgeon put in the final skin ties. "And when I go
back to finish my training some cocky chief resident will be
telling me the best way to sew up somebody in the emergency room."

"He'll tell you how to be calm in the O.R."

The doors to the operating hooch swung open. One of
the chiefs stuck his head in. "You guys all right?"

"Sure," I said. "Why, what's up, Chief?"

"What's up!" said the chief. "We just got the shit shelled
out of us. Three of them rounds landed right here in the
hospital compound."

"No kidding," said Jim. "Gee, we didn't hear anything."
Jim was beautiful.

The sidewalk outside the O.R. was destroyed. One of
the toilets in the head was blown away. One of the doctors
was sitting on that very toilet when the shelling began. He
dived and crawled toward the bunker just outside the head.

As he approached the bunker door, a blast wave threw him inside against the opposite wall. The worst he had to show for it were frazzled nerves and thoroughly messed up pants. Another round blasted the retaining wall just outside the operating rooms. It was that wall which prevented a direct hit on our operating room.

The afternoon fixed wing to Phu Bai took all the wounded and sick on hand. As long as we were receiving so many incoming rounds, we didn't want to keep anybody. The marine with the neck wound was stable enough to travel. The prison was taken south for more questioning, and the body of the air force major was being processed at Graves. Afternoon sick call was called off. We suddenly had nothing to do.

Jim found a football somewhere. He and I started tossing it around on the helicopter pad, and several others joined us for a touch football game. We divided up. Graves versus the stretcher bearers with two corpsmon and a doctor on each team. Jim went with the stretcher bearers; I joined the Graves.

We were winning eighteen to twelve when the game was interrupted by two helicopters approaching rapidly from the west. They were full of casualties and dead. Both teams returned to work. We hoped to finish the game later—but we never did.

Among the wounded were two brothers, one with a leg injury; the other with a head injury. It was difficult to believe that brothers would be assigned to the same outfit. I talked to one of the kids as I dressed his leg wound.

"Well, when my big brother found out I had joined the marines, he beat shit out of me, and then went and joined up himself. He told them he'd volunteer if they would let him be in my outfit. Said he wanted to look after me. How is he, Doc? How bad is my brother?"

"I don't know. Another doctor is looking after him. I'll go find out." I looked at the name on his medevac tag. "Hooker, William."

At the far end of triage I found a head injury with serious brain damage left to die. I felt a sinking emptiness as I approached and looked at the name tag. "Hooker, James." Big brother was going to die. A sweaty, nauseating weakness overcame me. I knew that every head injury waiting to die had a wife, or a child, or a brother. But ordinarily loved ones were fifteen thousand miles away at home. Family scenes just weren't part of my job. I waited a few minutes before I went back to little brother.

"Hi, kid. It looks like your brother is pretty bad. He got it in the head."

"Is he going to die, Doc?"

"It looks very bad, kid. I'm sorry."

"Jesus Christ, Doc, he was just trying to look out for his kid brother. Why does he have to die? I . . ." He clenched his jaw to keep from crying. I wanted to cry, too.

It was suppertime. I walked slowly to chow hall. One of the corpsmen came running up to me.

"Doctor Parrish, guess what? Tomorrow a USO show is coming. Rock and roll and dancing girls."

"That's great." I tried without success to sound enthusiastic.

"The girls are going to stay overnight. They'll be sleeping in the chief's club."

"That's nice." I walked on to the chow hall.

Liquid hamburger meat over bread, potato chips, and purple Kool-Aid. As usual, just about the time the tray hit the table, a helicopter landed outside on the pad. Maybe there were enough people in triage to handle it. Sometimes, even if you're not very hungry, it's nice just to sit by yourself for a couple minutes. A corpsman came back to the chow hall.

"There's a patient they want you to see in triage, Sir."

"I'll be right there." I finished off my Kool-Aid as I walked back to triage. It was not difficult for me to figure out which patient it was that the other doctor wanted me to see. There were four new arrivals. Only one did not have obvious signs of trauma. He lay on his back on the first litter, staring blankly at the ceiling. His breathing was slightly deeper and more rapid than normal. He made no attempt to help the two corpsmen undress him.

"His blood pressure is normal, Sir, but he seems to be paralyzed all over. His corpsman from the field is one of the wounded. Maybe he can tell you about this guy. He won't even hold a thermometer in his mouth. It keeps falling out."

It was apparent as the corpsmen tossed the patient about that his neck was supple and that the position of his head caused no obvious change in his neurological status. It was too late to suggest that his head and neck be kept stable according to the usual routine for a paralyzed patient. Many times before I had seen these same corpsmen carefully place sandbags on each side of a paralyzed soldier's head in order to prevent further damage to injured nerves. But today they not only failed to treat the boy with care, but also handled him with an air of contempt. They were almost abusive as they undressed him and obtained a rectal temperature. Though not moving a muscle, the boy's limp body somehow provoked the corpsmen to anger.

Lying completely nude on the green litter, he stared through the roof toward the sky. He was blond and average in build. His childlike face showed no sign of fear or concern about his paralysis. One arm hung awkwardly off the stretcher. I placed it at his side. His skin temperature was normal, and his peripheral pulses were strong.

"Hi, buddy. What's the trouble?" His eyes did not move toward me. The corpsmen walked away. "What's the trouble, buddy?" I repeated.

I shook him. He didn't respond. I squeezed his toes to induce a painful stimulus. No response. His extremities were flaccid. They offered no resistance to passive movement. But if his leg were raised and dropped, there was an unconscious, involuntary response to check its fall. Likewise, if his hand were held above his nose and dropped, the same response checked its fall as well. His deep tendon reflexes were intact. In fact, his ankle jerks were slightly exaggerated. There were no pathologic neurological signs.

"What's the trouble, buddy? Can you move your fingers if you try? Come on, move your fingers."

No response.

"We can help you if you try, buddy. Just move your fingers a little."

Nothing.

"Are you scared, buddy?"

His eyes flashed a suggestion of acknowledgment but quickly resumed a distant stare.

I went down the line to find the corpsman who had come in from the field at the same time. The corpsman had a few superficial shrapnel wounds of his hip and leg. Raised up on his elbow, he watched his leg being dressed and smoked a cigarette, obviously very proud of his red badge of courage.

"Hi, Doc. What's with Grady? He probably got a blast injury to his squash, 'cause he's completely paralyzed. He damn near got me killed, too."

"What happened?" Helping myself to one of the L & M's on the corpsman's litter, I propped one foot on the crossbar of the litter stand and leaned against the adjacent litter. The marine on that stretcher didn't mind. He was dead.

"Tell me about it."

The corpsman seemed happy to tell the story. "We were on a sweep, crossing a field of rice paddies, when our point stepped on a land mine and was blown away. We all froze in our tracks. Then the gooks opened up on us from the tree line on our right flank and wounded two. Two others ran for the road up ahead. One of them made it, but the other one stepped on another mine and was blown twenty feet in the air. We knew we couldn't charge the machine guns, because they had probably mined the area in front of them. We were trapped. That's when I got this scalp laceration. A round knocked my goddamn helmet off. Everytime somebody made a run for cover, he got hit by fire or blown up by a land mine.

"Our lieutenant started crawling for the road. He dragged his rifle butt on the ground to make a trail. Somehow he made it across the paddy, onto the road, and across to the far bank which offered some protection from the machine gun fire. The rest of us took turns following his trail and made it to safety. When we counted up, everybody was accounted for except Grady and his buddy who were still back somewhere in the goddamn rice paddy. The gunny went back a little way into the rice paddy to look for them. He called and cursed them just like at boot camp. Next thing I knew, there was a hell of an explosion and the gunny was silent. He didn't come back.

"The lieutenant called in a gunship on the tree line, and we set up mortars and blasted the shit out of the area for about twenty minutes. We either got the gooks, or they ran away. Those helicopter gunships did purely pound the shit out of that tree line. I mean, they kicked some ass.

"When it was quiet, I carefully followed the trail of the lieutenant's rifle butt back into the paddy. I found the gunny. He had both legs blown off, but was still alive. I dragged him back to the other side of the road."

The stretcher bearers came to move the litter I was leaning against.

"That's the gunny there." The corpsman pointed to the blanket-covered body as it was carried away. "Hell of a good man. He was going back to get Grady, and got his fucking legs blown off. Tough son-of-a-bitch, that gunny. He'd just as soon died, anyway, than not have any legs."

The corpsman paused to light another cigarette. His hands shook and he became less sure of himself.

"Well, anyway, then I went back to look for Grady and his buddy. The two of them were inseparable. They both came from Tennessee, but never met until the Nam. I kept calling for them, but there was no answer.

"Finally, I saw them. They were lying side by side in the tall grass off to the side of the dried up rice paddy. Neither one was moving. They were about fifteen meters from the lieutenant's line, and I was scared to go over and check them, because I might get blown up, too. But I got as close as I could and saw that Grady had his eyes open. He was lying on his side against a dirt bank, sort of half sitting. His buddy was face down with the back of his head all mashed and bloody. Looked like a round right through the middle of his face from the front. I called to Grady, but he wouldn't answer.

"I went back across the road and got a meat hook that we used to climb up hills and to hook trees to cross streams. After about five tries, I managed to hook Grady's buddy in the back and drag him toward me across the fifteen meters all the time expecting the whole world to blow up."

The corpsman's speech became shaky and rapid. He demonstrated with his arms how he cautiously pulled the body over the mined field.

"Well, nothing blew up, so I went over and got Grady and pulled him to the other side of the road. By that time the medevac chopper had arrived, and here we are."

I put my hand on his shoulder and nodded my head. I took another of his cigarettes. "You kept your cool. You did a good job."

"You know, Doc, I didn't even know my leg had been hit till I was loading these guys in the chopper. I mean, I knew when I got my helmet blown off, 'cause it knocked me on my ass. But I don't even know when I got all this shrapnel in my leg. Crazy! Right, Doc? I mean that's really crazy."

"This whole business is crazy. Thanks for the cigarettes."

"Anytime, Doc."

I went back to Grady. "I don't blame you for being scared, Grady," I said. "We'll fix you up, and you're going to be fine."

No response. I turned to a corpsman. "Give him fifty milligrams of Thorazine IM now, and another fifty milligrams in four hours. Give him a liter of sugar water overnight, and put him in a quiet corner of the ward. I'll be at the movies if you need me."

"Yes, Sir."

I had trouble sleeping that night even though I was very tired. Also, we were awakened twice in the middle of the night to receive casualties. Each time, I stopped by the ward to check on Grady.

"Vital signs are normal, Sir. He's sleeping soundly."

"Any problems with anybody else?"

"No, Sir. Quiet night tonight."

"Thank you."

"Yes, Sir. Good night."

During my run the next morning, the story of the corpsman and the gunny sergeant kept going through my mind. In this war it was impossible to predict who might cause you to die, and who might cause you to live. "Crazy. Right, Doc? I mean that's really crazy."

Grady was the first patient on my morning rounds. He was somnolent, but arousable and oriented. He sat up on the side of the bed as I approached.

"How are you, Grady?"

"Fine, Sir."

"Do you remember what happened to you?"

"Yes... well, sort of... when it came my turn to move... I couldn't."

"Another day's rest and you'll be okay. Then we'll talk about what happened to you. We can——"

"I want to go back to my outfit." He stood up, lost his balance, and sat down again. With another effort he started getting dressed.

"Right now?" I asked.

"Yes, Sir. Can I? Please."

"You stay for lunch. Then back to your outfit."

"Yes, Sir, and thanks. I've really got to go back to my outfit today. You understand. Don't you, Sir? I mean..."

"I understand completely. Now go shave and get cleaned up. The corpsman will find you some gear."

The hospital commander walked into the ward.

"John, we're having a USO show today and somebody has to cover triage. That somebody will be you. I hope you don't mind too much."

"When you have only four weeks left, you don't mind much of anything." I almost meant it.

"Try to handle it by yourself if you can. Just hold most of the work till the show is over."

"Sure."

"Of course, if anything urgent comes up, or if you get overwhelmed, just yell."

"Will do. I'll look after things."

Morning sick call was canceled because of the show.

The show was scheduled to begin at two o'clock, but, as usual, it was an hour late getting started. The stage was the platform from which we loaded casualties into ambulances. The roof was the sky. The audience sat on the ground. Patients in blue pajamas and white bandages made up the first four rows. The rest were green fatigues. At the back several large troop transport trucks provided balcony seats for those in the rear.

Three electric guitars, a bass, a small electric organ and a drum set were assembled and wired on the stage. Microphones were tested. The audience was expectant and noisy. I tried not to imagine the results of an artillery shell's landing in the midst of those smiling faces.

As the crowd grew more and more restless, a chief walked onto the stage. Three minutes of applause, whistles, and cheers welcomed him. The troops really needed something to be happy about.

"Today, we want to welcome some fine people from the Philippines who have been touring Vietnam to entertain the troops (loud cheering). Their well-known rock-and-roll group (more cheers) has spent four months touring Southeast Asia and entertaining mainly in the cities and big bases. But today they have come way out here to give a free show for D Med (prolonged cheers). I am proud to introduce The Sun Rocks."

The audience roared approval as six unattractive Philippino entertainers with inappropriate and artificial grins ran out onto the stage.

Three small, blousy-sleeved men approached the instruments, and three women in long skirts split on the side to the waist stepped up to the microphones. Two thin but sexy-looking girls took the side mikes. A slightly obese middle-aged woman with giant breasts and a painted face grabbed the center one. One of the electric guitar players ran the width of the stage, tripped as he approached his instrument, and plunged off the other side of the stage. A roar went up, and cheering persisted for five full minutes. Then there was total silence.

Awaiting their injured colleague's return to the stage, the entertainers shuffled about nervously. Finally, he limped back to the stage, strummed one chord on his guitar, and nodded to the drummer who banged out eight steady raps. Another chord by the lead guitar. Another eight raps. Another chord. The drummer suddenly went wild striking his drums and cymbals in a fast, rat-a-tat beat. The whole group erupted into loud, hard-core rock with a Fats Domino style. "I'm walking..." The troopers went wild. Hats flew in the air. "I'm walkin, yes indeed, I'm talking, talkin about you and me."

The fat mama could really sing. Her voice was low and loud. She enjoyed singing. Her whole body sang. The other two girls moved as if they had extra joints, especially in their pelvises. The guitar men did a short, side step with a little kick back and forth in unison. The lead guitar continued to limp. The troopers were ecstatic. They hugged each other and danced around to the music.

The song ended. The cheers were loud and long. People looked at one another with expressions emanating "this is the greatest." Somebody was smoking grass.

Silence. The lead guitar said something in another language to the drummer who threw both sticks into the air and skillfully juggled them as he stood over his drums. He stopped. All eyes were on him as he slowly raised one stick into the air. It came crashing down onto the drum, and with lightning speed he banged out an introduction that had everyone with legs up on his feet screaming. The group joined in with more loud rock. In perfect unison the two thin girls gyrated about at amazing speed. Soldiers who had two hands clapped in rhythm. Caught up in the mob euphoria everyone moved some part of his body or his brain to the beat of the music.

"Doctor Parrish, the MP's have a civilian casualty up in triage."

A thirty-year-old Vietnamese man in severe pain waited on a litter in triage. One entrance wound in his back. No exit wound. Also a through and through of the left flank. Paralyzed without sensation from the hips down. His grieving, hysterical wife and pulled at his shirt and embraced his head. An old Vietnamese woman stood in the corner looking sad, but resigned. She was no longer capable of fright or amazement. She seemed not to hear the loud music. Next to the old woman stood a nine-year-old boy who stared at me with distrust, curiosity, and hate.

Two young, all-American MP's stood next to the litter. "I don't know if he is VC or not. Caught him taking a big stack of clothing out of one of the huts in the ville. Told him to halt three times. He didn't, so I shot the fucker." The MP speaking was angry. The other grinned and side-shuffled back and forth to the music.

The Vietnamese man was very frightened. He flinched each time I reached out to touch him. Despite my reassurance in Vietnamese, he pleaded with me not to kill him or his family. The MP interrupted him.

"He wasn't armed. My Vietnamese isn't so good, so I said, 'Halt' in English and in Vietnamese. I gave him fair warning."

The Vietnamese man and the MP began talking at the same time. They spoke in different languages with different emotions, but they told the same story. They talked loudly to be heard above the music and above each other's voice. One was a pleading, weak, and broken victim. The other was an arrogant, powerful, but misinformed victim who suffered an equal but dissimilar fear. The core of the message was their helplessness. All of us in the room were victims although we coped with the war in different ways. The injured man was frightened, his wife hysterical, the old woman resigned, the boy stoic, the soldier overzealous, and I distraught.

"What the hell is he saying, Doc? Giving away any VC secrets?"

"He said that the hut was his own. The clothes were his wife's. He was taking them to an American soldier who told him that if he did not deliver the clothes before sundown his hut would be burned."

"You don't believe that do you, Doc?"

"Does it matter?"

"Well, if he's a VC then he should be shot. Right?"

"What's a VC?"

"A Viet Cong. They're the enemy. You know that, Sir. They're the bad guys. They have to be shot. Right?"

"I don't know, I don't know. I really don't know."

"What's that music all about? That's live music."

"It's a USO show. Go watch it. It's for soldiers like you."

"Thank you, Sir. Goodbye."

The MP turned to the boy in the corner and held his hand out to him. "Want to come hear some good old American music?"

The little boy stared at him. The MP walked toward the boy who did not move or change his stare. The MP held out gum and cigarettes. "Come on, don't be afraid."

"Will you get the hell out of here!" I screamed. "You just shot that boy's father in the back. He doesn't want your fucking gum. Just get the hell out of here!"

Shrugging his shoulders the surprised soldier left.

I followed the MP to the show. Noise and euphoria increased as the music grew louder. The people seemed to be in a dream. I found a surgeon.

"I have a civilian in triage with a surgical abdomen and a spinal cord injury. He needs his belly cracked."

"What's that, John?"

"Civilian O.R. case, now!"

"I can't hear you."

"Surgery, now!"

"Oh, okay, I'll be right there. Good show. I'll be right there. Hey, Chief. I need an O.R. crew."

"The moon stood stee-al."

The fat one sweated and held the microphone stand between her fat thighs. "I found mah three-al, on blueberry heee-al." Each of the thin ones pulled a GI from the audience to dance. One fellow struggled to get away, but the girl's insistence and his colleagues' pushes forced his embarrassed body to do a few jerky, self-conscious dance steps. The other

GI ran up and rhythmically dry-humped the girl. His buddies went wild with cheers and laughs of approval.

"On-a Blueberry Hee-al." The music and noise resounded in my head.

Helicopter noise is steady. It doesn't blend with music. When it grows loud and bothersome stretcher bearers bolt from the crowd and run.

Three bodies for Graves. Three wounded for triage.

Through and through of the wrist. Prepare him for the O.R. The orthopod can do him after the show. The beat goes on.

Third-degree burns of the face and hands. Debride it, dress it. Prepare him for the next medevac south. He is blind and thinks he hears live rock-and-roll music.

Shrapnel wound of the calf. X ray. Debride it under local anesthesia. Cut, probe around, irrigate. Keep time to the music. Cut, probe. Blunt dissection, probe around gently. Finally—the click! The hemostat hits the metal frag. That discovery click! Sometimes after long minutes of frustration. Sometimes after a few seconds of blind probing. The muffled click deep in the tissue that tells me I have scored. It tells me that I'm through cutting and tearing. Time to pinch the frag and pull it out. I hear the click with ears and fingers. It's a very familiar and welcome sound. It's more beautiful than a whole USO show. I hear it above helicopters, and above rock-and-roll music, and above screams of pain. I hear it above the sharp bang of outgoing shells. Lying on my stomach, I hear it when the world explodes around me. I hear it when I'm so tired that I hear nothing else.

Slowly open the hemostat and close it on the frag that is seen only with ears and fingers. A sixth sense reveals its shape and size. Pull it out of the living flesh and throw it sharply into the metal pan. The victory click! It's much louder, sharper, and higher pitched than the discovery click. The patient hears the victory click.

"Is it out, Doc?"

"Can I see it?"

"Thanks."

"I'm glad that's out."

Irrigate, dress the wound, make out medevac tags. The procedure is automatic. Today, one. Some days, one hundred.

Keeping time to the music, I sit for while tapping the

metal fragment with a hemostat. I can't resist throwing the fragment into the pan again.

The frenzy of music increases.

"Doctor Parrish, excuse me. We have some bodies at Graves. We need to get them ready for the four o'clock plane. Could you come and fill out some forms?"

"What's that?"

"Death certificates. Before four o'clock."

"Can't hear you."

"Pronounce the dead!"

"Oh yeah, be right there."

Washed down and identified. Papers in order. In green bags. Waiting in a row. Very efficient.

Graves marines tap their feet in time to the music. Blue Moon. Blue Moon.

Eleven bodies. A little more paperwork and their war is over. Bring in the dog and put out the cat.

Look 'em over. Find the cause of death. Yackity yak, don't talk back.

Gruesome, torn, mangled, destroyed. Kids, intestine, muscle. Waste! I said over and over and over again, this dance was gonna be a drag.

Zip up the green bags. Stack them up. Snap your fingers. Tap the pencil on the clip board. One and two and three and. . . . Get a job.

Use the hose to wash away the blood and feces and brains. Keep clean and leave no trace. The paperwork is done. Get off a my blue suede shoes.

Sweat causes make-up to run and blur and soaks armpits and giant breasts. She throws back her head. Her mouth opens. And right out of her fat guts comes "It's almost tomorrow."

Stand for a minute and sway with her. Clinched fists. Tears.

UNIT: 3rd Battalion, 3rd Marine Division
NAME: John Harrison Allan
SEX: Male
RACE: Caucasian
STATUS: Regular, active
LENGTH OF SERVICE: 10 months
AVIATION: No
FILE OR SERVICE NO: 2578901

RANK: Pfc.
BRANCH OF SERVICE: USMC
PLACE OF BIRTH: Chicago, Illinois
DATE OF BIRTH: 1/19/49
AGE: 19 years, 5 months, 17 days
RELIGION: Church of Christ
COLOR OF EYES: Blue
COLOR OF HAIR: Brown
COMPLEXION: Light
HEIGHT: 68 inches
WEIGHT: 136 pounds
MARKS AND SCARS: S 1½ right forehead
                         vacc. left upper arm
                         left inquinal hernia scar
                         circ.
FINGERPRINT: Right index finger
NEXT OF KIN: Mother Allan, Mrs. Richard D.
                    246 West Cedar, Payton, Illinois
ADMITTED TO SICK CALL: 3rd Med. Bt., 3rd Marines
DATE ADMITTED: 6 Jul 68
PLACE OF DEATH: Quang Tri Province, Vietnam
DATE OF DEATH: 6 Jul 68
DISEASE OR CONDITION DIRECTLY LEADING TO DEATH:
Penetrating missile wounds of chest, abdomen, neck.
APPROXIMATE INTERVAL BETWEEN ONSET AND DEATH:
Immediate
SUMMARY OF FACTS RELATING TO DEATH: While on
field maneuver in Quang Tri province the deceased
was felled by an enemy sniper bullet. While he lay
on the ground a mortar shell exploded at close range.

The medical officer at 3rd Medical Battalion
Dong Ha pronounced the deceased dead on arrival
of multiple penetrating missile wounds.

Identity of the remains was established by marks
and scars from the health record and from the
armed forces identification card.

Disposition of remains: transferred to U.S. Na-
val Hospital in Da Nang for preparation and
disposition.
DATE SIGNED: 6 Jul 68
SIGNATURE OF MEDICAL OFFICER: John A. Parrish
Lt./MC/USNR

## The drama, intensity
## and the horror of war:

- ☐ 24645-3 **MEDITATIONS IN GREEN**, Wright $3.95
- ☐ 25588-6 **BAT 21**, Anderson $3.50
- ☐ 26020-0 **THE 13th VALLEY**, Del Vecchio $4.50
- ☐ 25136-8 **GOSHAWK SQUADRON**, Robinson $3.50
- ☐ 25056-6 **PIECE OF CAKE**, Robinson $4.50

Look for them at your bookstore or use the coupon below:

*Relive the American Experience in Vietnam*

---

# BANTAM VIETNAM WAR BOOKS

---

## Join the Allies on the Road to Victory
# BANTAM WAR BOOKS